Also by M. Scott Peck, M.D.

THE ROAD LESS TRAVELED: A New Psychology of Love, Traditional Values and Spiritual Growth

PEOPLE OF THE LIE: The Hope for Healing Human Evil

WHAT RETURN CAN I MAKE?: Dimensions of the Christian Experience (with Marilyn von Waldner and Patricia Kay)

The Different Drum

COMMUNITY MAKING AND PEACE

M. Scott Peck, M. D.

A TOUCHSTONE BOOK
Published by Simon & Schuster

TOUCHSTONE
Rockefeller Center
1230 Avenue of the Americas
New York, New York 10020

First Touchstone Edition 1988
Second Touchstone Edition 1998

TOUCHSTONE and colophon are registered trademarks
of Simon & Schuster Inc.

Designed by Irving Perkins Associates

Manufactured in the United States of America

3 5 7 9 10 8 6 4 2

Library of Congress Cataloging-in-Publication Data
Peck, M. Scott (Morgan Scott), date.
The different drum.

Includes bibliographical references.
1. Community.   2. Peace.   3. Spiritual life.   I. Title.
HT65.P44 1987   307   87-4825

ISBN: 0-684-84858-9

*The names of individuals described herein have been changed,
wherever appropriate, to preserve confidentiality.*

To
the people of all nations
in the hope
that within a century
there will no longer be a
Veterans Day Parade
but
that there will be
lots of living people left
to
march to a different drum
because
all the world loves a parade.

ACKNOWLEDGMENTS

This work is the product of an almost lifelong journey, first toward and then ever deeper into community. There is no way I can list all the wonderful people who have led and accompanied me on this journey. Still, many stand out and deserve not only acknowledgment but my profound gratitude. They are in chronological order:

Carol Brandt, Dr. Earle Hunter, Fenno Hoffman, Tiny Drier, Lily Peck, Cynthia and William Weir, Belinda Peck, Julia Peck, Burke Hanschild, Mac Badgely, General John M. Finn, the "Tech Group" on Okinawa, Christopher Peck, Stewart Baker, Lindbergh Sata, Maria Dawson, Gene Kadish, Richard Slone, John Hoffman, Sister Ellen Stephen, Mary Ann Schmidt, Gerald McBrayer, John Keith Miller, "The People of the Kleenex," "The People of the Balloon," Vester Hughes, Tom Luce, Jerry Silverman, my editors Fred Hills and Burton Beals, the "Highly Disciplined Adhocracy," Pat White, the "Discovery Group," and the board and the staff of The Foundation for Community Encouragement.

Contents

9

Part II: The Bridge

Part III: The Solution

Prologue

There is a story, perhaps a myth. Typical of mythic stories, it has many versions. Also typical, the source of the version I am about to tell is obscure. I cannot remember whether I heard it or read it, or where or when. Furthermore, I do not even know the distortions I myself have made in it. All I know for certain is that this version came to me with a title. It is called "The Rabbi's Gift."

The story concerns a monastery that had fallen upon hard times. Once a great order, as a result of waves of antimonastic persecution in the seventeenth and eighteenth centuries and the rise of secularism in the nineteenth, all its branch houses were lost and it had become decimated to the extent that there were only five monks left in the decaying mother house: the abbot and four others, all over seventy in age. Clearly it was a dying order.

In the deep woods surrounding the monastery there was a little hut that a rabbi from a nearby town occasionally used for a hermitage. Through their many years of prayer and contemplation the old monks had become a bit psychic, so they could always sense when the rabbi was in his hermitage. "The rabbi is in the woods, the rabbi is in the woods again," they would whisper to each other. As he agonized over the imminent death of his order, it occurred to the abbot at one such time to visit the hermitage and ask the rabbi if by some possible chance he could offer any advice that might save the monastery.

The rabbi welcomed the abbot at his hut. But when the abbot explained the purpose of his visit, the rabbi could only commiserate with him. "I know how it is," he exclaimed. "The spirit has gone out of the people. It is the same in my town. Almost no one comes to the synagogue anymore." So the old

13

abbot and the old rabbi wept together. Then they read parts of the Torah and quietly spoke of deep things. The time came when the abbot had to leave. They embraced each other. "It has been a wonderful thing that we should meet after all these years," the abbot said, "but I have still failed in my purpose for coming here. Is there nothing you can tell me, no piece of advice you can give me that would help me save my dying order?"

"No, I am sorry," the rabbi responded. "I have no advice to give. The only thing I can tell you is that the Messiah is one of you."

When the abbot returned to the monastery his fellow monks gathered around him to ask, "Well, what did the rabbi say?"

"He couldn't help," the abbot answered. "We just wept and read the Torah together. The only thing he did say, just as I was leaving—it was something cryptic—was that the Messiah is one of us. I don't know what he meant."

In the days and weeks and months that followed, the old monks pondered this and wondered whether there was any possible significance to the rabbi's words. The Messiah is one of us? Could he possibly have meant one of us monks here at the monastery? If that's the case, which one? Do you suppose he meant the abbot? Yes, if he meant anyone, he probably meant Father Abbot. He has been our leader for more than a generation. On the other hand, he might have meant Brother Thomas. Certainly Brother Thomas is a holy man. Everyone knows that Thomas is a man of light. Certainly he could not have meant Brother Elred! Elred gets crotchety at times. But come to think of it, even though he is a thorn in people's sides, when you look back on it, Elred is virtually always right. Often very right. Maybe the rabbi did mean Brother Elred. But surely not Brother Phillip. Phillip is so passive, a real nobody. But then, almost mysteriously, he has a gift for somehow always being there when you need him. He just magically appears by your side. Maybe Phillip is the Messiah. Of course the rabbi didn't mean me. He couldn't possibly have meant me. I'm just an ordinary person. Yet supposing he did? Suppose I am the

Messiah? O God, not me. I couldn't be that much for You, could I?

As they contemplated in this manner, the old monks began to treat each other with extraordinary respect on the off chance that one among them might be the Messiah. And on the off, off chance that each monk himself might be the Messiah, they began to treat themselves with extraordinary respect.

Because the forest in which it was situated was beautiful, it so happened that people still occasionally came to visit the monastery to picnic on its tiny lawn, to wander along some of its paths, even now and then to go into the dilapidated chapel to meditate. As they did so, without even being conscious of it, they sensed this aura of extraordinary respect that now began to surround the five old monks and seemed to radiate out from them and permeate the atmosphere of the place. There was something strangely attractive, even compelling, about it. Hardly knowing why, they began to come back to the monastery more frequently to picnic, to play, to pray. They began to bring their friends to show them this special place. And their friends brought their friends.

Then it happened that some of the younger men who came to visit the monastery started to talk more and more with the old monks. After a while one asked if he could join them. Then another. And another. So within a few years the monastery had once again become a thriving order and, thanks to the rabbi's gift, a vibrant center of light and spirituality in the realm.

Introduction

In and through community lies the salvation of the world.

Nothing is more important. Yet it is virtually impossible to describe community meaningfully to someone who has never experienced it—and most of us have never had an experience of true community. The problem is analogous to an attempt to describe the taste of artichokes to someone who has never eaten one.

Still, the attempt must be made. For the human race today stands at the brink of self-annihilation.

Some of the victims of Hiroshima and Nagasaki are described as walking blindly down the street after the blasts, dragging bundles of their own skin behind them. I'm scared for my own skin. I'm even more scared for the skin of my children. And I'm scared for your skins. I want to save my skin. I need you, and you me, for salvation. We must come into community with each other. We need each other.

Because so few have a vision of community and so many know that peacemaking must be the first priority of civilization, initially I thought this book should be entitled "Peacemaking and Community." But that would put the cart before the horse. For I fail to see how we Americans will be able to communicate effectively with the Russians (or any peoples of other cultures) when generally we don't even know how to communicate with the neighbors next door, much less our neighbors on the other side of the tracks. True communication, like the charity it requires, begins at home. Perhaps peacemaking should start small. I am not suggesting for a moment that we should abandon global peacemaking efforts. I am dubious, however, as to how far we can move toward global community—which is the only way to achieve international peace—until we learn the basic principles of community in our own individual lives and personal spheres of influence.

In any case, this book will start small. The first section will focus entirely upon my personal experience of community. For there I discovered its extreme importance in my own life and in the lives of thousands of my fellow humans as we struggled together to communicate without superficiality or distortion or animosity.

The second section of this work will be much more "theoretical." It is a word I hesitate to use, because "theoretical" implies "impractical" to many. But here I will attempt to build a bridge between the basic concepts of community-making on a personal level and international, intercultural understanding. It is theoretical only because that bridge has largely been untried. But the fact that it is untried hardly means it is impractical. For the reality is that it is our traditional means of international relations that are impractical. They have been tried and are obviously and consistently to be found wanting. It is not impractical to consider seriously changing the rules of the game when the game is clearly killing you.

In the final section the theoretical becomes quite specific as I consider issues of community-making and peace as they relate to three particular institutions: the arms race (which has, indeed, become an institution), the Christian Church, and the government of the United States. Here again I will call for the rules to be changed. And here again, those who cannot think of the future in terms other than an extrapolation from the status quo will probably think: "Impractical."* But we must return to the reality that the status quo is murderous. If hu-

---

* Richard Bolles, author of *What Color Is Your Parachute?*, has succinctly addressed this issue in relation to the arms race in his booklet *The Land of Seven Tomorrows* (Ten Speed Press, P.O. Box 7123, Berkeley, CA 94707; $1.00, which is the cost to Bolles). He defines the arms race as solvable only by "new brain thinking" as opposed to "old brain thinking." Old brain thinking is characterized by the limited capacity to contemplate only those innovations that might logically evolve out of the current system. The old brain seems incapable of considering a radical change in the system itself—that is, the possibility of operating under a different set of rules.

mankind is to survive, the matter of changing the rules is not optional.

Already the word "salvation" has been used several times. It tends to have two different meanings in our Western civilization, where we traditionally separate, isolate, the physical from the spiritual. Physical salvation—as in "we want to save our skins"—refers to a rescue from death. But what is spiritual salvation, particularly when we think of the spirit as immortal? Here the word takes on more the meaning of healing (as with a salve that is used to heal the skin). Spiritual healing is a process of becoming whole or holy. Most specifically, I would define it as an ongoing process of becoming increasingly conscious. Even Freud, an atheist, said that the purpose of psychotherapy—healing of the psyche—was to make the unconscious conscious. And Jung ascribed human evil to the refusal to meet the Shadow—the Shadow being those aspects of ourselves that we do not want to own or recognize and that we continually attempt to sweep under the rug of consciousness. Indeed, one of the better definitions I know of evil is that it is "militant ignorance." But however the terms are defined, perhaps the most extraordinary result of nuclear technology is that it has brought the human race as a whole to the point at which physical and spiritual salvation are no longer separable. It is no longer possible for us to save our skins while remaining ignorant of our own motives and unconscious of our own cultures.

Issues of consciousness and unconsciousness will be touched on repeatedly in the chapters that follow. But this is inevitably a spiritual book. For we cannot save our skins without saving our souls. We cannot heal the mess we have made of the world without undergoing some kind of spiritual healing.

While inevitably a spiritual book, it is not a specifically Christian one. Andrew Marvell wrote to his "coy mistress" that he would love her "till the conversion of the Jews." Well, we cannot wait that long. Anyone who believes that world peace won't be established until religious and cultural differences are obliterated—until all Jews become Christians or all Christians Muslims or all Muslims Hindus—is thereby contributing to the problem rather than the solution. There simply isn't time for that. Even if there were—even if "one world" meant a melting pot in which everything comes out a bland mush instead of a salad of varied ingredients and textures—I'm not sure that outcome would be palatable. The solution lies in the opposite direction: in learning how to appreciate—yea, celebrate—individual cultural and religious differences and how to live with reconciliation in a pluralistic world.

After visiting the United Nations Meditation Room, which is unfinished so that offense is given to none of the world's great religions, Marya Mannes wrote: "It seemed to me standing there that the nothingness was so oppressive and disturbing that it became a sort of madness and the room a sort of padded cell. It seemed to me that the core of our greatest contemporary trouble lay here, that all this whiteness and shapelessness and weakness was the leukemia of noncommitment sapping our strength. We have found, finally, that only nothing could please all. . . . The terrifying thing about this room was that it made no statement whatever."*

I must write, therefore, out of the particularity of my culture as a citizen of the United States and my faith as a Christian. Should some take offense at this, I ask them to remember that it is their responsibility to embrace my particularity, my uniqueness, just as it is my responsibility to embrace theirs. And that community, which includes all faiths and all cultures without obliterating them, is the cure for "the core of our greatest contemporary trouble."

Actually, in these pages I am highly critical of many aspects of both my country and my Church, and that may offend still others. They may think that I am not a "true Christian" or a "true American." But I ask you to remember two things. One is that I focus more upon the sins of the United States and the Christian Church than upon those of Russia or Islam, for

* Marya Mannes, "Meditations in an Empty Room." *The Reporter* (February 23, 1956), p. 40.

example, because as they wisely teach in Alcoholics Anonymous, "the only person you change is yourself." The other is that I love my country and my Church so much that I expect much from them. The potential of each is glorious. I hope to see them significantly live up to their potential and promises.

Those promises have to do with community—with people living together in both freedom and love. "Freedom" and "love" are simple words. They are not simple actions. True freedom means something much more and different from a "me first" kind of individualism. Genuine love consistently requires some very hard decisions. Community neither comes naturally nor is it purchased cheaply. Demanding rules must both be learned and followed. But there are rules! Quite clear ones. Saving ones. They are not obscure. The purpose of this book is to teach these rules and encourage you to follow them. The hope of the book is that we will learn them first in our personal lives, then apply them universally. For that is how the world will be saved.

Scott Peck
Bliss Road
New Preston, Connecticut
06777

PART I

The
Foundation

CHAPTER I

Stumbling into Community

Community is currently rare.

Certain words become distorted over time. When people ask me to define myself politically, I tell them that I am a radical conservative. Unless it is Thursday, when I say I am a radical moderate. The word "radical" comes from the Latin *radix*, meaning "root"—the same word from which we get "radish." The proper radical is one who tries to get to the root of things, not to be distracted by superficials, to see the woods for the trees. It is good to be a radical. Anyone who thinks *deeply* will be one. In the dictionary the closest synonym to "radical" is "fundamentalist." Which only makes sense. Someone who gets down to the root of things is someone who gets down to the fundamentals. Yet in our North American culture these words have come to have opposite meanings, as if a radical were necessarily some left-wing, bomb-throwing anarchist and a fundamentalist automatically some right-wing primitive thinker.

"Community" is another such word. We tend to speak of our hometowns as communities. Or of the churches in our towns as communities. Our hometowns may well be geographical collections of human beings with tax and political structures in common, but precious little else relates them to each other. Towns are not, in any meaningful sense of the word, communities. And sight unseen, on the basis of my experience with many Christian churches in this country, I can be fairly confident that each of the churches in your hometown is not likely to be much of a community either.

While on one hand we bandy about the word "community" in such a shallow, meaningless way, many of us simultaneously long for the "good old days" when frontier neighbors gathered together to build one another's barns. We mourn the *loss* of community. I am not enough of a historian to know whether back then our forefathers did indeed enjoy the fruits of genuine community more than we do today or whether we are simply yearning for an imaginary "golden age" that never existed. Still, I know of some hints that indicate we humans may once have known more of community than we currently experience.

One such cue is contained in a sermon preached by John Winthrop, the first governor of the Massachusetts Bay Colony, in 1630. Speaking to his fellow colonists shortly before they set foot on land, he urged, "We must delight in each other, make others' conditions our own, rejoice together, mourn together, labor and suffer together, always having before our eyes our community as members of the same body."*

Two hundred years later the Frenchman Alexis de Tocqueville traveled through our young United States, and in 1835 he published what is still considered the classical work on the American character. In his *Democracy in America* he described those "habits of the heart," or mores, that gave citizens of the United States a unique new culture.† The one characteristic that impressed him most was our *individualism*. De Tocqueville admired this character trait immensely. He very clearly warned, however, that unless our individualism was continually and strongly balanced by other habits, it would inevitably lead to fragmentation of American society and social isolation of its citizens.

Very recently—another hundred and fifty years later—the highly respected sociologist Robert Bellah and his colleagues wrote a most striking follow-up, *Habits of the Heart.*†† In this work the authors compellingly argue that our individualism

* John Winthrop, "A Model of Christian Charity," *Puritan Political Ideas, 1558–1794,* ed. Edmund S. Morgan (Indianapolis: Bobbs-Merrill, 1965), p. 92.

† Alexis de Tocqueville, *Democracy in America,* trans. George Lawrence, ed. J. P. Mayer (New York: Doubleday Anchor Books, 1969), p. 287.

†† Robert Bellah et al., *Habits of the Heart: Individualism and Commitment in American Life* (Berkeley, Calif.: Univ. of California Press, 1985).

has not remained balanced, that De Tocqueville's direst predictions have come true, and that isolation and fragmentation have become the order of the day.

I personally know of this isolation and fragmentation. From the age of five until I left home at twenty-three I lived with my parents in an apartment building in New York City. There were two apartments to a floor, separated by a small foyer and elevator. As there were eleven stories above the first, this building was the compact home for twenty-two families. I knew the last name of the family across the foyer. I never knew the first names of their children. I stepped foot in their apartment once in those seventeen years. I knew the last names of two other families in the building; I could not even address the remaining eighteen. I did address most of the elevatormen and doormen by their first names; I never knew any of their last names.

More subtly yet devastatingly, the strange geographical isolation and fragmentation of the society of that building was reflected in a kind of emotional isolation and fragmentation within my own family. For the most part I feel blessed by my childhood home. It was both very stable and comfortable. Each of my parents was responsible and caring. There was plenty of warmth, affection, laughter, and celebration. The only problem was that certain emotions were unacceptable.

My parents had no difficulty being angry. On relatively infrequent occasions my mother would become sad enough to cry quietly and briefly—an emotionality that seemed to me then uniquely feminine. Never once in all my years of growing up did I ever hear either of my parents say that they were anxious or worried or scared or depressed or anything to indicate that they felt other than on top of things and in total control of their lives. They were good American "rugged individualists," and they very clearly wanted me to be one also. The problem was that I was not free to be me. Secure though it was, my home was not a place where it was safe for me to be anxious, afraid, depressed, or dependent—to be myself.

I had high blood pressure by my mid-teens. I was indeed

"hypertense." Whenever I was anxious I became anxious about being anxious. Whenever I felt depressed I got more depressed over being depressed. Not until after I had entered psychoanalysis at the age of thirty did I come to realize on an emotional level that, for me, anxiety and depression were acceptable feelings. Only through this therapy was I able to understand that I was in certain ways a dependent person who was in need of emotional as well as physical support. My blood pressure began to come down. But full healing is a lengthy journey. At fifty I am still completing the process of learning how to ask for help, how not to be afraid to appear weak when I am weak, how to allow myself to be dependent and unself-reliant when appropriate.

It was not just my blood pressure that was affected. Even though I yearned for intimacy, I had major difficulties *being* intimate, which was hardly surprising. Had someone asked my parents whether they had friends, they would have replied, "Do we have friends? Good gracious, yes. Why, we get over a thousand Christmas cards every Christmas!" On one level that answer would have been quite correct. They led a most active social life and were widely and deservedly respected—even loved. Yet in the deepest definition of the word, I am not sure they had any friends at all. Friendly acquaintances by the droves, yes, but no truly intimate friends. Nor would they have wanted any. They neither desired nor trusted intimacy. Moreover, as far as I can see, in an age of rugged individualism they were quite typical of their time and culture.

But I was left with a nameless longing. I dreamed that somewhere there would be a girl, a woman, a mate with whom I could be totally honest and open, and have a relationship in which the whole of me would be acceptable. That was romantic enough. But what seemed impossibly romantic was an inchoate longing for a society in which honesty and openness would prevail. I had no reason to believe that such a society existed—or ever had existed or ever could exist—until accidentally (or by grace) I began to stumble into varieties of real community.

FRIENDS SEMINARY, 1952–54

At the age of fifteen, much to my parents' dismay, I adamantly refused during my spring vacation to return to Phillips Exeter Academy, the New England boarding school that I had been unhappily attending for the preceding years. Exeter at the time was perhaps the nation's leading training school for rugged individualism. The administration and teachers quietly prided themselves on not coddling their students. "The race belongs to the swift," they might have said, "and if you can't cut the mustard, it's too bad." Occasionally something of a relationship might develop between a student and a faculty member, but such unusual instances were not encouraged. As inmates will in a prison, the students had their own society, with norms that were often as vicious. The pressures for social conformity were immense. At any given time at least half the student body occupied the status of outcasts. During my first two years there virtually all my energy was unsuccessfully expended in attempting to compete for a position as part of the "in" group.

In my third year I got "in." And as soon as I was in, I realized I didn't want to be there either. On my way to becoming a well-trained WASP, I dimly had the wisdom to know that I would soon suffocate in the exclusive air of that culture. It was not the thing to do at that time and place, but it was a matter of breathing for me: I dropped out.

In the fall of 1952 I began to repeat the eleventh grade at Friends Seminary, a little Quaker school on the edge of Greenwich Village in New York City. Neither my parents nor I can now remember how this fortuitous choice was made. In any case, Friends was the opposite of Exeter: it was a day school, whereas Exeter was a boarding school; it was small, whereas Exeter was large; it encompassed thirteen grades, from kindergarten up, whereas Exeter had four; it was coeducational, whereas Exeter was all male at the time; it was "liberal," whereas Exeter was purely traditional; and it had something of a sense of community, whereas Exeter had none. I felt I had come home.

Adolescence is, among other things, a strange blend of heightened consciousness and dramatic unconsciousness. During my two years at Friends Seminary I was surprisingly unconscious of the wonderfulness of that time and place. Within a week I felt immensely comfortable there but never gave a thought as to why. I began to thrive—intellectually, sexually, physically, psychologically, spiritually. But this thriving was no more conscious than that of a parched, drooping plant responding to the gift of rain. For the eleventh-grade compulsory American History course at Exeter, each student was expected to produce a ten-page, neatly typed original research paper by the end of the year, complete with footnotes and bibliography. I can remember what an impossible task it had seemed to me, a dreaded hurdle too high for my fifteen-year-old legs. The next year at Friends, repeating the eleventh grade at age sixteen, I encountered another mandatory American History course. For that course I effortlessly produced four forty-page papers, each neatly typed, with abundant footnotes and bibliographies. Within a mere nine months a dreaded hurdle had become an enjoyable form of study. I was glad of the difference, of course, but hardly aware of the almost miraculous nature of the change.

While at Friends, I awoke each morning eager for the day ahead. The fact that at Exeter I could barely crawl out of bed rapidly receded into the dimmer recesses of memory. I simply accepted my newfound lot in life as the natural course of things. I am afraid I took Friends for granted, never stopping to analyze my good fortune. It is only now in retrospect—more than thirty years later—that I am sufficiently aware to make that analysis. I wish I could remember more. I wish I had taken note at the time of sociological details, now forever lost, which might have helped to explain why or how Friends was gifted with such a unique culture. But I did not. I cannot tell you the whys and wherefores. But I can remember enough to tell you that it was indeed unique.

Despite the hardness of the wooden benches in the Quaker meetinghouse, which was an integral part of the school, I remember that all the boundaries between people were soft. We did not call our teachers by their first names, nor did we "socialize" with them. It was *Miss* Ehlers, *Doctor* Hunter. But they gently teased us, and we students gently, but gleefully, teased them in return. I was never afraid of them. In fact, most of them were able to laugh at themselves.

There were perhaps twenty in my class. A few of us boys wore ties; most did not. There was no dress code. (Strangely, I cannot remember any codes—possibly there were some— yet no one ever seemed to get in trouble.) We were twenty differently dressed adolescents—boys and girls—from every borough of New York City and from utterly different backgrounds. We were Jewish, agnostic, Catholic, Protestant. I remember no Muslims, but had there been, it would have made no difference. Our parents were physicians and lawyers, engineers and laborers, artists and editors. Some had splendid apartments; others lived in tiny, cramped walk-ups. This is what I remember most: how different we all were.

Some of us had A averages and some C–. Some of us were obviously brighter than others, prettier, handsomer, more physically mature, more sophisticated. But there were no cliques. There were no outcasts. Everyone was respected. There were parties on most weekends, but no one ever drew up a list of whom to invite and whom not to invite; it was assumed that everyone was welcome. Some hardly ever came to the parties, but that was because they lived far away or worked or had something better to do. Some of us dated; some did not. Some of us were closer than others, but no one was ever excluded. Subjectively, my profoundest memory is a nonmemory: I can never remember wanting or trying to be anyone other than myself. No one else seemed to want me to be different or want to be other than herself or himself. Perhaps for the first time in my life I was utterly free to be me.

I was also, unconsciously, part of a paradox that will pervade these pages. Friends Seminary created an atmosphere in which individualism flourished. Yet, regardless of our individ-

ual backgrounds or religious persuasion, we were in truth all
"Friends." I remember no divisiveness; I remember much cohesiveness. Some Quakers in a quaint way will refer to themselves as being "of the persuasion of Friends." Except for a
very occasional and brief silent meeting, Quaker principles
were not even taught, much less crammed down our throats.
It is a rather safe guess to conclude, however, that its identity
as a Quaker school profoundly contributed to its extraordinary atmosphere, although I have no idea how this came about.
Certainly we students—individuals all—were unconsciously
infected with a "friendly persuasion."

So there was individualism in all its glory, but there was
absolutely nothing "rugged" about it. The word "soft" comes
to me again. The competition associated with ruggedness was
totally absent. Even our own cohesiveness as a class was soft.
There was no interclass rivalry. One final detail returns to
mind about parties. A number of us dated people in the class
above us or below us, as well as graduates or people from
other schools. They were all included in our parties, as were,
not infrequently, older or younger siblings. The strange thing
is that, utterly unlike my previous mind-set, I cannot remember looking down on anyone who was younger or up to anyone older.

Even allowing for the distortion of memory, these were
indeed golden years. Yet if I said everything was perfect, it
would be a lie. Although wonderfully softened, all the usual
adolescent insecurities still plagued me. My blossoming
sexuality sometimes caused me agonizing confusion. One
teacher, although lovable, was blatantly alcoholic. Another,
although brilliant, was blatantly unlovable. And I could go on.
But even though it was unconscious, even though it was
muted by many factors, even though I had no idea what to
make of it at the time, one thing is clear in retrospect: during
those two years I experienced my first real taste of
community. It was a taste I would not have again for another
dozen years.

CALIFORNIA, FEBRUARY 1967

Midway through my three years of psychiatry training at the army's Letterman General Hospital in San Francisco, a senior career army psychiatrist, Mac Badgely, joined the faculty. His coming was preceded by rumors. Most indicated that he was incompetent, insane, or both. But one faculty member I highly respected described Mac as "the greatest genius in the army." I have previously recounted the difficulty I had coming to terms with this handsome man and remarkable teacher.* The fact that I was in analysis at the time—among other things because of an "authority problem"—helped me with this difficulty. In any case, by early autumn 1966 Mac had become for me a true mentor.

In December of that year Mac offered to run three marathon groups for those thirty-six of us on the staff—one in February, one in March, and one in April. Mac, we knew, had spent some time at the Tavistock Institute in England, where the theories of the British psychiatrist Wilfred Bion about the behavior of groups were taught and promoted. These groups, Mac announced, would be led according to "the Tavistock Model." Each would be limited to twelve participants. It was all voluntary. Until that time my training and experience in group therapy had been mediocre at best. But I had come to esteem Mac so much that I was eager to participate in anything with which he was involved. Consequently I was one of the twelve who signed up for the first available "group experience" in February. Twelve others volunteered for either the March or April group. Theirs was eventually held in April. The other eligible twelve decided to turn down the opportunity.

We first twelve—all relatively young male psychiatrists, psychologists, or social workers—began our weekend meeting with Mac at eight-thirty on a Friday evening in February in an empty barracks at an air base in nearby Marin County. Each of

* See M. Scott Peck, *The Road Less Traveled: A New Psychology of Love, Traditional Values and Spiritual Growth* (New York: Simon and Schuster, 1978), pp. 39–42.

us had worked all day and was already tired to begin with. We were told that the group would end early Sunday afternoon. It was not specified how much we would sleep, if at all. Nor was it specified what we would *do*. Yet three incidents occurred in the course of that weekend which made an indelible impression upon my very life. The first was the most profound mystical experience I have ever had.

Seated next to me in the group was a drafted young faculty psychiatrist from Iowa, who quickly made no bones about the fact that he disliked my East Coast mannerisms and "effete" clothes. I countered that I wasn't particularly keen either about his Midwestern boorishness and the big smelly cigars he smoked. About two o'clock Saturday morning this man fell asleep and began to snore loudly. At first it seemed a bit funny, but within a few minutes his guttural noises were repulsive to me. He was totally interfering with my concentration. Why couldn't he stay awake like the rest of us, I wondered. If he had wanted to volunteer for this experience, you'd think he'd at least have the grace and discipline not to fall asleep and disturb our work with his ugly snores. Wave upon wave of fury built up in me. The waves intensified as I looked at the ashtray next to him with its four stale-smelling dead cigars, their chewed ends still wet with his saliva. My hatred became pure white hot, utterly unforgiving and righteous.

But then a most odd thing happened. Just as I was looking at him with such disgust, he turned into *me*. Or did I turn into him? In any case, I suddenly saw myself sitting in his chair, *my* head rolling back, the snores coming out of *my* mouth. Sensing my own fatigue, I realized with equal suddenness that he was the sleeping part of me and I the waking part of him. He was doing my sleeping for me, and I was doing his waking for him. And I was overcome with love for him. The waves of fury, disgust, and hatred turned instantly into waves of affection and caring. And stayed that way. Within a few seconds he looked to me like his old self again, but it was never again the same. My affection for him continued after he awoke. Although we never became the very closest of friends, we deeply enjoyed playing tennis together the next six months until I was reassigned.

I do not know what creates a mystical experience. I know that fatigue can loosen "ego boundaries." I also know that I am now able to do voluntarily what happened to me then involuntarily: to see, whenever I remember to choose to do so, that all my enemies are my relatives and that all of us play roles for each other in the order of things. Perhaps I have not had so dramatic a mystical experience since because I no longer need one. But I needed that one eighteen years ago. There is no other way I could have loved the psychiatrist from Iowa. I had to be hit figuratively over the head with something, had to have my egocentric barriers broken by some force the like of which I could never have dreamed up by myself.

I told the others in the group of my mystical experience. Thereafter there was much hilarity and good fellowship. Exhausted by five in the morning, we broke for a very brief two hours of sleep. Around nine o'clock Saturday morning, however, the spirit seemed to go out of our group. I felt mildly depressed at the loss. During a lunch break at noon I confided my feelings to the two other members with whom I was eating. That was when the second memorable incident began.

"I don't see why you feel that way," each responded. "The group is going wonderfully, and we're having a marvelous time, even if you aren't."

I was disturbed by the discrepancy in our perceptions, so when the group reconvened at one o'clock Saturday afternoon, I spoke of it. One by one almost all of the other group members spoke of their delight in the group and the experience we were having. I was clearly the odd man out. I became more depressed as the group wondered what was wrong with me that I wasn't having the same wonderful time they were. They all knew that I was in psychotherapy at the time and inquired whether I might not be having some problem with my analyst which I was inappropriately bringing into the group.

It was now two o'clock in the afternoon. The only person

who had not spoken during the preceding hour other than Mac, our leader, was Richard, a rather distant, reserved, and detached individual. "Perhaps Scotty is the voice of the group's depression," Richard commented in his unemotional way.

The group members immediately turned on Richard. "What a weird statement," they proclaimed. "It doesn't make any sense. How could someone be a voice of the group's depression? What a peculiar thing to say. The group isn't depressed."

Then they turned back on me. "Obviously you've got a significant problem, Scotty," they told me in one way or another, "—in fact, a very major problem. Certainly not a problem a short-term group like this could deal with. Obviously you should talk about it with your analyst at the first possible opportunity. It's really a matter for your therapy, and you shouldn't have brought it in here and contaminated our group work with it. Probably you are so sick you really aren't ready for a group experience like this. Maybe the best thing for you and for the rest of us would be for you to pull out of the group right now. Even though it's Saturday afternoon, maybe your analyst would be willing to see you on an emergency basis this evening."

It was now three o'clock. Feeling more and more depressed—and, indeed, very much a pariah—I was on the point of offering to leave the group so as not to weigh it down with what seemed to be my psychopathology. But then Mac, the leader, spoke for the first time that day. "An hour ago Richard suggested that maybe Scotty was the voice of the group's depression," he said, "and you as a group chose to ignore that suggestion. Perhaps you were right in doing so. Perhaps you are correct in believing that Scotty's depression has nothing to do with the rest of us. But I would like to make one observation. Up until five o'clock this morning, when we broke for a nap, there was a great deal of laughter. If anything, the mood was one of hilarity. As you know, I haven't said anything since then, but I have been watching you, and I want to let you know that no one in this group has laughed since nine o'clock this morning. In fact, no one in the group has even smiled for the last six hours."

The group sat in stunned silence for several minutes. Then a member said, "I miss my wife."

"I miss my kids too," another added.

"The food here stinks," said a third.

"I don't know why we had to come all the way out here to this stupid air base for this stupid thing," added yet another, "when we could have saved time if we did it back at the Presidio, and we could have gone home to sleep."

"And your leadership has been lousy, Mac," chimed in yet another. "As you yourself acknowledged, you haven't said a word for six hours. You should have given us more leadership."

After everyone had expressed his feelings of anger, frustration, and resentment—the elements of depression—mirth and the spirit of joy returned to the group. I, of course, basked in the transformation of my status from pariah to prophet. Prophets are almost invariably the bearers of bad news. They proclaim that something is wrong with their society, as I had done in our little society. But people don't like to hear bad news about themselves, which is why prophets are so often stoned or otherwise scapegoated. This experience of being scapegoated as a minor prophet was so condensed, so clear and personal, as to be of great benefit to me. For ever since that time when I have been out of step in some way, I have never been totally certain I was wrong. And whenever I have been a member of a vigorous majority, I have never been able to be complacently certain I was right.

The third particularly memorable incident of that pregnant weekend was as gentle as the preceding one was potentially vicious.* After the group had ceased scapegoating and had dealt with its depression, it enjoyed Saturday evening suffused with quiet calm and lighthearted affection. We decided we had earned a reasonable night's sleep. We stopped at ten and agreed to resume at six Sunday morning. Our good spirits

* This incident was previously but only briefly described in M. Scott Peck, Marilyn von Waldner, and Patricia Kay, *What Return Can I Make?: Dimensions of the Christian Experience* (New York: Simon and Schuster, 1985), pp. 113–114.

prevailed as we greeted the California dawn together. Within an hour, however, a note of discord began to be subtly struck. Members started sniping at each other for no obvious reason. Only by this time we had become rather facile at being conscious of ourselves as a group organism and thereby able to contemplate our own health as a body. So it was not long before one of us remarked, "Hey, guys, we seem to have blown it. We've lost the spirit. What's going on?"

"I don't know about anyone else," another responded, "but I have been feeling irritated. I'm not sure what it's about. It just seems to me we've been going off into left field with a lot of airy-fairy talk about human destiny and spiritual growth."

Several members nodded their heads in vigorous agreement.

"What's so airy-fairy about human destiny and spiritual growth?" countered another. "It seems to me they're only *crucial.* That's where the action is. It's what life is all about. It's basic, for God's sake."

Several others of us now nodded in equally vigorous agreement.

"When you say 'for God's sake,' you put your finger right on the problem, as far as I'm concerned," said one of the earlier head-nodders. "I don't happen to believe in God. That's why you guys are out in left field. You're spouting off about God and destiny and spirit as if those things are real. None of them can be proved. They're ephemeral and leave me cold. What I'm interested in is the here and now of earning a living, my kid's measles, my wife getting overweight, how to cure schizophrenia, and whether or not I'm going to be assigned to Vietnam next year."

"One could say that we seem to be divided into two camps," another member mildly interjected.

Suddenly the whole group erupted into laughter at the mildness of his interpretation. "You might say that—yes, indeed, you just might," exclaimed one, slapping his thigh. "Just possibly seems that way," another said, guffawing.

So, rather gleefully, we set to work to elucidate further the division between us. It was equal. The camp I belonged to identified the other six as marching under the Sears, Roebuck banner. They, the materialists, in turn identified us as marching under the banner of the Holy Grail. Hence we came to be known as the Grailers. Mac refused to be sucked in as a tie-splitter.

Being efficient—having become what Mac said Bion called a "working group"—we quickly recognized that in the limited time left to us the Sears, Roebuckers would not be able to help us Grailers come to our senses and stop chasing after some spiritual will-o'-the-wisp. Similarly, we Grailers accepted the reality that we would be unable in the few remaining hours to convert the Sears, Roebuckers from their crass materialism. So we agreed to disagree, set our differences aside, and successfully got on with our work.

Which was the work of ending. We dealt with our impending demise as a group organism in a manner that was neither purely materialistic on the one hand nor blatantly spiritual on the other: we resorted to myth. Sad and happy at the same time, each member throwing in a new detail, we wove a myth of ourselves as a giant pregnant sea turtle that had come onto a beach to lay its eggs only to lumber back into the ocean to die. How many, if any, of our primitive eggs were to survive was left up to fate.

The resolution of the friction between the Sears, Roebuckers and the Grailers was my first experience with group-conflict resolution. I had not known before that it was possible for a group of people to acknowledge their differences, set them aside, and still love each other. What would have happened to those differences had we been able to work together for a longer time I do not know. But for that brief period of time I witnessed human beings both celebrating their differences and transcending them.

Those are the three incidents I particularly remember about that extraordinary marathon group that Mac Badgely led in February 1967. But what I remember even more clearly— what was even more important and potent for me—was not an incident. It was the feeling of joy.

Genuine communities vary extremely in their intensity. Friends Seminary was a relatively unintense community. There were separations between us students and faculty. We all lived in various parts of the city and were involved elsewhere dealing with our families and other friends. Most of the time, even when we were together, we were concentrating on academics and not on our relationships. When I was at Friends, as I have said, I awoke each morning with eagerness. It was a feeling somewhat akin to joy but so much more muted; the more accurate way of putting it would be to say simply that I was remarkably happy during those years.

Mac Badgely's group, on the other hand, was extremely intense. Brief, but intense. During the forty-two hours we thirteen spent together we were focusing on our interrelationships 75 percent of the time. There were major periods of depression, resentment, irritation, and even boredom during the experience. But these were interspersed with joy. The sort of happiness I experienced at Friends was condensed tenfold into a distillate no longer definable by the simple term "happiness" but only expressable by "joy."

I had felt joy of equal intensity before, but this was the first time I had ever known it with such frequency and constancy. Since it was a first experience for me, I was not at the time able to name it any further. But now I know it was the joy of community. Now I also know that, like lesser kinds of happiness, the joy of community is a by-product. Simply seek happiness, and you are not likely to find it. Seek to create and love without regard to your happiness, and you will likely be happy much of the time. Seeking joy in and of itself will not bring it to you. Do the work of creating community, and you will obtain it—although never exactly according to your schedule. Joy is an uncapturable yet utterly predictable side effect of genuine community.

There is an epilogue. All twelve of us in Mac Badgely's group agreed that the weekend was gloriously successful. On the other hand, from the reports I heard, the second marathon group that Mac led, in April, was a dismal failure. It was apparently a weekend of unresolved conflict and unceasing anger. I remain to this day curious as to the difference. The scientist in me picks up on the one variable of which I am aware: we in the first group were apparently sufficiently eager for the experience to elect the first possible date; those in the second group were apparently sufficiently ambivalent to opt for a later one. I would hypothesize that the eagerness—and perhaps openness—of our group accounted in significant part for its success. Other facts were involved. To my mind it is highly unlikely that we ever would have been able to achieve and briefly maintain community were it not for Mac's loving and highly disciplined—even brilliant—leadership and the Tavistock Model (about which more will be said in Chapter VI) that he employed. Nevertheless, it seems clear that his leadership and use of the Tavistock Model alone were not sufficient to ensure the creation of community by just any group.

OKINAWA, 1968–69

My next experience of community was of still a third kind.* It was as unintense as a community can be and still be a community. It again included another dozen males, but in this instance we met together on the average of no more than one hour a week for a year. A happy, fortuitous experience, it brought echoes of joy in its hilarity. And there were other connections between it and the much more intense community experience in Mac Badgely's group. The connection I want to focus on is the one of myth. Mythmaking seems to be a frequent characteristic of true community. And the "Tech Group" on Okinawa created the most elaborately beautiful myth it has ever been my joy to witness.

* My use of "third kind" has nothing to do with visitors from outer space or with Steven Spielberg's marvelous movie *Close Encounters of the Third Kind*. Yet, in a very real sense, the experience of genuine community is always a sort of close encounter of the third kind.

From the autumn of 1967 until the summer of 1970 I was responsible for virtually all psychiatric services provided to the hundred thousand or more military personnel and their families who were stationed on Okinawa. The largest part of our work was with outpatients. The department was seriously understaffed. Consequently I had to make maximum use of the young enlisted men assigned to our outpatient clinic. I learned that with a little training many of these young men, ranging in age from nineteen to twenty-five, were able to be remarkably effective psychotherapists.

The army job title (military occupational specialty or MOS) of these young men was "psychological technician." We came to call them simply "techs." They almost all arrived at this position through the same particular set of circumstances. At that time, as the Vietnam War was increasingly escalating, the draft was active. Service for students in college could be deferred until the end of their college education as long as they maintained a certain grade-point average. If a student failed to maintain that academic average, he had three choices. One was to flee to Canada. A second was to wait around helplessly until the draft struck, whereupon he would be assigned to whatever job the army decided on—including that of foot soldier. The third, and perhaps the smartest choice at that point, was to beat the draft by voluntarily enlisting. As an enlistee the student was allowed to choose an available job classification— one that somewhat suited his interests—and usually one unlikely to end up with him in combat in Vietnam. The latter was the route that almost all the techs had followed and that had placed them on Okinawa.

So they were smart and mature enough to have entered college, and they were sufficiently interested (though often only vaguely) in psychology to have chosen the job of psychological technician. From there they had gone through basic training and an additional two-month period of training in psychology before being assigned to Okinawa. Gradually I came to realize that they had two more things in common. One was a sense of helplessness over their condition. They had indeed been able to make some choices, but they were still choices that had been dictated to them by the mechanics of the draft and a war they did not believe in. The other was that they had all failed. Specifically, they had failed to maintain the grades in college required to make them draft-deferred. In no case, however, was this because of a lack of intelligence. For some it was because they had partied too much. Others had lost themselves in dating or drugs. Still others, for whatever reason, had simply been too apathetic to study enough. In any case, they had all failed, and this failure was a significant part of their identity at the time.

My experience in Mac Badgely's marathon group had whetted my appetite for group work. For my further experience, as well as to assist the techs in their adjustment, I asked them if they would be interested in meeting with me as a group for an hour each week. They were. The Tech Group began in mid-May 1968.

Two weeks later, in the beginning of June, I received a phone call from Colonel Cox, my commanding officer. "Scooott," he began in his wonderfully southern but not to be contradicted drawl, "Ah'd lahk to ask you to do a favah for me."

"Certainly, sir," I responded. "Just name it."

"Ah've got a good friend here on the island, another colonel, and he's got a son who's come from college. He's a nahce boy. He's majorin' in psychology back in the States. Won't be going back until after Christmas. He's feelin' at loose ends at the moment and would lahk to do something in this psychology business. Ah was wonderin' if you could just give him some volunteer job in yo clinic for a whahl."

"No problem, sir," I replied smartly. "Happy to do that. Just send him over at your convenience."

An hour later Henry showed up at the clinic. I was aghast. Henry had severe cerebral palsy. It was all he could do to jerk and shuffle his spastically way along the clinic corridor. One side of his face drooped, and his speech was so slurred it was almost unintelligible until one became accustomed to it. Much

of the time he drooled. Inwardly I cursed Colonel Cox for
saddling me and my public clinic with such a monstrosity. And
I cursed God as well for creating such a seeming ogre. But I
was stuck with Henry. So, wincing, I made him a clerk-
receptionist, and since he was at least a temporary part of the
team and was interested in psychology, I invited him into the
Tech Group.

Within the group I realized in short order that Henry was
one of the most intelligent, sensitive, and beautiful human
beings I have ever encountered. After but a few sessions—and
very much with Henry's help—our weekly group became a
community. And shortly thereafter it began to weave the myth
of "Albert."

Albert was the deformed, illegitimate son of the mayor of
Fresno. He was so deformed he had only one hand, and that
grew out of the center of his forehead. Which was the reason
why, the group discerned, Albert was one of the few people in
this world who could hear "the sound of one hand clapping."*
Perhaps because of this unique ability, or perhaps because of
his father's influence, Albert had become a dramatically successful labor organizer, the first ever to be able to unionize the
homosexual shrimp fishermen of Fresno. It was left ambiguous as to whether the shrimp fishermen of Fresno were homosexuals themselves or whether they were "straight"
fishermen who simply caught homosexual shrimp. In any case,
it was because of this success that Albert was requested by the
government to come to Okinawa to organize Local 89 of the
Homosexual Shrimp Fishermen's Union. (Article 89 was the
legal article under which, at the time, discovered homosexuals
were dismissed from the army.) And so the myth grew on,
layer upon layer, with the group each week hilariously developing a new chapter of Albert's adventures.

It was a lovely thing to witness the self-acceptance and acceptance of each other in this weekly community, which allowed the crippled Henry and the crippled enlisted men

* A famous Zen Buddhist koan, or riddle, is: "What is the sound of one hand
clapping?"

(remember, they had all been college failures) and crippled me to participate together in the weaving of this wonderful myth. Please forgive the psychiatrist in me if I also note how the myth not only helped us to deal with our own crippledness but also our anxieties about our parentage, our impotence in being in the army on Okinawa, our distaste for the army's maltreatment of homosexuals, and our own sexuality.

By Christmas time the Adventures of Albert could have filled a book. Sad to say, we never wrote them down. In January 1969 Henry returned to the States, as did several of the techs whose enlistment had been completed. Simultaneously the clinic moved to a newly built medical complex of which I became the officer in charge. Those factors and additional responsibilities led us to disband the Tech Group. But I will always remember its camaraderie and creativity. Moreover, when my own crippledness is most brought home to me, when my afflictions seem great and I am badly in need of mirth, through my heaviness I can still recall at least a chuckle over Albert's triumphs.

The subject of myth will continue to surface. This is because myths speak more eloquently to the truth of the human condition than do other kinds of prose. I never had a short-term community experience more pregnant than Mac Badgely's group. So the "myth of ourselves as a giant pregnant sea turtle that had come onto a beach to lay its eggs only to lumber back into the ocean to die" poignantly expressed the fecund reality of our so brief time together. Albert, the crippled hero, speaks of the reality that many of both the strongest and weakest of us are indeed crippled heroes. It is not a sine qua non that a community create its own myth, but most eventually do, and this fact reflects a collective creative genius of genuine community which is quite routine.

BETHEL, MAINE, JUNE 1972

I have recounted how, as a child, I was trained in the precepts of rugged individualism. Anxiety, depression, and helplessness were feelings that were not supposed to be expressed. "Big boys don't cry." It was inevitable that for me, a male, crying was discouraged.

One night when I was approximately six years old, my parents were out for an evening on the town. They strolled past an area of Broadway in the theater district that at the time was lined with joke gift stores, the kind that could in a few minutes produce a mock paper with some fake headline such as "Harry and Phyllis Hit Town." The next morning I was presented with one such "gift" newspaper. The headline read: "Scott Peck Hired by Circus as World's Greatest Crybaby."

That was effective if injudicious training. I can't say that I never cried after that. I have always been a sucker for movies with corny sentimental endings. But the few tears I did allow myself to shed were always carefully wiped away before the theater lights came on. The worst time came at age nineteen, when I had to take the responsibility for breaking off a three-year relationship with a once beloved girl friend who not only cared for me deeply but had given me a whole new world. Then the tears streamed down my face. The street where we finally parted was dark, however, and the tears noiseless. I never *really* cried until age thirty-six.

Never really crying, I went through Exeter, Friends, Middlebury College, Harvard, Columbia, medical school, internship in Hawaii, residency training in San Francisco, Okinawa, and then hit Washington, D.C. Having become an objector to the Vietnam War, I elected to stay in the army in order to go to Washington as one who would "fight from within." At first the fight was exciting. Then it began to become heavy. And heavier. No big battles were won, and most little ones were lost. Half of the few that were won were shortly nullified by this or that countermanding action of the vagaries of the official powers above or those of penny-ante history. I grew tired. After two years of this it so happened that I was dispatched to the National Training Laboratories (NTL) headquarters in Bethel, Maine, in June 1972, to experience one of their twelve-day "sensitivity groups" as part of exploring a potential contract between NTL and the army.

There were approximately sixty trainees at our lab. More or less equally divided between men and women, we spent a third of our working time in various kinds of psychological exercises, either as a total group, in pairs, or in very small groups. These exercises were interesting and often quite useful or educational. But the real payoff came in the so-called "T-group," where we spent the greater part of our time. The lab was divided into four T-groups of approximately fifteen trainees each, in addition to its trainer. Our trainer was Lindy, a mature, experienced psychiatrist.

We were a very diverse group of people, we sixteen. The first three days were spent in intense struggle. It was not boring. But it was often anxious, often unpleasant, and there was much anger expressed, at times almost viciously. But on the fourth day something happened, and I remember the suddenness of the shift. Suddenly we all cared for each other. Thereafter some cried and a couple wept. Much of the time I had tears in my eyes, although of course I did not let them flow. For me they were tears of joy as I observed much healing taking place. We continued to have moments of struggle, but it was never again vicious. I felt very safe in the T-group. It was a place where I had no trouble being authentically myself. Once more I felt as if I had come home. My emotions ranged all over the map, but I knew that for this limited period we members loved one another, and the predominant thing I felt was joy.

On the afternoon of the tenth day I became depressed. At first I tried to shrug it off with a nap, thinking of how intense and exhausting our work had been. But soon I could no longer deny the fact that what was truly bothering me was the impending demise of the experience. It felt so right to be there in Maine bathed in an atmosphere of love, and in a mere two days I would have to return to the heaviness of my job in Washington. I did not want to leave.

It was at this point, in the late afternoon, that I received notice to call my office. It was a minor matter. But in the course of the conversation with my chief I learned that the selections had been made for promotions to general officer grade. The Medical Corps colonel I had strongly hoped would be promoted to brigadier general—a visionary man who had been something of a mentor to me—was not selected, and I knew his career was essentially at an end. In his stead the physician in the medical bureaucracy I most distrusted was the one promoted. I became more depressed.

I was the first one to speak in the T-group that night. I told the group that I was feeling depressed and explained why: that I was upset about the promotion selection and sad that the group would soon dissolve and I would have to return to Washington. When I was finished, one of the members commented, "Scotty, your hands are shaking."

"My hands frequently shake," I responded. "They've done that since I was an adolescent."

"It's sort of like your arms are all tensed up to fight," another member said. "Are you angry?"

"No, I don't feel angry," I answered.

Lindy, our trainer, stood up from where he was sitting, picked up his pillow, came over, and sat down in front of me, his pillow now between us. "You're a psychiatrist, Scotty," he said. "You know perfectly well that depression is usually related to anger. I really suspect you are angry."

"But I don't feel angry," I numbly replied.

"I'd like you to do something for me," Lindy said in his gentle way. "You probably won't want to, but I'd like you to do it anyway. It's an exercise we sometimes use called 'pounding the pillow.' I'd like you to pound this pillow. I want you to pretend that the pillow is the army, and I want you to pound it with your fist just as hard as you can. Will you do that for me?"

"It seems stupid, Lindy," I answered, "but I love you, so I'll try."

I made a fist and weakly hit the pillow a couple of times. "It really feels embarrassing."

"Hit it harder," Lindy commanded.

I hit a little harder, but it seemed to take all my energy.

"Harder," Lindy ordered. "The pillow's the army. You're angry at the army. Hit it."

"I'm not angry," I proclaimed forlornly as I feebly pounded the pillow.

"Yes, you *are* angry," Lindy said. "Now, hit it. Really hit it. You're angry at the army."

Obediently I hit the pillow still a little harder, at the same time saying, "I'm really not angry at the army. The system maybe, but not the army. It's just a little part of the whole system."

"You're angry at the army," Lindy shouted. "Now, hit it. You're angry."

My voice rose in resistance. "I'm *not* angry. What I feel is tired, not angry."

And then it began to happen. Weakly, methodically hitting that pillow, I continued speaking almost as if in a trance: "I'm tired. I'm not angry, I tell you. I'm tired. I'm unbelievably tired."

"Keep hitting," Lindy said.

"I'm not angry. I'm just tired. You can't believe how tired I am. I'm so tired of it all." A few tears began to flow down my cheek.

"Keep going," Lindy encouraged.

"It's the system," I moaned. "I don't hate the army. I can't fight the system anymore. I'm so tired. I've been tired for so long. For so long I've been so tired."

Waves of fatigue began to sweep over me. I started to sob. I knew I was doing it. I wanted to stop. I didn't want to make a fool of myself. But the fatigue was too much. I didn't have the energy to stop. The sobs escaped from my throat, at first as rasps and gasps. The waves grew stronger. All the battles lost, all the energy going nowhere, all the wasted struggle. I let go. I sobbed and sobbed. "But I can't quit," I blurted out. "Someone has to stay in Washington. How can I help out? Somebody has to be willing to work within the system. I'm so tired. But I can't cop out."

My face was drenched with tears. Mucus was pouring out of my nose, but I no longer cared. Lindy was holding me as I now lay on the pillow. Others had come to hold me as well. Through my tears their faces were a blur. But it didn't matter who they were. I just knew I was loved, snot and all. And I completely surrendered to the waves. The first waves were of Washington, of the "in" box three feet high, the talking papers written late at night, the lies I had seen perpetrated, the mixture of apathy, self-interest, and conniving callousness against which I struggled. But as I let them come in, there were far older waves of fatigue, of struggling to make a marriage work, of almost endless nights in emergency rooms, thirty-two-hour tours of duty throughout medical school and internship, pacing the floor with colicky babies—wave after wave.

I sobbed for half an hour. It frightened one woman in the group. "I've never seen anyone cry like that," she said. "It's terrible what we do to men in our society."

I grinned at her through my still wet eyes, but I was no longer crying; indeed, I felt light as a feather. "Please bear in mind," I said, "that I've been saving it up for thirty years."

Lindy had now retired across the room to his regular seat. "I'm going to do something I don't ordinarily do in these groups," he said. "I want to tell you, Scott, a couple of things. One is that we are very much alike, you and I. I do not want to tell you what you should do. But the other thing I do want to tell you is that I spent three years working in an inner-city ghetto. Then I had to leave. I felt what you are feeling. I felt that I owed it to society to stay in that ghetto, that someone had to be there, that it would be a cop-out if I quit. But you see, I had to get out; it was killing me. I wanted to let you know, Scotty, that I wasn't strong enough to stick it out any longer."

I began to cry again gently and with gratitude for the permission Lindy gave me. What I would decide to do with that permission I did not know.

It didn't take me long to decide.

Within a month my wife, Lily, and I were house-hunting in an area where I could establish a private practice. By Labor

Day we had found our house, and I submitted my resignation. We left Washington on November 4, four and a half months after that night I had first sobbed.

Once again I had stumbled into community; and quite apart from the joy I felt, the freedom to be myself, the experience had changed the course of my life. For the first time I became aware of the healing power of genuine community. Many are aware of this power. Many have had "peak experiences" in such settings; but since we all must return to the valley, we question whether such healing ever lasts. Many times it does not. But I can tell you that I have never been ashamed to cry since that night. Furthermore, I can now really cry—even sob again—whenever it is appropriate. On a certain level my parents were correct. I am the "world's greatest crybaby."

The vast majority of groups are not particularly healing, just as they are not genuine communities. My T-group experience was a part of the "sensitivity group movement" that swept this country in the sixties and early seventies. That movement has largely died. One of the reasons for its death is that a great many people found their sensitivity group experiences profoundly unpleasant. In the name of "sensitivity," confrontation was more encouraged than love. Frequently that confrontation was vicious. There is no doubt in my mind that the leaders of the movement were struggling toward community, but the term had not yet been defined, and they had not yet discerned the rules. Therefore community was a happenstance. Sometimes it happened, and sometimes it didn't. Just as Mac Badgely's second marathon group had failed, so I heard enough to know that the other three T-groups had been much less successful than ours. What made the difference I have no idea. I am sure that Lindy's fine, instructive leadership played a significant role. Otherwise it seemed to be simply a fortunate accident.

Although I still did not know then how or why, I did know enough by the end of June 1972 to realize that I had experienced community. I did not call it that yet, but I knew there was a connecting thread running through Friends Seminary,

Mac Badgely's group, the Tech Group on Okinawa, and Lindy's T-group in Bethel, Maine. Four times I had been a member of a group of different people who loved one another in a sustained fashion. It might never happen to me again. But I did have a dim sense that it could be a replicable phenomenon. And ever since knowing that a group of very different people loving one another was potentially repeatable, I have never been able to feel totally hopeless about the human condition.

CHAPTER II

Individuals and the Fallacy of Rugged Individualism

I am lonely.

To a degree my loneliness—and yours—is inevitable. Like you, I am an individual. And that means I am unique. There is no one else like me in this whole wide world. This "I-entity" that is me is different from each and every other "I-entity" that ever lived. Our separate *identities*, like fingerprints, make all of us unique individuals, identifiable one from another.

This is the way it must be. The very genetic code is such that (except for the rare aberration of identical twins) each of us is not only subtly different biologically from any other human being who ever existed but is substantially dissimilar. From the moment of conception. And if that were not enough, all of us are born into different environments and develop differently according to a unique pattern throughout our own individual lives.

Indeed, many believe this is not only the way it must be but is also the way it *should* be. Most Christians believe God designed it that way; He designed each soul differently. Christian theologians have reached a well-nigh universal conclusion: God loves variety. In variety He delights. And nowhere is that variety more apparent and inevitable than among the human species.

Psychologists may or may not agree with notions of divine creation, but almost all agree with the theologians that the uniqueness of our individuality is called for. They envision it as the goal of human development that we should become fully ourselves. Theologians sometimes speak of this as the call to "freedom"—the freedom to be our true individual selves as

God created us to be. The psychiatrist Carl Jung named this goal of human development "individuation." The process of human development is one of becoming fully individual.

Most of us never totally complete the process and may never get very far at all. Most, to a greater or lesser degree, fail to individuate—to separate—ourselves from family, tribe, or caste. Even into old age we remain figuratively tied to the apron strings of our parents and culture. We are still dictated to by the values and expectations of our mothers and fathers. We still follow the direction of the prevailing wind and bow before the shibboleths of our society. We go with the crowd. From laziness and fear—fear of loneliness, fear of responsibility, and other nameless dreads—we never truly learn to think for ourselves or dare to be out of step with the stereotypes. But in light of all we understand, this failure to individuate is a failure to grow up and become fully human. For we are called to be individuals. We are called to be unique and different.

We are also called to power. In this individuation process we must learn how to take responsibility for ourselves. We need to develop a sense of autonomy and self-determination. We must attempt, as best we can, to be captains of our own ships if not exactly masters of our destiny.

Furthermore, we are called to wholeness. We should use what gifts or talents we are given to develop ourselves as fully as possible. As women, we need to strengthen our masculine sides; as men, our feminine sides. If we are to grow, we must work on the weak spots that prevent growth. We are beckoned toward that self-sufficiency, that wholeness required for independence of thought and action.

But all this is only one side of the story.

It is true that we are called to wholeness. But the reality is that we can never be completely whole in and of ourselves. We cannot be all things to ourselves and to others. We cannot be perfect. We cannot be doctors, lawyers, stockbrokers, farmers, politicians, stonemasons, and theologians, all rolled into one. It is true that we are called to power. Yet the reality is that there is a point beyond which our sense of self-determination not only becomes inaccurate and prideful but increasingly self-defeating. It is true that we are created to be individually unique. Yet the reality is that we are inevitably social creatures who desperately need each other not merely for sustenance, not merely for company, but for any meaning to our lives whatsoever. These, then, are the paradoxical seeds from which community can grow.

Let me cite an experience that many of us have shared. Lily and I have struggled together for years to make our marriage something of a community of two. From the beginning of our marriage Lily was mildly disorganized. Not infrequently she would become so engrossed in smelling the flowers that she would forget an appointment or neglect to write a promised letter. I, on the other hand, from the beginning was what has been called "goal oriented"—to put it mildly. I never had time to sniff a flower unless its bloom happened to coincide with my schedule, according to which every third Thursday afternoon from two to two-thirty was designated for flower sniffing, barring rain. I used to berate Lily for her inclination to speak in what I considered to be irrelevancies as well as to ignore civilization's most significant instrument: the clock. She was equally harsh about my maddening punctuality and my stodginess and pedantic insistence on speaking in paragraphs that began "First of all," "Second," "Third," or "In conclusion." Lily believed hers was the superior psychology; I upheld the excellence of mine.

Then Lily began to raise our children and I began to write books. I do not mean to imply that I had nothing whatsoever to do with the children, but I can't pretend that I was a very good parent. I was particularly inadequate when it came to playing with them. Have you ever tried to play well with children on schedule? Or when you get off schedule and all you can think about is the chapter on religious ecstasy you had promised to write? Lily, however, played with our children with an unending grace that laid a foundation I could never have given them. I also do not mean to imply that Lily did not contribute to my books. As I wrote in the introduction to the first, "She has been so giving that it is hardly possible to distinguish her wisdom . . . from my own."* But she could not have organized her time to write (and rewrite) sentences, paragraphs, and chapters week after week, month after month.

Gradually, therefore, Lily and I have come to accept what once looked like vices as virtues, curses as blessings, liabilities as gifts. Lily has the gift of flowing; I have the gift of organization. I have not yet learned to flow with the children the way a good parent should, nor will Lily ever be completely organized. But as we have come to appreciate each other's very different styles as gifts, we have slowly begun to incorporate the other's gifts into ourselves—with great moderation of course. As a consequence she and I, as individuals, are gradually becoming more whole. Yet this would not have been possible had we not first come to terms with our individual limitations and recognized our interdependence. In fact, it is unlikely that our marriage could even have survived without this recognition.

So we are called to wholeness and simultaneously to recognition of our incompleteness; called to power *and* to acknowledge our weakness; called to both individuation *and* interdependence. Thus the problem—indeed, the total failure—of the "ethic" of rugged individualism is that it runs with only one side of this paradox, incorporates only one half of our humanity. It recognizes that we are called to individuation, power, and wholeness. But it denies entirely the other part of the human story: that we can never fully get there and that we are, of necessity in our uniqueness, weak and imperfect creatures who need each other.

This denial can be sustained only by pretense. Because we cannot ever be totally adequate, self-sufficient, independent beings, the ideal of rugged individualism encourages us to fake it. It encourages us to hide our weaknesses and failures. It teaches us to be utterly ashamed of our limitations. It drives

* *The Road Less Traveled* (New York: Simon and Schuster, 1978), p. 12.

us to attempt to be superwomen and supermen not only in the eyes of others but also in our own. It pushes us day in and day out to look as if we "had it all together," as if we were without needs and in total control of our lives. It relentlessly demands that we keep up appearances. It also relentlessly isolates us from each other. And it makes genuine community impossible.

On my lecture tours across the country the one constant I have found wherever I go—the Northeast, Southeast, Midwest, Southwest, or West Coast—is the lack of—and the thirst for—community. This lack and thirst is particularly heartbreaking in those places where one might expect to find real community: in churches. Speaking to my audiences, I often say, "Please don't ask me questions during the break times. I need those times to get my thoughts together. Besides, it has invariably been my experience that the questions you have represent concerns that others have as well and that they are best addressed in the group as a whole." But more often than not someone will come to me during the break with a question. When I say, "I thought I requested you not to," the usual response is "Yes, but, Dr. Peck, this is terribly important to me, and I can't ask it in the group because some of the members of my church are here." I wish I could say this was an exception. There are, of course, exceptions and exceptional churches. But such a remark speaks of the normal level of trust and intimacy and vulnerability in our churches and other so-called "communities."

Yes, I am lonely. Since I am an utterly unique individual, there is no one who can totally understand me, who can know exactly what it is like to walk in my shoes. And there are parts of my journey—as there are in everyone's journey—that must be walked alone. Some tasks can be accomplished only in solitude. But I am infinitely less lonely than I used to be before I learned that it was human to have feelings of anxiety and depression and helplessness, before I learned that there were places where I could share such feelings without guilt or fear and people would love me all the more for it, before I knew I could be weak in my strength and strong in my weakness, before I had experienced real community and learned how to find it or create it again.

Trapped in our tradition of rugged individualism, we are an extraordinarily lonely people. So lonely, in fact, that many cannot even acknowledge their loneliness to themselves, much less to others. Look at the sad, frozen faces all around you and search in vain for the souls hidden behind masks of makeup, masks of pretense, masks of composure. It does not have to be that way. Yet many—most—know no other way. We are desperately in need of a new ethic of "soft individualism," an understanding of individualism which teaches that we cannot be truly ourselves until we are able to share freely the things we most have in common: our weakness, our incompleteness, our imperfection, our inadequacy, our sins, our lack of wholeness and self-sufficiency. It is the understanding expressed by those in the Fellowship of Alcoholics Anonymous when they say: "I'm not OK and you're not OK, but that's OK." It is a kind of softness that allows those necessary barriers, or outlines, of our individual selves to be like permeable membranes, permitting ourselves to seep out and the selves of others to seep in. It is the kind of individualism that acknowledges our interdependence not merely in the intellectual catchwords of the day but in the very depths of our hearts. It is the kind of individualism that makes real community possible.

CHAPTER III

The True Meaning of Community

In our culture of rugged individualism—in which we generally feel that we dare not be honest about ourselves, even with the person in the pew next to us—we bandy around the word "community." We apply it to almost any collection of individuals—a town, a church, a synagogue, a fraternal organization, an apartment complex, a professional association—regardless of how poorly those individuals communicate with each other. It is a false use of the word.

If we are going to use the word meaningfully we must restrict it to a group of individuals who have learned how to communicate honestly with each other, whose relationships go deeper than their masks of composure, and who have developed some significant commitment to "rejoice together, mourn together," and to "delight in each other, make others' conditions our own." But what, then, does such a rare group look like? How does it function? What is a true definition of community?

We can define or adequately explain only those things that are smaller than we are. I have in my office, for instance, a very handy little electrical space heater. If I were an electrical engineer, I could take it apart and explain to you—define—exactly how it works. Except for one thing. That is the matter of the cord and plug that connect it with something called electricity. And there are certain questions about electricity, despite its known physical laws, that even the most advanced electrical engineer cannot answer. That is because electricity is something larger than we are.

There are many such "things": God, goodness, love, evil, death, consciousness, for instance. Being so large, they are many-faceted, and the best we can do is describe or define one facet at a time. Even so, we never seem quite able to plumb their depths fully. Sooner or later we inevitably run into a core of mystery.

Community is another such phenomenon. Like electricity, it is profoundly lawful. Yet there remains something about it that is inherently mysterious, miraculous, unfathomable. Thus there is no adequate one-sentence definition of genuine community. Community is something more than the sum of its parts, its individual members. What is this "something more?" Even to begin to answer that, we enter a realm that is not so much abstract as almost mystical. It is a realm where words are never fully suitable and language itself falls short.

The analogy of a gem comes to mind. The seeds of community reside in humanity—a social species—just as a gem originally resides in the earth. But it is not yet a gem, only a potential one. So it is that geologists refer to a gem in the rough simply as a stone. A group becomes a community in somewhat the same way that a stone becomes a gem—through a process of cutting and polishing. Once cut and polished, it is something beautiful. But to describe its beauty, the best we can do is to describe its facets. Community, like a gem, is multifaceted, each facet a mere aspect of a whole that defies description.

One other caveat. The gem of community is so exquisitely beautiful it may seem unreal to you, like a dream you once had when you were a child, so beautiful it may seem unattainable. As Bellah and his coauthors put it, the notion of community "may also be resisted as absurdly Utopian, as a project to create a perfect society. But the transformation of which we speak is both necessary and modest. Without it, indeed, there may be very little future to think about at all."* The problem is that the lack of community is so much the norm in our society, one without experience would be tempted to think, How could we possibly get there from here? It *is* possible; we *can* get there from here. Remember that to the uninitiated eye it would seem impossible for a stone ever to become a gem.

* Robert Bellah et al., *Habits of the Heart* (Berkeley, Calif.: Univ. of California Press, 1985), p. 286.

The facets of community are interconnected, profoundly interrelated. No one could exist without the other. They create each other, make each other possible. What follows, then, is but one scheme for isolating and naming the most salient characteristics of a true community.

INCLUSIVITY, COMMITMENT, AND CONSENSUS

Community is and must be inclusive.

The great enemy of community is exclusivity. Groups that exclude others because they are poor or doubters or divorced or sinners or of some different race or nationality are not communities; they are cliques—actually defensive bastions against community.

Inclusiveness is not an absolute. Long-term communities must invariably struggle over the degree to which they are going to be inclusive. Even short-term communities must sometimes make that difficult decision. But for most groups it is easier to exclude than include. Clubs and corporations give little thought to being inclusive unless the law compels them to do so. True communities, on the other hand, if they want to remain such, are always reaching to extend themselves. The burden of proof falls upon exclusivity. Communities do not ask "How can we justify taking this person in?" Instead the question is "Is it at all justifiable to keep this person out?" In relation to other groupings of similar size or purpose, communities are always relatively inclusive.

In my first experience of community at Friends Seminary, the boundaries between grades, between students and teachers, between young and old, were all "soft." There were no outgroups, no outcasts. Everyone was welcome at the parties. There was no pressure to conform. So the inclusiveness of any community extends along all its parameters. There is an "allness" to community. It is not merely a matter of including different sexes, races, and creeds. It is also inclusive of the full range of human emotions. Tears are as welcome as laughter, fear as well as faith. And different styles: hawks and doves, straights and gays, Grailers and Sears, Roebuckers, the talkative and the silent. All human differences are included. All "soft" individuality is nurtured.

How is this possible? How can such differences be absorbed, such different people coexist? Commitment—the willingness to coexist—is crucial. Sooner or later, somewhere along the line (and preferably sooner), the members of a group in some way must commit themselves to one another if they are to become or stay a community. Exclusivity, the great enemy to community, appears in two forms: excluding the other and excluding yourself. If you conclude under your breath, "Well, this group just isn't for me—they're too much this or too much that—and I'm just going to quietly pick up my marbles and go home," it would be as destructive to community as it would be to a marriage were you to conclude, "Well, the grass looks a little greener on the other side of the fence, and I'm just going to move on." Community, like marriage, requires that we hang in there when the going gets a little rough. It requires a certain degree of commitment. It is no accident that Bellah et al. subtitled their work *Individualism and Commitment in American Life*. Our individualism must be counterbalanced by commitment.

If we do hang in there, we usually find after a while that "the rough places are made plain." A friend correctly defined community as a "group that has learned to transcend its individual differences." But this learning takes time, the time that can be bought only through commitment. "Transcend" does not mean "obliterate" or "demolish." It literally means "to climb over." The achievement of community can be compared to the reaching of a mountaintop.

Perhaps the most necessary key to this transcendence is the appreciation of differences. In community, instead of being ignored, denied, hidden, or changed, human differences are celebrated as gifts. Remember how I came to appreciate Lily's "gift of flowing," and she my "gift of organization." Marriage is, of course, a small, long-term community of two. Yet in short-term communities of even fifty or sixty, while the timing and depth are almost opposite, I have found that the dynamics are the same. The transformation of attitudes toward each other that allowed Lily and me to transcend our differences took twenty years. But this same transcendence can routinely occur within a community-building group over the course of eight hours. In each case alienation is transformed into appreciation and reconciliation. And in each case the transcendence has a good deal to do with love.

We are so unfamiliar with genuine community that we have never developed an adequate vocabulary for the politics of this transcendence. When we ponder on how individual differences can be accommodated, perhaps the first mechanism we turn to (probably because it is the most childlike) is that of the strong individual leader. Differences, like those of squabbling siblings, we instinctively think can be resolved by a mommy or daddy—a benevolent dictator, or so we hope. But community, encouraging individuality as it does, can never be totalitarian. So we jump to a somewhat less primitive way of resolving individual differences which we call democracy. We take a vote, and the majority determines which differences prevail. Majority rules. Yet that process excludes the aspirations of the minority. How do we transcend differences in such a way as to include a minority? It seems like a conundrum. How and where do you go beyond democracy?

In the genuine communities of which I have been a member, a thousand or more group decisions have been made and I have never yet witnessed a vote. I do not mean to imply that we can or should discard democratic machinery, any more than we should abolish organization. But I do mean to imply that a community, in transcending individual differences, routinely goes beyond even democracy. In the vocabulary of this transcendence we thus far have only one word: "consensus." Decisions in genuine community are arrived at through consensus, in a process that is not unlike a community of jurors, for whom consensual decision making is mandated.

Still, how on earth can a group in which individuality is

encouraged, in which individual differences flourish, routinely arrive at consensus? Even when we develop a richer language for community operations, I doubt we will ever have a formula for the consensual process. The process itself is an adventure. And again there is something inherently almost mystical, magical about it. But it works. And the other facets of community will provide hints as to how it does.

REALISM

A second characteristic of community is that it is realistic. In the community of marriage, for example, when Lily and I discuss an issue, such as how to deal with one of our children, we are likely to develop a response more realistic than if either of us were operating alone. If only for this reason, I believe that it is extremely difficult for a single parent to make adequate decisions about his or her children. Even if the best Lily and I can do is to come up with two different points of view, they modulate each other. In larger communities the process is still more effective. A community of sixty can usually come up with a dozen different points of view. The resulting consensual stew, composed of multiple ingredients, is usually far more creative than a two-ingredient dish could ever be.

We are accustomed to think of group behavior as often primitive. Indeed, I myself have written about the ease with which groups can become evil.* "Mob psychology" is properly a vernacular expression. But groups of whatever kind are seldom real communities. There is, in fact, more than a quantum leap between an ordinary group and a community; they are entirely different phenomena. And a real community is, by definition, immune to mob psychology because of its encouragement of individuality, its inclusion of a variety of points of view. Time and again I have seen a community begin to make a certain decision or establish a certain norm when one of the

* M. Scott Peck, *People of the Lie: The Hope for Healing Human Evil* (New York: Simon and Schuster, 1983).

members will suddenly say, "Wait a minute, I don't think I can go along with this." Mob psychology cannot occur in an environment in which individuals are free to speak their minds and buck the trend. Community is such an environment.

Because a community includes members with many different points of view and the freedom to express them, it comes to appreciate the whole of a situation far better than an individual, couple, or ordinary group can. Incorporating the dark and the light, the sacred and the profane, the sorrow and the joy, the glory and the mud, its conclusions are well rounded. Nothing is likely to be left out. With so many frames of reference, it approaches reality more and more closely. Realistic decisions, consequently, are more often guaranteed in community than in any other human environment.

An important aspect of the realism of community deserves mention: humility. While rugged individualism predisposes one to arrogance, the "soft" individualism of community leads to humility. Begin to appreciate each others' gifts, and you begin to appreciate your own limitations. Witness others share their brokenness, and you will become able to accept your own inadequacy and imperfection. Be fully aware of human variety, and you will recognize the interdependence of humanity. As a group of people do these things—as they become a community—they become more and more humble, not only as individuals but also as a group—and hence more realistic. From which kind of group would you expect a wise, realistic decision: an arrogant one, or a humble one?

CONTEMPLATION

Among the reasons that a community is humble and hence realistic is that it is contemplative. It examines itself. It is self-aware. It knows itself. "Know thyself" is a sure rule for humility. As that fourteenth-century classic on contemplation, *The Cloud of Unknowing*, put it: "Meekness in itself is nothing else than a true knowing and feeling of a man's self as he is. Any man who truly sees and feels himself as he is must surely be meek indeed."*

The word "contemplative" has a variety of connotations. Most of them center upon awareness. The essential goal of contemplation is increased awareness of the world outside oneself, the world inside oneself, and the relationship between the two. A man who settles for a relatively limited awareness of himself could hardly be called contemplative. It is also questionable whether he could be called psychologically mature or emotionally healthy. Self-examination is the key to insight, which is the key to wisdom. Plato put it most bluntly: "The life which is unexamined is not worth living."†

The community-building process requires self-examination from the beginning. And as the members become thoughtful about themselves they also learn to become increasingly thoughtful about the group. "How are *we* doing?" they begin to ask with greater and greater frequency. "Are *we* still on target? Are *we* a healthy group? Have *we* lost the spirit?"

The spirit of community once achieved is not then something forever obtained. It is not something that can be bottled or preserved in aspic. It is repeatedly lost. Remember how, toward the end of Mac Badgely's Tavistock group in 1967, after enjoying hours of nurturing fellowship, we began to squabble again. But remember also that we were quick to recognize it because we had become aware of ourselves as a group. And because we were rapidly able to identify the cause of the problem—our division into Grailers and Sears, Roebuckers—we were rapidly able to transcend that division and recapture the spirit of community.

No community can expect to be in perpetual good health. What a genuine community does do, however, because it is a contemplative body, is recognize its ill health when it occurs and quickly take appropriate action to heal itself. Indeed, the longer they exist, the more efficient healthy communities be-

* Trans. Ira Progoff (New York: Julian Press, 1969), p. 92.
† J. W. Mackail, ed., *The Greek Anthology* (1906), Vol III, *Apology*, p. 38.

come in this recovery process. Conversely, groups that never learn to be contemplative either do not become community in the first place or else rapidly and permanently disintegrate.

A SAFE PLACE

It is no accident that I relearned "the lost art of crying" at the age of thirty-six while I was in a true community setting. Despite this relearning, my early training in rugged individualism was sufficiently effective that even today I can cry in public only when I am in a safe place. One of my joys, whenever I return to community, is that the "gift of tears" is returned to me. I am not alone. Once a group has achieved community, the single most common thing members express is: "I feel safe here."

It is a rare feeling. Almost all of us have spent nearly all of our lives feeling only partially safe, if at all. Seldom, if ever, have we felt completely free to be ourselves. Seldom, if ever, in any kind of a group, have we felt wholly accepted and acceptable. Consequently, virtually everyone enters a new group situation with his or her guard up. That guard goes very deep. Even if a conscious attempt is made to be open and vulnerable, there will still be ways in which unconscious defenses remain strong. Moreover, an initial admission of vulnerability is so likely to be met with fear, hostility, or simplistic attempts to heal or convert that all but the most courageous will retreat behind their walls.

There is no such thing as instant community under ordinary circumstances. It takes a great deal of work for a group of strangers to achieve the safety of true community. Once they succeed, however, it is as if the floodgates were opened. As soon as it is safe to speak one's heart, as soon as most people in the group know they will be listened to and accepted for themselves, years and years of pent-up frustration and hurt and guilt and grief come pouring out. And pouring out ever faster. Vulnerability in community snowballs. Once its members become vulnerable and find themselves being valued and appreciated, they become more and more vulnerable. The walls come tumbling down. And as they tumble, as the love and acceptance escalates, as the mutual intimacy multiplies, true healing and converting begins. Old wounds are healed, old resentments forgiven, old resistances overcome. Fear is replaced by hope.

So another of the characteristics of community is that it is healing and converting. Yet I have deliberately not listed that characteristic by itself, lest the subtlety of it be misunderstood. For the fact is that most of our human attempts to heal and convert prevent community. Human beings have within them a natural yearning and thrust toward health and wholeness and holiness. (All three words are derived from the same root.) Most of the time, however, this thrust, this energy, is enchained by fear, neutralized by defenses and resistances. But put a human being in a truly safe place, where these defenses and resistances are no longer necessary, and the thrust toward health is liberated. When we are safe, there is a natural tendency for us to heal and convert ourselves.

Experienced psychotherapists usually come to recognize this truth. As neophytes they see it as their task to heal the patient and often believe they succeed in doing so. With experience, however, they realize that they do not have the power to heal. But they also learn that it is within their power to listen to the patient, to accept him or her, to establish a "therapeutic relationship." So they focus not so much on healing as on making their relationship a safe place where the patient is likely to heal himself.

Paradoxically, then, a group of humans becomes healing and converting only after its members have learned to stop trying to heal and convert. Community is a safe place precisely because no one is attempting to heal or convert you, to fix you, to change you. Instead, the members accept you as you are. You are free to be you. And being so free, you are free to discard defenses, masks, disguises; free to seek your own psychological and spiritual health; free to become your whole and holy self.

A LABORATORY FOR PERSONAL DISARMAMENT

Toward the end of a two-day community experience in 1984 a late-middle-aged lady announced to the group: "I know Scotty said we weren't supposed to drop out, but when my husband and I got home yesterday evening we were seriously considering doing just that. I didn't sleep very well last night, and I almost didn't come here this morning. But something very strange has happened. Yesterday I was looking at all of you through hard eyes. Yet today for some reason—I don't really understand it—I have become soft-eyed, and it feels just wonderful."

This transformation—routine in community—is the same as that described in the story of the rabbi's gift. The decrepit monastery, a dying group, came alive (and into community) once its members began looking at each other and themselves through "soft eyes," seeing through lenses of respect. It may seem strange in our culture of rugged individualism that this transformation begins to occur precisely when we begin to "break down." As long as we look out at each other only through the masks of our composure, we are looking through hard eyes. But as the masks drop and we see the suffering and courage and brokenness and deeper dignity underneath, we truly start to respect each other as fellow human beings.

Once when I was speaking about community to the governing body of a church, one of the members wisely commented: "What I hear you saying is that community requires the confession of brokenness." He was correct of course. But how remarkable it is that in our culture brokenness must be "confessed." We think of confession as an act that should be carried out in secret, in the darkness of the confessional, with the guarantee of professional priestly or psychiatric confidentiality. Yet the reality is that every human being is broken and vulnerable. How strange that we should ordinarily feel compelled to hide our wounds when we are all wounded!

Vulnerability is a two-way street. Community requires the ability to expose our wounds and weaknesses to our fellow creatures. It also requires the capacity to be affected by the wounds of others, to be wounded by their wounds. This is what the woman meant by "soft eyes." Her eyes were no longer barriers, and she did, indeed, feel wonderful. There is pain in our wounds. But even more important is the love that arises among us when we share, both ways, our woundedness. Still, we cannot deny the reality that this sharing requires a risk in our culture—the risk of violating the norm of pretended invulnerability. For most of us it is a new—and, seemingly, potentially dangerous—form of behavior.

It may seem odd to refer to community as a *laboratory*. The word implies a sterile place filled not with softness but with hardware. A laboratory can better be defined, however, as a place designed to be safe for experiments. We need such a place, because when we experiment we are trying out—testing—new ways of doing things. So it is in community: it is a safe place to experiment with new types of behavior. When offered the opportunity of such a safe place, most people will naturally begin to experiment more deeply than ever before with love and trust. They drop their customary defenses and threatened postures, the barriers of distrust, fear, resentment, and prejudice. They experiment with disarming themselves. They experiment with peace—peace within themselves and within the group. And they discover that the experiment works.

An experiment is designed to give us new *experience* from which we can extract new wisdom. So it is that in experimenting with personally disarming themselves, the members of a true community *experientially* discover the rules of peacemaking and learn its virtues. It is a personal experience so powerful that it can become the driving force behind the quest for peace on a global scale.

A GROUP THAT CAN FIGHT GRACEFULLY

It may at first glance seem paradoxical that a community that is a safe place and a laboratory for disarmament should also be a place of conflict. Perhaps a story will help. A Sufi master was strolling through the streets one day with his students. When they came to the city square, a vicious battle was being fought between government troops and rebel forces. Horrified by the bloodshed, the students implored, "Quick, Master, which side should we help?"

"Both," the Master replied.

The students were confused. "Both?" they demanded. "Why should we help both?"

"We need to help the authorities learn to listen to the aspirations of the people," the Master answered, "and we need to help the rebels learn how not to compulsively reject authority."

In genuine community there are no sides. It is not always easy, but by the time they reach community the members have learned how to give up cliques and factions. They have learned how to listen to each other and how not to reject each other. Sometimes consensus in community is reached with miraculous rapidity. But at other times it is arrived at only after lengthy struggle. Just because it is a safe place does not mean community is a place without conflict. It is, however, a place where conflict can be resolved without physical or emotional bloodshed and with wisdom as well as grace. A community is a group that can fight gracefully.

That this is so is hardly accidental. For community is an amphitheater where the gladiators have laid down their weapons and their armor, where they have become skilled at listening and understanding, where they respect each others' gifts and accept each others' limitations, where they celebrate their differences and bind each others' wounds, where they are committed to a struggling together rather than against each other. It is a most unusual battleground indeed. But that is also why it is an unusually effective ground for conflict resolution.

The significance of this is hardly slight. There are very real conflicts in the world, and the worst of them do not seem to go away. But there is a fantasy abroad. Simply stated, it goes like this: "If we can resolve our conflicts, then someday we shall be able to live together in community." Could it be that we have it totally backward? And that the real dream should be: "If we can live together in community, then someday we shall be able to resolve our conflicts"?

A GROUP OF ALL LEADERS

When I am the designated leader I have found that once a group becomes a community, my nominal job is over. I can sit back and relax and be one among many, for another of the essential characteristics of community is a total decentralization of authority. Remember that it is antitotalitarian. Its decisions are reached by consensus. Communities have sometimes been referred to as leaderless groups. It is more accurate, however, to say that a community is a group of all leaders.

Because it is a safe place, compulsive leaders feel free in community—often for the first time in their lives—to *not* lead. And the customarily shy and reserved feel free to step forth with their latent gifts of leadership. The result is that a community is an ideal decision-making body. The expression "A camel is a horse created by a committee" does not mean that group decisions are inevitably clumsy and imperfect; it does mean that committees are virtually never communities.

So it was in 1983 when I needed to make some difficult major decisions in my life—so difficult that I knew I was not intelligent enough to make them alone even with expert advice. I asked for help, and twenty-eight women and men came to my aid from around the country. Quite properly, we spent the first 80 percent of our three days together building ourselves into a community. Only in the last few hours did we turn our attention to the decisions that needed to be made. And they were made with the speed and brilliance of lightning.

One of the most beautiful characteristics of community is what I have come to call the "flow of leadership." It is because of this flow that our community in 1983 was able to make its decisions so rapidly and effectively. And because its members felt free to express themselves, it was as if their individual gifts were offered at just the right moment in the decision-making process. So one member stepped forward with part A of the solution. And since the community recognized the wisdom of the gift, everyone deferred to it so that instantly, almost magically, a second member was free to step forward with part B of the solution. And so it flowed around the room.

The flow of leadership in community is routine. It is a phenomenon that has profound implications for anyone who would seek to improve organizational decision making—in business, government, or elsewhere. But it is not a quick trick or fix. Community must be built first. Traditional hierarchical patterns have to be at least temporarily set aside. Some kind of control must be relinquished. For it is a situation in which it is the spirit of community itself that leads and not any single individual.

A SPIRIT

Community *is* a spirit—but not in the way that the familiar phrase "community spirit" is usually understood. To most of us it implies a competitive spirit, a jingoistic boosterism, such as that displayed by fans of winning football teams or the citizens of a town in which they take great pride. "Our town is better than your town" might be taken as a typical expression of community spirit.

But this understanding of the spirit of community is profoundly misleading as well as dreadfully shallow. In only one respect is it accurate. The members of a group who have achieved genuine community do take pleasure—even delight— in themselves as a collective. They know they have won something together, collectively discovered something of great value, that they are "onto something." Beyond that the similarity ends. There is nothing competitive, for instance, about the spirit of true community. To the contrary, a group possessed by a spirit of competitiveness is by definition not a community. Competitiveness is always exclusive; genuine community is inclusive. If community has enemies, it has begun to lose the spirit of community—if it ever had it in the first place.

The spirit of true community is the spirit of peace. People in the early stages of a community-building workshop will frequently ask, "How will we know when we are a community?" It is a needless question. When a group enters community there is a dramatic change in spirit. And the new spirit is almost palpable. There is no mistaking it. No one who has experienced it need ever ask again "How will we know when we are a community?"

Nor will one ever question that it is a spirit of peace that prevails when a group enters community. An utterly new quietness descends on the group. People seem to speak more quietly; yet, strangely, their voices seem to carry better through the room. There are periods of silence, but it is never an uneasy silence. Indeed, the silence is welcomed. It feels tranquil. Nothing is frantic anymore. The chaos is over. It is as if noise had been replaced by music. The people listen and can hear. It is peaceful.

But spirit is slippery. It does not submit itself to definition, to capture, the way material things do. So it is that a group in community does not always feel peaceful in the usual sense of the word. Its members will from time to time struggle with each other, and struggle hard. The struggle may become excited and exuberant with little, if any, room for silence. But it is a productive, not a destructive, struggle. It always moves toward consensus, because it is always a loving struggle. It takes place on a ground of love. The spirit of community is inevitably the spirit of peace and love.

The "atmosphere" of love and peace is so palpable that almost every community member experiences it as a spirit. Hence, even the agnostic and atheist members will generally report a community-building workshop as a spiritual experience. How this experience is interpreted, however, is highly variable. Those with a secular consciousness tend to assume that the spirit of community is no more than a creation of the group itself; and beautiful though it may be, they will leave it at that. Most Christians, on the other hand, tend toward a more complicated understanding.

In the latter frame of reference the spirit of community is not envisioned as a purely human spirit or one created solely by the group. It is assumed to be external to and independent of the group. It therefore is thought of as descending upon the group, just as the Holy Spirit is said to have descended upon Jesus at his baptism in the form of a dove. This does not mean, however, that the spirit's visitation is accidental or unpredictable. It can fall upon and take root only in fertile, prepared ground. Thus for those of Christian orientation the work of community building is seen as preparation for the descent of the Holy Spirit. The spirit of community is a manifestation of the Holy Spirit.

This does not mean that community is solely a Christian phenomenon. I have seen community develop among Christians and Jews, Christians and atheists, Jews and Muslims, Muslims and Hindus. People of any religious persuasion or none whatever can develop community. Nor does it mean that a belief in Christianity is a guarantee of community. It is reported that some men saw Jesus' disciples casting out demons in his name, and they thought that this was an easy formula. So with no more thought, they went up to some demoniacs and shouted, "Jesus, Jesus, Jesus." But absolutely nothing happened, except that the demons laughed at them.

So it is with groups. A group of Christians who are not prepared can sit around shouting "Jesus, Jesus, Jesus" until they are blue in the face, and nothing will happen. They will move no closer to community. On the other hand, any group of people (no matter what their religious persuasion or whether the word "Jesus" is ever spoken) who are willing to practice the love, discipline, and sacrifice that are required for the spirit of community, that Jesus extolled and exemplified, will be gathered together in his name and he will be there.

My own frame of reference is Christian, and for me, therefore, the spirit of community, which is the spirit of peace and love, is also the spirit of Jesus. But the Christian understanding of community would go even beyond this. The doctrine of the Trinity—of three in one—holds that Jesus, God, and the Holy Spirit, while separate in one sense are the same in another. So when I talk of Jesus being present in community, I am also speaking of the presence of God and the Holy Spirit.

In Christian thought the Holy Spirit is particularly identified with wisdom. Wisdom is envisioned as a kind of revelation. To the secular mind we humans, through thought, study, and the assimilation of experience, arrive at wisdom. It is our own achievement. We somehow earn it. While Christian thinkers hardly denigrate the value of thought, study, and experience, they believe that something more is involved in the creation of wisdom. Specifically, they believe wisdom to be a gift of God and the Holy Spirit.

The wisdom of a true community often seems miraculous. This wisdom can perhaps be explained in purely secular terms as a result of the freedom of expression, the pluralistic talents, the consensual decision making that occur in community. There are times, however, when this wisdom seems to my religious eye to be more a matter of divine spirit and possible divine intervention. This is one of the reasons why the feeling of joy is such a frequent concomitant of the spirit of community. The members feel that they have been temporarily—at least partially—transported out of the mundane world of ordinary preoccupations. For the moment it is as if heaven and earth had somehow met.

CHAPTER IV

The Genesis of Community

CRISIS AND COMMUNITY

Genuine communities of a sort frequently develop in response to crisis. Strangers in the waiting room of an intensive-care ward suddenly come to share each other's hopes and fears and joys and griefs as their loved ones lie across the hall on the "critical list."

On a larger scale, in the course of a minute a distant earthquake causes buildings to crumble and crush thousands of people to death in Mexico City. Suddenly rich and poor alike are working together night and day to rescue the injured and care for the homeless. Meanwhile men and women of all nations open their pocketbooks and their hearts to a people they have never seen, much less met, in a sudden consciousness of our common humanity.

The problem is that once the crisis is over, so—virtually always—is the community. The collective spirit goes out of the people as they return to their ordinary individual lives, and community is lost. Yet community is so beautiful that the time of crisis is often mourned. Many Russians speak with great feeling about the brutal days of the siege of Leningrad, when they all pulled together. American veterans still remember the muddy foxholes of World War II, when they had a depth of comradeship and meaning in their lives they have never since been quite able to recapture.

The most successful community in this nation—probably in the whole world—is Alcoholics Anonymous, the "Fellowship of AA." In June 1935 Bill W. started the first AA group in Akron, Ohio. Today, a mere two generations later, there are AA groups—and Alanon groups and Alateen groups and Overeaters Anonymous groups and Emotions Anonymous groups, and other such groups—in every hamlet of the country. Through the community of AA and similar fellowships modeled on it, millions upon millions have received healing, millions upon millions have found meaning in their lives. And all this has been done with virtually no organization, the founders having brilliantly sensed that excessive organization is antithetical to community. There are no dues, no budgets, no buildings. Yet no other phenomenon has had such an impact for good in the nation.

As with the victims of a natural disaster, AA starts with people in crisis. Men and women come to it in a moment of breaking. They come to it because they realize that they do not "have it all together," that they are in need, that they can no longer go it alone. Yet it would be a mistake to think of alcoholics as a truly special breed. Because it has become a safe place in which to reveal themselves, all men and women in genuine community sooner or later confess their brokenness. We are all wounded. None of us really has it all together. None of us can really go it alone. We are all in need, in crisis, although most of us still seek to hide the reality of our brokenness from ourselves and one another. The men and women of AA can no longer hide their alcoholism; they must confess their brokenness. Crisis is a built-in condition of the AA community, and in that sense alcoholism may be a blessing.

The men and women in the Fellowship of AA have chosen with great grace and wisdom to augment this blessing. For they early developed the tradition of referring to themselves not as "former alcoholics" or "recovered alcoholics" but always as "recovering alcoholics." What they mean by this term is that the crisis is omnipresent. Recovery is never complete. The danger of relapse is always there. So also is the need for community and the omnipresent opportunity for psychospiritual growth. Recognition of the continuing crisis of alcoholism is part of the genius of AA.

The remarkable success of AA suggests that if we recognized that crisis is an everyday event in our lives, it would make community a matter of routine. It may seem strange that we should want to look at our lives as an everyday crisis. But I am reminded of the Chinese word for crisis, which consists of two characters: one represents "danger" and the other "hidden opportunity." Certainly we should like our lives to be ones of daily opportunity. Moreover, there is a profound although little understood reality of psychological health. Contrary to what many might believe, the healthy life is hardly one marked by an absence of crises. In fact, an individual's psychological health is distinguished by how *early* he or she can meet crisis.

The word crisis is fashionably used these days in the term "midlife crisis." But long before this term was invented the phenomenon was recognized in women as a frequent element of the menopause. While it was common for some women to become depressed during menopause, it was hardly inevitable. What happens to a psychologically healthy woman, to cite an admittedly oversimplified example, is that one day in her mid-twenties, perhaps, she looks in the mirror, sees the beginning of crow's feet at the corners of her eyes, and thinks to herself, You know, I don't think that the Hollywood talent scout is going to come around. That same woman in her mid-thirties, when her youngest child starts kindergarten, muses, Maybe I ought to start doing something other than make the children the sole focus of my life. So she begins the difficult process of developing a second career. Then, in her mid-fifties when her periods cease, with the exception of hot flashes (which can be annoying enough), she is likely to sail easily and happily through menopause because she had negotiated the crisis twenty years before.

The woman likely to get into serious difficulty, however, is the one who tries to put off the crisis, who holds onto the fantasy that the Hollywood talent scout is still going to come around, and who does not work on developing any significant interest in her life beyond her children. Is it any wonder, then, that around the time her periods stop (which is also the time when no amount of makeup can hide the wrinkles and her children have departed home, leaving her not only with an empty nest but also an empty life style) she should fall apart?

I use the above example not to stereotype either women or the problems of midlife. While the flavor may be different, the problems of midlife are as intense for men and can be handled equally well or equally poorly. These are not easy problems. But they demonstrate the point that the healthy life consists of meeting and resolving crises as early as possible so that we can get on to the next one. Oddly, the best measure of psychospiritual health is how many crises we can cram into a lifetime.

There is a dreadful form of psychiatric disorder that compels its victims to lead destructively histrionic lives. The far more common curse, however, is for us human beings to fail to live our lives with a proper sense of drama. Here those people with an active religious bent have another advantage. Secular people have plain ups and downs in their lives, while we religious get to have "spiritual crises." It is much more dignified, or so it would seem, to have a spiritual crisis than a depression. It is also often the more appropriate way of looking at things. But, in fact, all psychological problems can be seen as crises of the human spirit. In my practice of psychotherapy, more often than not I have to work quite hard to teach people a sense of their own importance and dramatic significance.

We do not have to manufacture crises in our lives; we have merely to recognize that they exist. Indeed, we must recognize that we live in a time in which our need for community has itself become critical. But we have a choice. We can keep on pretending that this is not so. We can continue refusing to face the crisis until the day when we individually and collectively destroy ourselves and our planet. We can avoid community until the end. Or we can wake up to the drama of our lives and begin to take the steps necessary to save them.

COMMUNITY BY ACCIDENT

Because our need—our subliminal yearning—for it is so compelling, we sometimes fall into community by accident, even when there is no apparent crisis. This is what happened to me and others in Mac Badgely's group, in the Tech Group in Okinawa, and in Lindy's T-group in Bethel, Maine. It was a hit-or-miss sort of affair, however. Remember that Mac's other group and the other T-groups did not become communities. Sometimes it happened; sometimes it didn't.

It was one such accidental happening that revived my interest in the concept of community. In 1981 I was invited by George Washington University to conduct a workshop on the subject of "spiritual growth." Never having been an academician or serious scholar, I felt uneasy about my qualifications in an academic environment. Serendipitously, however, several months before this workshop I had occasion to read an article in an impressively scholarly journal which had some bearing on the subject. Entitled "Education as Transformation: Becoming a Healer Among the ! Kung and Fijians," the article, written by anthropologist Richard Katz, depicted the spiritual journey of those designated as healers in these two "primitive" societies at opposite ends of the world.* The theologies of these cultures were remarkably different. What therefore struck me was that the dynamics of the spiritual journey of the two types of healers were the same. Not only that, they were also the same as the dynamics of the spiritual journey undertaken by many Christian monks and nuns and others in our own culture. It occurred to me that this article was not only relevant to the workshop I was scheduled to conduct but also that it would duly

* Richard Katz, "Education and Transformation: Becoming a Healer Among the ! Kung and Fijians," *Harvard Educational Review*, Vol. 51, No. 1 (1981).

impress the sixty scheduled participants with my erudition. I ordered sixty copies and took them with me.

I began the workshop by giving each participant a copy of the article and half an hour to read it. Then I asked them to meditate upon it in silence for ten minutes. Finally, as we all sat around in a circle, I requested them to begin discussing the article among themselves and told them I would pick up on the themes of their discussion.

I thought it would be very safe and intellectual.

As the discussion began, the members of the group immediately appreciated the similarity of the dynamics of the spiritual journeys of the ! Kung, the Fijians, and themselves. But that was not the theme. It barely interested them. What rapidly emerged, however, was their profound *envy* of the healers in these "primitive" societies.

It turned out that virtually all the participants in this workshop were teachers, nurses, therapists, or ministers: professional healers themselves. Living and working in urban Washington or its "bedroom communities," they felt profoundly isolated from their own society and those they served. The ! Kung and the Fijian healers, as they were described in the article, lived with their patients in small, integrated rural groupings. As the members of the group spoke of the ! Kung and Fijians, their eyes were filled with yearning. The focus of the workshop quickly became their own shrieking loneliness.

It was not intellectual.

It was, however, powerful, moving, healing, and deeply satisfying. Because, yearning for community, we stumbled, under the guise of an intellectual workshop, into just what our hearts were most thirsting for. We *became* a community, and even though it was only for a few brief, wonderful hours, we experienced a surcease of our loneliness.

In fact, all the previous intellectual workshops I had conducted paled in significance, power, and educational value before this one, where we had accidentally—almost miraculously—achieved community. And from that moment on, I was confronted with a challenge: Could I lead future workshops in such a manner that the miracle of community would predictably happen again? Could groups be brought into community not by crisis, not by accident, but by deliberate design?

COMMUNITY BY DESIGN

The answer is yes.

I have referred to community as a miracle. Almost by definition we do not think of miracles as being predictable or controllable. Rather, they are intrusions of the extraordinary into the ordinary. And in our society the occurrence of community is still rare—indeed, an extraordinary happening in the ordinary course of things. A miracle is also defined as a phenomenon not explainable by natural law. But that does not mean they are unlawful. Perhaps miracles simply obey laws that we humans generally and currently do not understand.

Whether the occurrence of community is or is not a miracle, after that Sunday workshop in Washington, I deliberately set out to replicate the occurrence whenever I had the opportunity. I began to conduct "community-building workshops" with frequency. And although a lot of what I have done in this regard has been by trial and error (and I am still learning), I have been able to reach a number of conclusions with such a degree of certainty that I know them to be facts.

The most basic are these:

1. The process by which a group of human beings becomes a community is a lawful process. Whenever a group functions in accord with certain quite clear laws or rules it will become a genuine community.

2. The words "communicate" and "community," although verb and noun, come from the same root. The principles of good communication are the basic principles of community-building. And because people do not naturally know how to communicate, because humans have not yet learned how to talk with each other, they remain ignorant of the laws or rules of genuine community.

3. In certain situations people may unconsciously stumble onto the rules of communication or community. That is what occurred in the communities I have already described. Since the process is unconscious, however, people do not consciously learn these rules as a result and therefore immediately forget how to practice them.

4. The rules of communication and community-building can be simply taught and learned with relative ease. This conscious learning allows people to remember the rules and practice them at a later date.

5. Learning can be passive or experiential. Experiential learning is more demanding but infinitely more effective. As with other things, the rules of communication and community are best learned experientially.

6. The vast majority of people are capable of learning the rules of communication and community-building and are willing to follow them. In other words, if they know what they are doing, virtually any group of people can form themselves into a genuine community.

I am able to state the above conclusions as facts because, since the George Washington University experience in 1981, I have conducted scores of community-building workshops. Almost all of them have had their difficult moments. Ultimately, however, every one was a success; each and every group succeeded in becoming a community—unlike the sensitivity-group days, when community seemed to be a hit-or-miss sort of affair. This success has little or nothing to do with my particular personality. While it may be true that not everyone can be a successful community-building leader, other selected women and men whom I have trained in the principles of community have not only had similar success but are themselves already engaged in training others.

What are these principles, these laws and rules? The basic ones can best be elucidated by describing the stages of the community-making process. To these stages we now turn. However, beware. It has always been quite common—and perhaps comfortable—for people to complain, "I don't have any community in my life." As long as community is an accidental happening, such complaints may well be justified. But with the knowledge of these rules—demanding though they are—it may no longer be so pardonable to yearn for community without doing something about it.

CHAPTER V

Stages of Community-Making

Communities, like individuals, are unique. Still we all share the human condition. So it is that groups assembled deliberately to form themselves into community routinely go through certain stages in the process. These stages, in order, are:

> Pseudocommunity
> Chaos
> Emptiness
> Community

Not every group that becomes a community follows this paradigm exactly. Communities that temporarily form in response to crisis, for instance, may skip over one or more stages for the time being. I do not insist that community development occur by formula. But in the process of community-making by design, this is the natural, usual order of things.*

PSEUDOCOMMUNITY

The first response of a group in seeking to form a community is most often to try to fake it. The members attempt to be an instant community by being extremely pleasant with one another and avoiding all disagreement. This attempt—this pre-

---

* Others who have worked extensively with groups that have become communities have discerned that there are stages of the developmental process. Among group leaders there is even a mnemonic about such stages: "Forming, Storming, Norming, Performing." But this simple formula, while not useless, is at best incomplete.

tense of community—is what I term "pseudocommunity." It never works.

I was quite nonplussed when I first encountered pseudocommunity—particularly since it was created by experts. It occurred during a workshop in Greenwich Village, in lower Manhattan, whose members, to a person, were highly sophisticated, achievement-oriented New Yorkers. Many had undergone extensive psychoanalysis, and they were all accustomed to being "unspontaneously vulnerable." Within minutes they were sharing deep, intimate details of their lives. And during the very first break they were already hugging. Poof—instant community!

But something was missing. At first I was delighted, and I thought, Boy, this is a piece of cake. I don't have to worry about a thing. But by the middle of the day I began to grow uneasy, and it was impossible to put my finger on the problem. I didn't have the wonderful, joyful, excited feeling I had always had in community. I was, in fact, slightly bored. Yet to all intents and purposes the group seemed to be behaving just like a real community. I didn't know what to do. I didn't even know whether I ought to do anything. So I let it slide for the rest of the day.

I did not sleep well that night. Near dawn, still having no idea whether it was the right thing to do, I decided I owed it to the group to disclose my sense of unease. When we assembled the second morning I began by saying, "You're an unusually sophisticated group of people. I think that's why we seemed to become a community so quickly and easily yesterday morning. But perhaps it was too quick and too easy. I have a strange feeling that something's missing, that we're really not a community yet. Let's have a period of silence now and see how we will respond to it."

Respond the group did! Within five minutes of the end of the silence these seemingly mellow, affectionate people were almost at one another's throats. Dozens of interpersonal resentments from the previous day surfaced practically simultaneously. Fast and furiously the members began clobbering each other with their different ideologies and theologies. It was glorious chaos! And finally we were able to begin the work of building real community, which, by the end of the workshop we succeeded in doing. But until that point of chaos the group, with all its sophistication, had succeeded only in delaying the process for a whole day.

There are two morals to this story. One is: Beware of instant community. Community-making requires time as well as effort and sacrifice. It cannot be cheaply bought. The other moral is that it is at least as easy to build community among unsophisticated people as among the sophisticated. I have never seen the community-making process work more rapidly and effectively, for instance, than among a group of civic leaders of a small Midwestern city who had almost no psychological training. The sophisticated, on the other hand, may be more adept at faking.

In pseudocommunity a group attempts to purchase community cheaply by pretense. It is not an evil, conscious pretense of deliberate black lies. Rather, it is an unconscious, gentle process whereby people who want to be loving attempt to be so by telling little white lies, by withholding some of the truth about themselves and their feelings in order to avoid conflict. But it is still a pretense. It is an inviting but illegitimate shortcut to nowhere

The essential dynamic of pseudocommunity is conflict-avoidance. The absence of conflict in a group is not by itself diagnostic. Genuine communities may experience lovely and sometimes lengthy periods free from conflict. But that is because they have learned how to deal with conflict rather than avoid it. Pseudocommunity is conflict-avoiding; true community is conflict-resolving.

What is diagnostic of pseudocommunity is the minimization, the lack of acknowledgment, or the ignoring of individual differences. Nice people are so accustomed to being well mannered that they are able to deploy their good manners without even thinking about what they are doing. In pseudocommunity it is as if every individual member is operating according to the same book of etiquette. The rules of this book are: Don't do or say anything that might offend someone else; if someone does or says something that offends, annoys, or irritates you, act as if nothing has happened and pretend you are not bothered in the least; and if some form of disagreement should show signs of appearing, change the subject as quickly and smoothly as possible—rules that any good hostess knows. It is easy to see how these rules make for a smoothly functioning group. But they also crush individuality, intimacy, and honesty, and the longer it lasts the duller it gets.

The basic pretense of pseudocommunity is the denial of individual differences. The members pretend—act as if—they all have the same belief in Jesus Christ, the same understanding of the Russians, even the same life history. One of the characteristics of pseudocommunity is that people tend to speak in generalities. "Divorce is a miserable experience," they will say. Or "One has to trust one's instincts." Or "We need to accept that our parents did the best they could." Or "Once you've found God, then you don't need to be afraid anymore." Or "Jesus has saved us from our sins."

Another characteristic of pseudocommunity is that the members will let one another get away with such blanket statements. Individuals will think to themselves, I found God twenty years ago and I'm still scared, but why let the group know that? To avoid the risk of conflict they keep their feelings to themselves and even nod in agreement, as if a speaker has uttered some universal truth. Indeed, the pressure to skirt any kind of disagreement may be so great that even the very experienced communicators in the group—who know perfectly well that speaking in generalities is destructive to genuine communication—may be inhibited from challenging what they know is wrong. The effect of this inhibition is such that the proverbial observer from Mars would conclude from pseudocommunity that while human beings look very different on the outside, they are all the same on the inside. The observer might also conclude that human beings are boring.

In my experience most groups that refer to themselves as

"communities" are, in fact, pseudocommunities. Think about whether the expression of individual differences is encouraged or discouraged, for instance, in the average church congregation. Is the kind of conformism I have described in the first stage of community-making the norm or the exception in our society? Could there be many people who do not even know that there is anything beyond pseudocommunity?

Since that workshop in Greenwich Village I've found it not only easy to recognize pseudocommunity but also to nip it in the bud. Often all that is required is to challenge the platitudes or generalizations. When Mary says, "Divorce is a terrible thing," I am likely to comment: "Mary, you're making a generalization. I hope you don't mind my using you as an example for the group, but one of the things people need to learn to communicate well is how to speak personally—how to use 'I' and 'my' statements. I wonder if you couldn't rephrase your statement to 'My divorce was a terrible thing for me.' "

"All right," Mary agrees. "My divorce was a terrible thing for me."

"I'm glad you put it that way, Mary," Theresa is likely to say, "because my divorce was the best thing that ever happened to me in the last twenty years."

Once individual differences are not only allowed but encouraged to surface in some such way, the group almost immediately moves to the second stage of community development: chaos.

CHAOS

The chaos always centers around well-intentioned but misguided attempts to heal and convert. Let me cite a prototypical example. After a period of uneasy silence a member will say, "Well, the reason I came to this workshop is that I have such-and-such a problem, and I thought I might find a solution to it here."

"I had that problem once," a second member will respond. "I did such-and-such, and it took care of the difficulty."

"Well, I tried that," the first member answers, "but it didn't solve anything."

"When I acknowledged Jesus to be my Lord and Savior," a third member announces, "it took care of that problem and every other problem I had."

"I'm sorry," says the first member, "but that Jesus Lord-and-Savior stuff just doesn't grab me. It's not where I'm at."

"No," says a fourth member. "As a matter of fact, it makes me want to puke."

"But it's *true*," proclaims a fifth member.

And so they're off.

By and large, people resist change. So the healers and converters try harder to heal or convert, until finally their victims get their backs up and start trying to heal the healers and convert the converters. It is indeed chaos.

Chaos is not just a state, it is an essential part of the process of community development. Consequently, unlike pseudocommunity, it does not simply go away as soon as the group becomes aware of it. After a period of chaos, when I remark, "We don't seem to be doing very well at community, do we?" someone will reply, "No, and it's because of this."

"No, it's because of that," someone else will say. And so they're off again.

In the stage of chaos individual differences are, unlike those in pseudocommunity, right out in the open. Only now, instead of trying to hide or ignore them, the group is attempting to obliterate them. Underlying the attempts to heal and convert is not so much the motive of love as the motive to make everyone *normal*—and the motive to win, as the members fight over whose norm might prevail.

The desire to convert, however, does not necessarily center around issues of theology. The stage of chaos in the group of civic leaders I previously mentioned revolved around the different plans of the members to benefit their city. One felt her plan to house the homeless was the way. Another saw the labor-management relations board as the most critical focus. Another believed the program to curb child abuse was more essential. So these well-motivated men and women clobbered each other over the head with their own pet projects; each wanted his or her particular project to win or prevail, and each attempted to convert the others to his or her way.

The stage of chaos is a time of fighting and struggle. But that is not its essence. Frequently, fully developed communities will be required to fight and struggle. Only they have learned to do so effectively. The struggle during chaos is chaotic. It is not merely noisy, it is uncreative, unconstructive. The disagreement that arises from time to time in a genuine community is loving and respectful and usually remarkably quiet— even peaceful—as the members work hard to listen to each other. Still, upon occasion in a fully mature community the discussion might become heated. Yet even then it is vivacious, and one has a feeling of excitement over the consensus that will be hammered out. Not so in chaos. If anything, chaos, like pseudocommunity, is boring, as the members continually swat at each other to little or no effect. It has no grace or rhythm. Indeed, the predominant feeling an observer is likely to have in response to a group in the chaotic stage of development is despair. The struggle is going nowhere, accomplishing nothing. It is no fun.

Since chaos is unpleasant, it is common for the members of a group in this stage to attack not only each other but also their leader. "We wouldn't be squabbling like this if we had effective leadership," they will say. "We deserve more direction than you've been giving us, Scotty." In some sense they are quite correct; their chaos is a natural response to a relative lack of direction. The chaos could easily be circumvented by an authoritarian leader—a dictator—who assigned them specific tasks and goals. The only problem is that a group led by a dictator is not, and never can be, a community. Community and totalitarianism are incompatible.

In response to this perceived vacuum of leadership during the chaotic stage of community development, it is common for one or more members of the group to attempt to replace the designated leader. He or she (usually it is a he) will say, "Look, this is getting us nowhere. Why don't we go around the circle counterclockwise and each person say something about himself or herself?" Or "Why don't we break into small groups of six or eight, and then we can get somewhere?" Or "Why don't we form a subcommittee to develop a definition of community? Then we will know where we're going."

The problem of the emergence of such "secondary leaders" is not their emergence but their proposed solutions. What they are proposing, one way or another, is virtually always an "escape into organization." It is true that organizing is a solution to chaos. Indeed, that is the primary reason for organization: to minimize chaos. The trouble is, however, that organization and community are also incompatible. Committees and chairpeople do not a community make. I am not implying that it is impossible for a business, church, or some other organization to have a degree of community within itself. I am not an anarchist. But an organization is able to nurture a measure of community within itself only to the extent that it is willing to risk or tolerate a certain lack of structure. As long as the goal is community-building, organization as an attempted solution to chaos is an unworkable solution.

The duration of the chaotic stage of community development varies, depending on the nature of the leader and the nature of the group. Some groups will leave it behind almost as soon as I point the way out. Even though chaos is unpleasant, other groups will resist its proper resolution for a number of painful hours. Back in the sensitivity-group days there were a number of groups that languished in unproductive chaos for their entire existence.

The proper resolution of chaos is not easy. Because it is both unproductive and unpleasant, it may seem that the group has *degenerated* from pseudocommunity into chaos. But chaos is not necessarily the worst place for a group to be. Several years ago I had the opportunity to consult briefly with a large church that was in chaos. A few years before, the congregation had chosen a dynamic new minister to lead it. His style of leadership turned out to be even more assertive than they had bargained for. By the time I visited, over a third of the congregation had been deeply alienated by this style, but the majority was delighted with it. The disagreement was quite vocal, and the membership was in real pain over the schism. Yet in their outspokenness, their open suffering, and their commitment to hang in there as they struggled with each other I sensed a great deal of vitality. I was hardly able to suggest any immediate solution. But I was at least able to offer some consolation by telling them that I sensed more vitality in their congregation than most church bodies. "Your chaos," I explained to them, "is preferable to pseudocommunity. You are not a healthy community, but you are able to confront the issues openly. Fighting is far better than pretending you are not divided. It's painful, but it's a beginning. You are aware that you need to move beyond your warring factions, and that's infinitely more hopeful than if you felt you didn't need to move at all."

EMPTINESS

"There are only two ways out of chaos," I will explain to a group after it has spent a sufficient period of time squabbling and getting nowhere. "One is into organization—but organization is never community. The only other way is into and through emptiness."

More often than not the group will simply ignore me and go on squabbling. Then after another while I will say, "I suggested to you that the only way from chaos to community is into and through emptiness. But apparently you were not terribly interested in my suggestion." More squabbling, but finally a member will ask with a note of annoyance, "Well, what is this emptiness stuff anyway?"

It is no accident that groups are not generally eager to pick up on my suggestion of emptiness. The fact that "emptiness" is a mystical sort of word and concept is not the deterrent. People are smart, and often in the dimmer recesses of their consciousness they know more than they want to know. As soon as I mention "emptiness," they have a presentiment of what is to come. And they are in no hurry to accept it.

Emptiness is the hard part. It is also the most crucial stage of community development. It is the bridge between chaos and community.

When the members of a group finally ask me to explain what I mean by emptiness, I tell them simply that they need to empty themselves of barriers to communication. And I am able to use their behavior during chaos to point out to them specific things—feelings, assumptions, ideas, and motives—that have so filled their minds as to make them impervious as billiard balls. The process of emptying themselves of these barriers is the key to the transition from "rugged" to "soft" individualism. The most common (and interrelated) barriers to communication that people need to empty themselves of before they can enter genuine community are:

Expectations and Preconceptions. Community-building is an adventure, a going into the unknown. People are routinely terrified of the emptiness of the unknown. Consequently they fill their minds with generally false expectations of what the experience will be like. In fact, we humans seldom go into any situation without preconceptions. We then try to make the experience conform to our expectations. Occasionally this is useful behavior, but usually (and always in regard to community-building) it is destructive. Until such time as we can empty ourselves of expectations and stop trying to fit others and our relationships with them into a preconceived mold we cannot really listen, hear, or experience. "Life is what happens when you've planned something else," someone once wisely put it. But despite this wisdom, we still do not go easily into new situations with an open (and empty) mind.

Prejudices. Prejudice, which is probably more often unconscious than conscious, comes in two forms. One is the judgments we make about people without any experience of them whatsoever, as when you or I might say to ourselves on meeting a stranger, "He's effeminate. I bet he's a real creep." Or "My God, she looks like she's ninety—probably senile." Even more common are the judgments we make about people on the basis of very brief, limited experience. Not a workshop goes by when I don't quickly conclude that some member is a real "nerd," only to discover later that that person has enormous gifts. One reason to distrust instant community is that community-building requires time—the time to have sufficient experience to become conscious of our prejudices and then to empty ourselves of them.

Ideology, Theology, and Solutions. Obviously we cannot move very far toward community with our fellow human beings when we are thinking and feeling, She clearly has no appreciation of Christian doctrine; she has a long way to go before she will be saved like me. Or else, Well, it's clear he's a Republican businessman hawk. I hope there'll be someone here worth relating to. It is not only such ideological and theological rigidities that we need to discard, it is any idea that assumes the status of "the one and only right way." So it was that the group of Midwestern civic leaders I mentioned had to empty themselves of their pet plans, which each thought was *the* solution for their city.

In speaking of this emptying process, however, I do not mean to imply we should utterly forsake our sometimes hardwon sentiments and understandings. A community-building workshop in Virginia several years ago offered an example of the distinction between emptying and obliteration. The group was the most dedicated band of converters I have ever encountered. Everyone wanted to talk about God; everyone had a different idea of God; and everyone was certain she or he knew exactly who God was. It didn't take us long to get into chaos of magnificent proportions. But thirty-six hours later, after the group had made its miraculous transition from chaos to community, I told them, "It's fascinating. Today you are still talking just as much about God as you were yesterday. In that respect you haven't changed. What has happened, however, is the way in which you talk. Yesterday each of you was talking as if you had God in your back pocket. Today you are all talking about God with humility and a sense of humor."

The Need to Heal, Convert, Fix, or Solve.   During the stage of chaos, when the members of a group attempt to heal or convert each other, they believe they are being loving. And they are truly surprised by the chaos that results. After all, isn't it the loving thing to do to relieve your neighbor of her suffering or help him to see the light? Actually, however, almost all these attempts to convert and heal are not only naïve and ineffective but quite self-centered and self-serving. It hurts me when my friend is in pain. If I can do something to get rid of this pain I will feel better. My most basic motive when I strive to heal is to feel good myself. But there are several problems here. One is that my cure is usually not my friend's. Indeed, offering someone my cure usually only makes that person feel worse. So it was that all the advice that Job's friends gave him in his time of affliction served only to make him more miserable. The fact of the matter is that often the most loving thing we can do when a friend is in pain is to *share* that pain—to be there even when we have nothing to offer except our presence and even when being there is painful to ourselves.

The same is true with the attempt to convert. If your theology or ideology is different from mine, it calls mine into question. It is uncomfortable for me to be uncertain of my own understanding in such basic matters. On the other hand, if I could convert you to my way of thinking, it would not only relieve my discomfort, it would be further proof of the rectitude of my beliefs and cast me in the role of savior to boot. How much easier and nicer that would be than extending myself to understand you as you are.

As they enter the stage of emptiness the members of a group come to realize—sometimes suddenly, sometimes gradually—

that their desire to heal, convert, or otherwise "solve" their interpersonal differences is a self-centered desire for comfort through the obliteration of these differences. And then it begins to dawn on them that there may be an opposite way: the appreciation and celebration of interpersonal differences. No group ever got the message more quickly than those unsophisticated Midwestern civic leaders. Because we had little time to work together, I was blunt with them. "I told you at the beginning," I reminded them, "that our purpose in being together is to form ourselves into a community, and not to solve the problems of your city. Yet here you are in short order not talking about yourselves but about your proposed solutions. They all sound to me like very fine ideas, but the fact is that you are clobbering each other over the head with them. Now, if you want, you can keep on doing that for the next twenty-four hours, but I honestly don't think it's going to get you or the city any further than when you walked in here this morning. And it certainly isn't going to get you to community. If you want to get to community, on the other hand, you're going to have to empty yourselves of your fine proposals and your need to see them triumph. And maybe, just maybe, if you become a true community, you will be able to work together in such a way that it will help your city. I don't know. But let's take an extra-long break—forty minutes—and let's see if during that time each of you can possibly empty yourself of your solutions sufficiently for us at least to get to know each other as different human beings."

We became a community within the hour.

The Need to Control.   This barrier to community is my own prime bugaboo. As the designated leader of a workshop I am supposed to see to it that the group does not get out of control—that it comes to no harm. Furthermore, even though I have told the group that each member is no more and no less responsible than any other member for the success of the group, I don't really feel that way in my heart. If the workshop fails, I feel, I'm the one who is going to look bad. Consequently

I am constantly tempted to *do* things—manipulations or maneuvers—that will ensure the desired outcome. But the desired outcome—community—cannot be achieved by an authoritarian leader who calls the shots. It must be a creation of the group as a whole. Paradoxically, then, to be an effective leader I must spend most of the time sitting back, *doing nothing,* waiting, letting it happen. As a basically overcontrolling person I don't do that very easily.

The need for control—to ensure the desired outcome—is at least partially rooted in the fear of failure. For me to empty myself of my overcontrolling tendencies I must continually empty myself of this fear. I must be willing to fail. Indeed, a significant number of workshops have succeeded in becoming communities only after I have said to myself, "Well, it looks as if this one is going to fail, and I'm helpless to do anything about it." I am not sure such timing is accidental.

The learning that occurs in community-building is frequently extended to day-to-day living. My experience in emptying myself of my need to control has begun to improve some of my everyday relationships, including my relationship to life itself. Others have joined me, through community, in learning an increased capacity for surrender and how to appreciate the truth that often "Life is not a problem to be solved but a mystery to be lived."

I have hardly exhausted the list of things that individuals may need to give up in order to form themselves into a community. I routinely ask the members of a group to reflect in silence, during a break period or overnight, on what they as individuals most need to empty themselves of in their own unique lives. When they return, their reports are as varied as the topography of our globe: "I need to give up my need for my parents' approval," "my need to be liked," "my resentment of my son," "my preoccupation with money," "my anger at God," "my dislike of homosexuals," "my concern about neatness," and so on, and so on. Such giving up is a sacrificial process. Consequently the stage of emptiness in community development is a time of sacrifice. And sacrifice hurts. "Do I have to give up everything?" a group member once wailed during this stage.

"No," I replied, "just everything that stands in your way."

Such sacrifice hurts because it is a kind of death, the kind of death that is necessary for rebirth. But even when we realize this intellectually, such dying is still a fearsome adventure into the unknown. And many group members during the stage of emptiness often seem almost paralyzed between fear and hope, because they will incorrectly think and feel about emptiness not in terms of rebirth but in terms of "nothingness" or annihilation.

The terror that may be involved was never more dramatically illustrated than in Martin's "rebirth." Martin was a slightly hard and depressed-appearing sixty-year-old man whose "workaholism" had made him extremely successful, even famous. During the stage of emptiness in a workshop he and his wife attended, and when the group was still attempting to deal with emptiness on the level of an intellectual concept, Martin suddenly began to tremble and shake. For a brief moment I thought he might be having a seizure. But then, almost as if he were in a trance, he began to moan, "I'm scared. I don't know what's happening to me. All this talk about emptiness. I don't know what it means. I feel I'm going to die. I'm terrified."

Several of us gathered around Martin, holding him for comfort, still uncertain whether he was in a physical or emotional crisis.

"It feels like dying," Martin continued to moan. "Emptiness. I don't know what emptiness is. All my life I've done things. You mean I don't have to do anything? I'm scared."

Martin's wife took his hand. "No, you don't have to do anything, Martin," she said.

"But I've always done things," Martin continued. "I don't know what it's like not to do anything. Emptiness. Is that what emptiness is? Giving up doing things? Could I really not do anything?"

"It's all right to do nothing, Martin," his wife responded.

Martin stopped shaking. We held him for about five minutes. Then he let us know that his fear of emptiness, his terror of dying, had subsided. And within an hour his face began to radiate a soft serenity. He knew that he had been broken and had survived. He also knew that through his brokenness he had somehow helped the whole group toward community.

Because the stage of emptiness can be so painful, there are two questions I am routinely asked with agony. One is, "Isn't there any way into community except through emptiness?" My answer is "No." The other question is, "Isn't there any way into community except through the sharing of brokenness?" Again my answer is "No."

As a group moves into emptiness, a few of its members begin to share their own brokenness—their defeats, failures, doubts, fears, inadequacies, and sins. They begin to stop acting as if they "had it all together" as they reflect on those things they need to empty themselves of. But the other members generally do not listen to them very attentively. Either they revert to attempts to heal or convert the broken members or else they ignore them by quickly changing the topic. Consequently those who have made themselves vulnerable tend to retreat quickly into their shells. It is not easy to confess your weakness when others are apt to try immediately to change you or else behave as if you haven't said anything worth listening to.

Sometimes the group by itself will soon come to recognize that it is blocking expressions of pain and suffering—that in order to truly listen they have to *truly* empty themselves, even of their distaste for "bad news." If they don't, it becomes necessary for me to point out to its members that they are discouraging the sharing of brokenness. Some groups will then immediately correct their callousness. But other groups toward the end of the stage of emptiness will wage their final last-ditch struggle against community. Typically, there will be a spokesman who will say, "Look, I have my own burdens at home. There's no need to pay good money and spend a whole weekend just to take on more burdens. I'm all for this community business, but I don't see why we have to focus so much on negative things all the time. Why can't we talk about the good things, the things we have in common, our successes instead of our failures? I'd like this to be a joyful experience. What's the point of community if it can't be joyful?"

Basically this final resistance is an attempt to flee back into pseudocommunity. But here the issue at stake is no longer over whether individual differences will be denied. The group has moved too far for that. Instead the struggle is over wholeness. It is over whether the group will choose to embrace not only the light of life but also life's darkness. True community *is* joyful, but it is also realistic. Sorrow and joy must be seen in their proper proportions.

I have spoken of the stage of emptiness largely as if it were something that occurs solely within the minds and souls of the individuals who compose a group. But community is always something more than the sum total of the individuals present. Pseudocommunity, chaos, and emptiness are not so much individual stages as group stages. The transformation of a group from a collection of individuals into genuine community requires little deaths in many of those individuals. But it is also a process of group death, group dying. During the stage of emptiness my own gut feeling is often not so much the pain of watching individuals here and there undergoing little deaths and rebirths as it is the pain of witnessing a group in its death throes. The whole group seems to writhe and moan in its travail. Individuals will sometimes speak for the group. "It's like we're dying. The group is in agony. Can't you help us? I didn't know we'd have to die to become a community."

Just as the physical death of some individuals is rapid and gentle while for others agonizing and protracted, so it is for the emotional surrender of groups. Whether sudden or gradual, however, all the groups in my experience have eventually succeeded in completing, accomplishing, this death. They have all made it through emptiness, through the time of sacrifice, into community. This is an extraordinary testament to the human spirit. What it means is that given the right circumstances and knowledge of the rules, on a certain but very real level we human beings are able to die for each other.

COMMUNITY

When its death has been completed, open and empty, the group enters community. In this final stage a soft quietness descends. It is a kind of peace. The room is bathed in peace. Then, quietly, a member begins to talk about herself. She is being very vulnerable. She is speaking of the deepest part of herself. The group hangs on each word. No one realized she was capable of such eloquence.

When she is finished there is a hush. It goes on a long time. But it does not seem long. There is no uneasiness in this silence. Slowly, out of the silence, another member begins to talk. He too is speaking very deeply, very personally, about himself. He is not trying to heal or convert the first person. He's not even trying to respond to her. It's not she but he who is the subject. Yet the other members of the group do not sense he has ignored her. What they feel is that it is as if he is laying himself down next to her on an altar.

The silence returns.

A third member speaks. Perhaps it will be to respond to the previous speaker, but there will be in this response no attempt to heal or convert. It may be a joke, but it will not be at anyone's expense. It may be a short poem that is almost magically appropriate. It could be anything soft and gentle, but again it will be a gift.

Then the next member speaks. And as it goes on, there will be a great deal of sadness and grief expressed; but there will also be much laughter and joy. There will be tears in abundance. Sometimes they will be tears of sadness, sometimes of joy. Sometimes, simultaneously, they will be tears of both. And then something almost more singular happens. An extraordinary amount of healing and converting begins to occur—now that no one is trying to convert or heal. And community has been born.

What happens next? The group has become a community. Where does it go from here? What, then, is its task?

There is no one answer to those questions. For the groups that have assembled specifically for a short-term experience of community, its primary task may be no more than simply to enjoy that experience—and benefit from the healing that accompanies it. It will have the additional task, however, of ending itself. Somehow there must be closure. Women and men who have come to care for each other deeply need time to say goodbyes. The pains of returning to an everyday world without community need expression. It is important for short-term communities to give themselves the time for ending. This is often done best when the community is able to develop for itself a joyous sort of funeral, with some kind of liturgy or ritual for conclusion.

If the group has assembled with the ultimate goal of solving a problem—planning a campaign, healing a division within a congregation, engineering a merger, for example—then it should get on with that task. But only after it has had the time to enjoy the experience of community for itself sufficiently to cement the experience. Such groups should always bear in mind the rule: "Community-building first, problem-solving second."

Or the task of the community may be the difficult one of deciding whether it will or will not maintain itself. This decision usually should not be made quickly. In the joy of the moment members may make commitments that they shortly discover they are unable to fulfill. The consequences of long-term commitment are major and should not be taken lightly.

If a community—or part of it—does decide to maintain itself, it will have many new tasks. Community maintenance requires that multiple major decisions be made or remade over extensive periods of time. The community will frequently fall back into chaos or even pseudocommunity in the process. Over and again it will need to do the agonizing work of reemptying itself. Many groups fail here. Many convents and monasteries, for instance, while referring to themselves as "communities," long ago allowed themselves to become rigid authoritarian organizations. As such they may continue to fill useful roles in society, but they do so without joy and fail to be a "safe place" for their membership. They have forgotten that maintaining themselves as a true community should take priority over all the other tasks of their community.

Because I have spoken so glowingly of its virtues, it worries me that some might conclude that life in community is easier or more comfortable than ordinary existence. It is not. But it is certainly more *lively*, more intense. The agony is actually greater, but so is the joy. The experience of joy in community, however, is hardly automatic. During times of struggle the majority of the members of a true community will not experience joy. Instead, the prevailing mood may be one of anxiety, frustration, or fatigue. Even when the dominant mood is one of joy, a few members, because of individual worries or conflicts, may still be unable to feel a part of the community spirit. Yet the most common emotional response to the spirit of community is the feeling of joy.

It is like falling in love. When they enter community, people in a very real sense do fall in love with one another en masse. They not only feel like touching and hugging each other, they feel like hugging everyone all at once. During the highest moments the energy level is supernatural. It is ecstatic. Lily provided one community myth during a workshop in a Knoxville hotel when she pointed to an electrical outlet in the center of the floor and commented: "It's as if we're connected to the entire electrical energy output of the TVA."

Great power, however, can sometimes hold potential danger. The danger of the power of true community is never the creation of mob psychology but of group sexuality. It is only natural when a group of people fall in love with one another that enormous sexual energy should be released. Usually this is not harmful, but it is wise for communities to be aware of their great potential sexuality in order that it does not get out of hand. It may need to be suppressed. It should not, however, be repressed. And it is wise to remember that the experience of the other forms of love, "phila" and "agape" (brother or sister love, and divine love) can be even deeper and more rewarding than simple erotic or romantic bonding. The sexuality of community is an expression of its joy, and its energy can be channeled to useful and creative purpose.

If it is so channeled, life in community may touch upon something perhaps even deeper than joy. There are a few who repeatedly seek out brief experiences of community as if such episodes were some sort of "fix." This is not to be decried. We all need "fixes" of joy in our lives. But what repeatedly draws me into community is something more. When I am with a group of human beings committed to hanging in there through both the agony and the joy of community, I have a dim sense that I am participating in a phenomenon for which there is only one word. I almost hesitate to use it. The word is "glory."

CHAPTER VI

Further Dynamics of Community

Community-making is always an adventure. But we learn what is significantly new only through adventures. However, going into the unknown is invariably frightening. Each new time, even as an experienced leader, I am just as scared as the rest of the participants in a community-building group.

There is no way that the process of community-making can be reduced to a complete set of formulas that would relieve either leaders or participants from the anxiety of the unexpected. Each community-making experience is unique, just as each individual member of the group is unique. But there are certain patterns in the behavior of the group as a whole that strongly influence and often impede the process. An experienced leader is aware of these patterns, and the group must be led to a similar awareness, whether conscious or unconscious, in order to achieve community.

PATTERNS OF GROUP BEHAVIOR

Out of his group therapy work with military patients during World War II, the British psychiatrist Wilfred Bion developed a remarkably comprehensive understanding of group behavior. His work led to the development in Great Britain of the Tavistock Institute, where many group leaders have been trained. For this reason the use of Bion theory in group leadership or leadership style is sometimes referred to as the "Tavistock Model."*

* See Margaret J. Rioch, "The Work of Wilfred Bion on Groups," *Psychiatry* (Washington, D.C.), Vol. 33, No. 1 (Feb. 1970), pp. 56–66.

Bion discerned that every group—whether a therapy group, a "sensitivity" group, or an organizational group or committee of any kind—has a task. The task may be conscious, stated, and explicit, as when an engineering group meets to design a new telephone system. Or it may be less conscious and implicit. For instance, while all individual members of a therapy group are likely to be quite conscious of their own desires for healing, they may be entirely unconscious of the fact that it is their task *as a group* to create an atmosphere of safety and acceptance in which healing can occur.

Bion stated that sooner or later (and usually very soon) all groups attempt to avoid their tasks, and he pointed out that there are several ways in which groups do this. He called these ways "task-avoidance assumptions" and distinguished four: "Flight," "Fight," "Pairing," and "Dependence." He used the term "assumptions" rather than "styles" because, when operating under them, groups behave as if they assume their purpose is to avoid their tasks in accord with particular assumptions.

Bion further noted that if a group becomes aware of its own particular task-avoidance assumption, it is likely to switch immediately to one of the other modes of avoidance. Whenever a group manages to be free from any of these task-avoidance assumptions—that is, when it is working effectively and appropriately on its task or toward its completion—it becomes what Bion called a "working group."

A community might also be called a working group, but the term "community" is, on the whole, preferable. Tavistock leaders frequently failed to mold their clients into a working group. "Working group" suggests efficiency and effectiveness, but it does not imply the love and commitment, the sacrifice, and the transcendence required to build community. Had Tavistock leaders spoken of the necessity for such values, I believe they would have been more successful in forming their clients into effective working groups—that is to say, communities.

Although I believe it had its imperfections, the Tavistock Model is of profound importance in understanding the dynamics of community-making. Bion's foremost ground-breaking contribution was his recognition of a group not simply as a collection of individuals but as an organism with a life of its own. His "task-avoidance assumptions" are realities that do in fact shape peoples' behavior in both community-building and maintenance. It is virtually impossible for a group to become or stay in genuine community without understanding these realities and coming to terms with them.

Flight. In the task-avoidance assumption of flight, groups show a strong tendency to flee from troublesome issues and problems. Rather than confront these issues and problems, groups will act as if they *assume* it is their purpose to avoid them. In a sense all task-avoidance assumptions are a form of flight, and such behavior on the part of groups is just as neurotic as it is for individuals.

An example of how neurotically destructive group flight can be was provided when Mac Badgely's group attempted to scapegoat me. I had announced that I was feeling depressed. It ultimately turned out that the whole group was also depressed. But it did not want to deal with the pain of its depression. In order to flee from its own depression, the group was quite willing both to label me sick and then to ostracize me. Scapegoating is always a form of the task-avoidance assumption of flight.

The most familiar form of group flight is found in what I have termed "pseudocommunity." The basic assumption of pseudocommunity is that the problem of individual differences should be avoided. The boring mannerliness of pseudocommunity is a pretense devoted to fleeing from anything that might cause healthy as well as unhealthy conflict.

Another frequent variety of flight occurs during the period of chaos when the group attempts to avoid the path of emptiness by fleeing into organization. A common way in which this occurs is the proposal to split into subgroups. This proposal is particularly seductive because of the prevailing false dogma that fifteen or so is the "ideal" maximum group size.

But in my experience it is invariably an attempt to flee from the group as a whole and its task of building itself into a genuine community.

Another common form of flight in community-building groups is the ignoring of emotional pain. It occurs repeatedly. In the midst of the pleasantries of pseudocommunity, the squabbling of chaos, or the death throes of emptiness, one of the group members (generally a true leader)—let's call her Mary—speaks of something very personal and painful. Tears will fill her eyes. "I know I shouldn't be crying," she says, "but what was just said reminds me of my father. He was an alcoholic. When I was a child I felt he was the only one who really cared for me. He liked to play with me. He was always ready to have me sit on his lap. He died from cirrhosis of the liver when I was thirty-one. He just drank himself to death. I was furious with him for killing himself. I felt he had abandoned me. I felt that if he really loved me he would somehow have stopped drinking. I've become reconciled to his death now. I don't know what his pain was—maybe just having to live with my mother—but I think probably he needed to go the way he did. But I haven't been able to become reconciled to myself." Now Mary is crying openly. "You see," she finished, "I never told him when he was dying how much I loved him. I was so angry at him, I never got around to thanking him. And now it's too late. Forever too late."

Exactly five seconds pass before Larry says irritably, "I still don't understand how we can become a community when we don't even have a definition of it."

"We have a community in our church," Marilyn comments cheerfully. "Almost twenty of us get together the last Thursday of every month for a potluck supper."

"We used to do that in the army," Virginia adds, "some of us in our housing area. Each month we'd make dishes from a different country. One month it would be Mexican, another Chinese. Once we even had Russian. I must say I didn't like borscht though."

With luck, one of the other members will perceive what's

happening. "Hey," Mark may say, "Mary's crying, and we're acting like nothing happened. She just poured her heart out, and you people are talking about potluck suppers. I wonder how she feels."

If this doesn't happen, the leader may feel it necessary to intervene. "The group has apparently not learned to listen to its members' pain," I might say. "It chose to ignore Mary rather than share her suffering—to talk about intellectual definitions of community while avoiding the opportunity to *be* in community with her." Often this kind of intervention needs to be repeated. "You keep asking what 'emptiness' means," I might say. "One of the things it means is to shut up long enough—to be empty long enough—to digest what someone has just said. Whenever someone says something painful, the group runs away from it into noisiness."

The task-avoidance assumption of flight can also occur *after* genuine community has been achieved. Perhaps the most dramatic example of this I have ever witnessed occurred in the 1972 sensitivity group of the National Training Laboratory where I first openly wept. Under the remarkably able leadership of Lindy, sixteen of us rapidly became a community. For the next ten days we experienced great love and joy and learning and healing together. But the last day was boring. We sat around on our usual pillows talking of nothing. A mere half hour before the end, one of us commented, almost offhandedly, "It feels a little bit strange that this is our last group meeting." But by then it was too late. We did not have the time to deal with the problem of reentry or grieve properly over the demise of ourselves as a community.

In retrospect, it was a very remarkable phenomenon. In almost two weeks sixteen of us human beings had come not only to have a most vivacious, life-changing experience together but to love and care for one another very deeply. Yet on this last day we acted as if nothing had happened. We utterly avoided the issue of our death as a group. We were in total flight from our mortality. Our very success as a community contributed to our motivation to pretend that it was not the end of us. Unconsciously we sought to flee from the reality of our expiration. During that last day we assumed it was our purpose together to avoid the issue. To this day I do not know whether Lindy allowed us this flight out of his own pain at the loss of our togetherness or consciously gave us one final experience of task avoidance. In either case, we all participated willingly in it.

Fight.   This is the task-avoidance assumption that predominates during the second stage of the community-building process, the period I have labeled "chaos." As soon as it moves out of pseudocommunity, a group will usually start behaving like a conglomeration of amateur psychotherapists and preachers, all attempting to heal or convert one another. But of course it doesn't work. And the less it seems to work, the harder group members try to make it work. The process of attempting to heal and convert instantaneously becomes a process of fighting. The group is operating under the task-avoidance assumption of fighting. It *assumes* that its purpose in being together is to squabble in this manner, although as individual members they do not think of themselves as fighting. Usually they think, I'm only trying to help. But the group process becomes very angry and chaotic.

Here it becomes the job of the community-building leader not only to expose to the group the task-avoidance assumption of fighting but also to point the way to the solution. "We are supposedly trying to build community," I may say, "but all we seem to be doing is fighting. I wonder why?" This kind of intervention should not be made too early. If it is, the group is likely to retreat into pseudocommunity by attempting to avoid fighting without ever asking itself why it was fighting in the first place. If it has spent enough time in chaos, however, it is more likely to ask itself, "What are we doing wrong?" Once this question is seriously asked, groups can occasionally figure out the answer by themselves. More often they need a little—but only a little—help. So I may say, if their self-analysis seems to be floundering, "As I was listening to all the squabbling, it seemed to me you were all trying to heal or convert one another. It might help if you examined your motives for acting as if it were your task to heal or convert."

In this way in the course of a mere hour or two an entire group can come to learn what it usually takes professional psychotherapists years to learn: that we cannot, by ourselves, heal or convert. What we can do is examine our own motives at the deepest possible level. The more we do this, the more we empty ourselves of our desires to fix people, the more we become able and willing and even eager to allow others to be themselves, thereby creating an atmosphere of respect and safety. In such an atmosphere, which is the essence of community, healing and converting will effortlessly begin to occur without anyone pushing it.

Groups that have achieved community also fight. There are many times when they must indeed struggle together toward the resolution of significant issues. For that reason I have given the name "chaos" to the period when a group is bogged down in the task-avoidance assumption of fighting. "Chaos" specifically implies a fruitless conflict going nowhere, an utterly uncreative kind of fighting. It centers around attempts to convert or heal rather than the attempt to incorporate individual differences. The struggles of a true community, on the other hand, involve the creative emptying process that allows the ultimate arrival at genuine consensus.

Pairing. The tendency to lose sight of the central task of building community is profound. And pairing is indeed a common pitfall in this regard. Alliances, conscious or unconscious, between two or more members are highly likely to interfere with a group's mature development.

One or more married couples or pairs or groups of friends almost always attend community-building groups together. Frequently—particularly during the period of chaos—some such pair will start whispering to each other. Then, if the group ignores this behavior, I must say, "I wonder if the group isn't curious about what Jane and Betty are whispering? Does the group feel excluded—are Jane and Betty behaving as if the rest of us didn't exist?"

Often during a community-building experience two members of the group will develop a romantic relationship. Indeed, some come to workshops hoping to find romance. This is not necessarily to be discouraged. But limits do need to be put on this conduct if it begins to interfere with the integrity of the community as a whole. "John and Mary," I may say, "we're delighted that you've developed such an affection for each other. But maybe it seems to the group you're so busy making moon eyes at each other that you're not paying attention to the rest of us. Since you can be together all you want during the break times, maybe the group might want you to consider sitting apart from each other while we're here in session."

The problem of pairing can be particularly intense in those workshops that are designed to build community among previously disparate groups. For example, my colleagues and I have been requested on several occasions to "bring together" students and faculty or faculty and administration or administration and parents or any such combination. Generally these subgroups will begin by sitting with one another as a block. It is not usually necessary to direct them to rearrange their seating. But it is essential to point out just when and how they are excluding each other. In fact it is a real joy in community to see disparate groups actually break up, students sitting among the faculty, administrators among students, the old among the young.

Pairing is equally destructive in long-term communities. Religious communes—convents and monasteries—have dramatic staying power in relation to secular communes. The greatest reason for this is that monks and nuns clearly gather for some purpose higher than the mere pleasure of being together. Still, they frequently forget that higher purpose. Two novices, Sisters Susan and Clarissa, for instance, may strike up a firm friendship. They spend as much of their free time together as they can, finding each other's company more enjoyable than that of the other nuns. But soon things subtly start going wrong.

The other nuns become irritable with them. The two find themselves left out of important decisions. Finally, in distress, Sister Susan complains to the novice mistress that she and Clarissa are being excluded by the community.

"Perhaps it is the other way around," the novice mistress will tell her. "You and Clarissa have developed such an intense friendship that you seem to care only about each other. Maybe by focusing so much attention on your relationship, it is the two of you who are excluding your sisters. You're depriving them of your attention and energy. At least, that's what they report to me. Wonderful though friendship can be, in the old days we used to tell the postulants that excessively close friendships were forbidden. Now we generally prefer that you find out the dangers for yourselves. It's not easy, Susan, but I would suggest that you and Clarissa ask yourselves whether in your friendship you haven't forgotten about the community as a whole and your deepest purposes in being here."

Dependency.   Of all the task-avoidance assumptions that of dependency is the most devastating to community development. It is also the most difficult—often excruciatingly difficult—for community leaders to combat.

My colleagues and I must engage in this combat from the beginning of building community. In advance literature we inform the participants that the experience will be participatory and experiential rather than didactic. At the start of a workshop we remind them of this. "A community cannot exist if the members depend upon a leader to lecture them or carry their load," we say. "Each one of us has no more and no less responsibility than any other for the success of our work together."

But groups do not at first take kindly to being even relatively leaderless. Although it does nothing to develop their maturity—indeed, it interferes with their development—people would generally much rather depend upon a leader to tell them what to do than determine that for themselves. All instructions to the contrary, groups rapidly slip into the task-avoidance assumption of dependency. And until the group grows out of it—until it becomes a community, a group of all leaders—its members will almost invariably misunderstand and resent their nonauthoritarian leader. Indeed, their desire for an authority figure or father figure may be so strong that they will figuratively crucify the leader who refuses to accede to their demands.

It is not easy to be crucified—even figuratively. Yet it is usually necessary. Crucifixion is not simply some dynamic that happened to a uniquely great leader two thousand years ago. It is a strange kind of law. In the training of community-building leaders I tell them over and again, "You must be willing and able to die for the group." But there are no words that can prepare them for the agonizing experience of the vilification a group may heap upon a leader who refuses to be a "Big Daddy." The issue calls into question our very definitions of "strength" and "weakness" in leadership. To lead people into community a true leader must discourage their dependency, and there may be no way to do this except to refuse to lead. Paradoxically, the strong leader in these instances is she or he who is willing to risk—even welcome— the accusation of failing to lead. The accusation is always made. Sometimes it is mild. Sometimes it is almost murderous.

At one such time a rabbinical story came to the mind of a colleague. It has been added to our compendium for use during that dreadful period when groups, refusing emptiness, flounder in chaos and blame the leader for their condition. "A rabbi was lost in the woods," my colleague told his workshop. "For three months he searched and searched but could not find his way out. Finally, one day in his searching he encountered a group from his synagogue who had also become lost in the forest. Overjoyed, they exclaimed, 'Rabbi, how wonderful we have found you. Now you can lead us out of the woods!' 'I am sorry, I cannot do that,' the rabbi replied, 'for I am as lost as you. What I can do, because I have had more experience being lost, is to tell you a thousand ways you cannot get out of the woods. With this poor help, working with each other, perhaps we shall be able to find our way out together.' "

The moral is hardly obscure. Yet it is amazing how little the story helps. As likely as not the group will use it to add one more to their list of charges: "Besides which," they will inform their leader, "you tell stupid stories."

Still, the hardest part for the leader is not the nails driven in by others; it is the self-crucifixion. It is refusing the temptation to be the leader the group clamors for. Those of us who gravitate to such positions are quite accustomed to lead. It is far easier for us to teach and preach than to not speak. Continually we must empty ourselves of our need to control. More often than not a group will become a community only after I have given up, when I have decided, This is the time it will be a failure. I do not think this timing is accidental. Community-building requires that those accustomed to leadership be genuinely willing to enter a state of helplessness. It demands that I empty myself of my need to talk, my need to help all the time, my need to be a guru, my desire to look like a hero, my quick and easy answers, my cherished notions. But a group can learn how to go into emptiness only when its leader is able to practice emptiness.

The difficulty was well expressed by a highly successful middle-aged Protestant clergyman whom I had helped to train. After leading his first community-building workshop he wrote: "I remembered that you told us these things often succeed only after you concluded you had failed. But it didn't help. Saturday night I called my wife and told her I was not cut out for the job. I moved my car so I could be the first one out of the parking lot. Still, I clung on. I am a master minister manipulator. During the night I kept thinking there must be some trick I could still pull off. Just after dawn I finally realized that I didn't know anything about Christianity. I didn't know anything about sacrifice. I didn't know anything about dying to my own ego. And at that moment I did die. After breakfast we became community."

It is an old rule, however, that the more you put into some-

thing, the more you get out of it. Thus the designated leader
of a community-building group may benefit even more than
other participants. His sacrifice may be greater, but so may be
his gain. My friend concluded the above letter by saying: "People report that I am more mellow—softer—since my return. I
feel strangely well. I may be crazy, but yes, I am willing to do
it again."

INTERVENTIONS IN GROUP BEHAVIOR

Since a group is more than the sum of its parts—it is a living
organism in its own right—leaders should keep their focus on
the group as a whole. They usually need not concern themselves with the problems or personalities of individual members. In fact, such concern is likely to interfere with community
development. The general rule, therefore, is that leaders
should restrict their interventions to interpretations of group
rather than individual behavior. And the purpose of all such
interventions is not to *tell* the group what to do or not to do but
to awaken it to awareness of its behavior.

Typical examples of such group interventions would be for
the leader to say: "The group seems to be acting as if everyone
has the same religious faith"; or "All this chaos seems to center
around attempts to change each other"; or "It looks to me as
if the younger and the older members are dividing themselves
into different factions"; or "The group seems to change the
subject every time someone says something painful, as if we
didn't want to hear of one another's suffering"; or "I wonder
whether the group doesn't need to empty itself of its resentment of my weak leadership before we can become a community."

One effect of this style of leadership is to teach the other
members also to think in terms of the group as a whole. In the
beginning few have any group consciousness, but by the time
they reach community, most of the participants have learned
to be aware of themselves as a body. Indeed, they will also start

to make effective group interventions. Thus a businessman who tagged along to a workshop with his wife simply to please her may come to say, "I feel that the group has become bogged down again. I wonder if there isn't something we should be looking at about ourselves." As this occurs, the designated leader can more and more assume the pleasant role of "just another member."

Abiding by another general rule of community-building leadership, the designated leader should make only those interventions that the other members are not yet capable of making. Otherwise the group could not become a community—a group of all leaders. Conversely, a fully developed community is quite capable of solving its own problems without a single designated leader. This requires, however, that the designated leader must do a lot of waiting—waiting to see if the other members will pick up on a problem already visible to herself or himself. Such necessary waiting (which often appears to be weak leadership) is possible only when designated leaders are willing to empty themselves of their need to be in control. One of the agonizing tasks of community-building leaders is to continually discern just how long to wait before concluding that the group is not yet ready to handle the problem by itself.

General rules have exceptions. Occasionally, for instance, it is necessary for the designated leader to focus on the behavior of an individual member. This should be done, however, not so much for the needs of the individual as for those of the group: that is, when the individual's behavior is clearly interfering with the development of the community and the group as a whole seems not yet capable of confronting the problem. By way of example, let me recount two such instances when I felt compelled to make individual interventions.

As a result of a careless slipup on my part the brochure for one of my workshops did not make clear that its primary purpose, without question, was community-building. It was explained at the very start of the workshop, however, that this was my desire, and the members seemed enthusiastic at the prospect. Shortly after we became a community one of the members, Marshall, a middle-aged, highly intellectual Christian, kept trying to get the group into a discussion of abstract theology. When the group rebuffed him, he complained that the brochure had not stated this was a community-building group and that he had come to it because he wanted to learn more about my particular theology. The group pointed out that while the brochure had not mentioned anything about community-building, it had, in fact, said that it would be a participatory workshop in which the meaning of Christian love, discipline, and sacrifice would be clarified *experientially*. Marshall persisted in wanting intellectual discussion. I said, "You are quite correct, Marshall, that I did not make it clear in the brochure that this was to be a community-building experience. It was a careless oversight on my part. I should have been more clear. I can understand that you feel misled, and you deserve an apology from me. I'm sorry that I misled you."

During the break that shortly followed, Marshall accosted me. "I'm quite upset about this weekend. I feel I've wasted my time and money. I wouldn't have come if I had known it was going to be one of these community-building things."

"I don't know what to do except apologize to you again, Marshall," I responded. "I'm not going to try to turn it into a theological discussion, because that's not what the group as a whole wants. I hope you will be able to make the adjustment. But as I told you, I did make a mistake, and I'm truly sorry for it and for the fact that I disappointed you."

When the group reconvened, Marshall was sullenly silent for an hour. The group ignored him. He was becoming the group pariah. I wasn't sure what to do. I didn't like the way things were going, but I waited. Just before lunch Marshall began again with several statements of high theology. The group was outspokenly hostile to him, but there was not enough time before lunch to deal with the problem. After lunch we would begin the final third of the workshop. Marshall was sufficiently proud, I sensed, that if I were to confront him in the group, it would be profoundly humiliating for him. Yet if something was not done, it also seemed that Marshall's and the group's resentments would seriously undermine the finale and success of the workshop. As we broke, I asked Marshall if he would have lunch with me alone.

I did not waste time with amenities. "We've got a real problem, Marshall," I said as soon as we were seated. "I apologized to you in the group this morning for the brochure, but during the morning break time you criticized me for it again. Clearly you had not accepted my apology. So I apologized to you a second time. Yet you are still trying to turn the group into a theology discussion, and it seems clear you still haven't forgiven me for the group's being different from what you expected. How many times do I have to apologize, Marshall? While the brochure did not say anything about this being a community-building experience, it did say that the learning about Christian love, discipline, and sacrifice would be experiential. I am sure you would agree that the issue of forgiveness is quite a central one in Christian theology. Now, you are either going to have an experience here this weekend of forgiving me or an experience of not forgiving me. Which it is will be up to you. Also, as you know, we've talked a lot about emptiness, and that's quite related to sacrifice. The only way you're going to forgive me for this group's not being what you expected is to empty yourself of your expectation, to sacrifice your preconceptions and desires. Again, Christianity has something to say about sacrifice, and, again, it is up to you whether you are going to make that sacrifice or not. Experiential learning is tough learning. But the reality is that the experience of this workshop for you is going to depend upon your actual practice of Christian theology."

It worked. Marshall worked. He attempted no more intellectual discussion. As we took our midafternoon break, one of the male members, who had been highly critical of Marshall's intellectualizing, was hugging several other men. Marshall said, "Aren't you going to hug me?" The man did hug him. Several of us cried. During the final session that followed, Marshall confessed it was the first time he had ever hugged another man. Several of us cried again. Marshall learned a lot of theology that day.

One of the reasons that interventions with individuals are so difficult is that they are usually required when a group member, like Marshall, does not easily get the message. Because of the member's resistance, the intervention must often take the form of a kind of clobbering. I didn't like to clobber Marshall. I don't like to clobber anyone. Because people usually don't like to be clobbered, and it is hard to predict how they will respond, such interventions are potentially dangerous and should be made only after considerable agonizing analysis of the situation.

On another occasion, during the first third of our nine hours together, when a workshop was in its usual chaos, I realized that one of the members—we will call him Archie—posed a potential problem. Archie had spoken about three times with great passion and eloquence of a sort. The problem was, I didn't understand a thing that he was saying. I knew that the other group members didn't understand him either but that out of kindness they would have difficulty telling him so. At the end of the afternoon I asked the group, still floundering in chaos, to spend the night reflecting on where we were going wrong. I spent the night thinking about Archie. He was such a confusing person. I knew that if we succeeded in becoming a community, Archie would likely destroy it unless I made some kind of intervention. I hoped it wouldn't happen, but I suspected it would, and I wasn't sure what I should do or how it would work.

When we reassembled the next morning the group immediately went into emptiness and rapidly thereafter into community. We were just beginning to appreciate the joy of it when Archie made one of his poetic, impassioned contributions. "I understand exactly how you feel, Archie," one woman said. "That's the way I felt when my husband died—real angry at first." "But that wasn't what Archie was saying," another member protested. "He was talking about how sad he was." Archie gave another poetic speech. "Maybe Archie was both sad and angry," someone commented. "I heard anger," said another. "No, it was sadness," proclaimed a fifth a bit loudly. "I didn't hear either," rebuked a sixth. The group was back into chaos.

"The group is confused," I said, "and there's a reason for it. Archie, I have very mixed feelings about you," I went on, with my heart in my throat. "On the one hand, I like you. I sense that you have the soul of a poet. I resonate to your passion. I think you're a good and deep man. But I also think you have a problem with self-discipline in relation to words. For some reason—I have no idea why—you have never learned the discipline of translating your passion, the poetry of your soul, into words that other people can understand. Consequently, while people get turned on when you talk, they also get confused, just as the group is confused now. I think you can learn that self-discipline, and I dearly hope you will, because I suspect you've got some wonderful things to say. But learning that kind of discipline takes a lot of time, and I very much doubt that in the space of the one day left to us you will be able to learn it."

There was a moment of dreadful silence as I waited to see— as everyone waited to see—how Archie would respond. "Thank you," he answered. "You're one of the few people, Scotty, who has ever understood me."

For the remainder of the workshop Archie said nothing. But in his saying nothing the community felt loved by him, and I could sense him basking in their love in return.

I do not know whether Archie has ever succeeded in developing the discipline to translate the poetry of his soul into words that others can understand. But there is a follow-up to the story. A year and a half later I was conducting a similar community-building workshop in the same city under the same auspices. Archie phoned the sponsor of the workshop. "I'd like to attend again," he told her, "but I don't have the money. But will you tell Scotty that if he needs a bodyguard, I'll be over."

These interventions were successful—both for the commu-

nity and for the individuals concerned—largely because of
Marshall's and Archie's capacity to change, to give up a pattern of behavior. But what would have happened if they had
refused to make these sacrifices? In my experience, groups
can handle all varieties of individual psychopathology except
one. Indeed, it is often the "sickest" members who contribute
the most to the community-building process. There are, however, rare individuals who are not only unwilling to subordi-
nate any of themselves to the needs of the group but also seem
consciously or unconsciously motivated to actively destroy
community. It is these few I have previously dared to call
"evil."*

Such individuals are highly likely to avoid the community-
building process in the first place. Consequently I have encountered only two of them in the course of over a hundred of
such workshops involving five thousand people. In one, the
person did succeed in destroying the community. In the other
the community excluded the individual, a most difficult decision, since, by definition, community is inclusive. Yet if the life
of the community itself is threatened, it is a decision that must
be made.

The task of dealing with an evil member should not, however, be solely undertaken by a designated leader. Evil individuals are powerful people and more than a match for any
single person, no matter how skilled. The instance in which an
evil individual succeeded in destroying community occurred
early in my experience, and, as the designated leader, I regarded it as my responsibility to do battle with her single-
handedly in order to rescue the group. The problem was that
she was quite capable of fighting back with sufficient clever-
ness to gain enough allies against me to polarize the group and
keep it that way.

It should, therefore, be the responsibility of the group as a
whole to solve the problem of an evil member. This is what
happened in the other workshop, which ultimately required

* M. Scott Peck, *People of the Lie* (New York: Simon and Schuster, 1983).

that an evil man leave. In this instance I kept insisting he was the group's problem, and while the group suffered greatly because of its guilt over excluding him, ultimately the process facilitated its becoming a community.

If a group does decide on exclusion, it should be minimal. The above group requested the man to leave for a mere half day, with the option to return and try again. He did not take that option. I once consulted with a long-term intentional ("live in") community that an evil woman had joined. The community finally told her she was so disruptive she could no longer live in the house. However, they also informed her that she would continue to be welcome at their social hour and that if she demonstrated any real change, they would take her back into the house for another try. She also did not elect to take the option. While both members chose not to seek their way back, they at least were not totally banished, and if nothing else, the partial nature of their exclusion diminished the guilt of the excluding communities to reasonable proportions.

While it should not be incapacitating, guilt is inevitable for any community that even partially excludes an evil member. For exclusion is the violation of the number-one principle of community: inclusivity. Moreover, having been excluded, the evil person is simply likely to bedevil another community. Exclusion is no solution to the problem of evil. No matter how necessary it might be to maintain itself, the true community will always recognize that in excluding anyone, it has failed in a significant dimension. Without this sense of failure and accompanying guilt, a community would, in fact, cease to be a community; it would have degenerated into exclusivity as a way of being. If it no longer agonized over the question of whether or not exclusion of a member might represent scapegoating, it would become prone to scapegoating. It would no longer itself be immune to evil. To be in true community means to be in constant pain and tension over the problem of human evil.

On the other side of the coin, the problem of human evil, however vexing, is statistically insignificant at the small-group level. In my experience only two individuals out of the roughly five thousand could not be successfully incorporated into the community-building process. The reality is that human beings are sufficiently good that, if properly guided, all but a very tiny fraction of them can participate creatively in that process at the level on which we have been speaking. On a larger scale, such as that of a government or nation, the problem of human evil begins to assume a different magnitude. The issue of institutional evil is a far more haunting specter.

COMMUNITY SIZE

The success of a group seeking to achieve community does not seem to be related to its size. I have led several groups of three to four hundred people at a time into community. A huge retreat center, a conference coordinator, twenty trained small-group leaders, and five days' time were required. Such an elaborate organization is usually not practical. With that caveat, however, the upper limit to the size of a group that can be guided into community is unknown. Otherwise the number of participants in my community-building workshops have ranged between twenty-five and sixty-five, with that limit set simply because it is the largest group that can squeeze itself into a facsimile of an intimate circle.

This size may be surprising to psychotherapists or others knowledgeable about group behavior. There is a prevalent professional assumption that the "ideal group size" ranges between eight and fifteen and that any group over twenty is unmanageable. I believed this too until that day in 1981 in Washington, D.C., when our "intellectual workshop" of sixty participants suddenly became a community.

In my experience a major factor that makes community-building with large groups feasible is that I do not require every participant to speak. For the typical therapy or sensitivity group leader the totally silent member is an anathema. But I have become profoundly impressed by the power of nonverbal behavior. Professional lecturers know that in many an audience there will be a man or woman who by his or her facial expression or simple posture will lift them up, empower them to speak with greater courage, confidence, and forcefulness. Conversely, there may be a single individual in an audience who by means of a constant frown or glare will pull them down and sap them of their spirit. So it is in community-building groups. Members who speak not a word may contribute as much to the group as the most voluble.

It requires no expertise to ascertain whether a silent member is participating emotionally in the group. Simply his or her facial expressions or postures over time will be enough to let you know. Should someone—let's say a young woman, Mary—sit pulled away from the group, staring out the window for two hours with a blank, bored, or depressed expression, I am likely to comment: "The group seems to be ignoring the fact that Mary looks pretty withdrawn." But as long as members are emotionally "with it," I am under no compulsion whatever to solicit their words.

Not only do the nonverbal contribute to the community in ways that are powerful but they also receive as much as they give. Margaret, for instance, had entered individual therapy with me at age twenty-six, with a chief complaint of excessive shyness. After we had worked together for a year and a half and she had made some progress, I was scheduled to conduct a small community-building workshop in a lovely setting nearby. It seemed like an ideal opportunity for Margaret to have an experience of becoming comfortable in a group. I suggested it to her. She reluctantly agreed. But to my dismay, when the time came, Margaret did not speak a single word throughout the entire two days. It seemed the experience had been a failure for her.

Five days later, her face glowing, Margaret came for her individual session and told me it had been the most joyful experience of her life. "I've had that feeling before," she said, "but this was different. Before it had always been very fleeting—a moment here, a moment there months later. This past weekend I was expecting the joy to go away. But it kept coming back and back and back."

COMMUNITY DURATION

In my experience two days provide just the right amount of time for a group of thirty to sixty to become a true community. It is possible to do it more rapidly. Genuine community of sorts can usually be established in a few hours when the group is instructed from the outset to refrain from generalizations, to speak personally, to be vulnerable, to avoid attempting to heal or convert, to empty itself, to listen wholeheartedly, and to embrace the painful as well as the pleasant. But it is like being lifted to a mountaintop by helicopter. The glory can hardly be appreciated as it is when one has had to wade through the swamps and scramble over the boulders to get there. One of the briefest community myths was offered by a young clergywoman in reference to this problem of "quickie" community. As people were saying their last words at the end of such a one-day workshop, she summed it up by noting, "For me the day has had all the benefits and liabilities of a one-night stand."

An odd sort of converse is true. In two-day workshops some groups reach community by midafternoon of the first day, others halfway through, others with only four hours to go. A few, clinging to their old traditional ways of relating, did not achieve community until the last two hours. Yet the members of these last few leave with complete satisfaction. "This has been the most valuable experience of my life," they are likely to say. How can this be when all they have received is a mere two hours of reward for twelve hours of the hardest work? But who at the end of true lovemaking would regret that it finally occurred only after weeks of courtship?

COMMITMENT TO COMMUNITY

Because it is so important to community-making, participants should be prepared for the commitment they will be required to make. Participants in my workshops are given advance notice in writing not only that the purpose of their gathering will be to build themselves into a community but also that the process of doing so is likely to be difficult or painful at first. They are instructed before they arrive concerning the need to stay with the process and ride out the storm.

As soon as they convene I repeat this instruction: "There is only one major rule. You can't drop out." Since some people need an escape route, I am careful to add that I have no guns, whips, chains, or shackles to enforce this commitment. "But each one of us is responsible for the success of this group," I continue. "If you are unhappy with the way things are going—and you will be—it is your responsibility to speak up and voice your dissatisfaction rather than simply pick up your marbles and quietly leave. The expectation is that we will hang in together through periods of doubt, anxiety, anger, depression, and even despair."

In my experience an average of 3 percent of the participants break this commitment. Roughly half do so during the difficult stage of chaos or emptiness. An example is that of a sophisticated and successful middle-aged psychologist who announced one third of the way through a workshop of fifty-nine participants: "I know I committed myself to staying here, but I'm going to break that commitment. I'm going to leave at the end of this session tonight, and I won't be back in the morning."

The rest of us were immediately concerned. "Why?" we clamored.

"Because this is all foolishness," she replied. "I've been leading groups for twenty years, and it's impossible for a group of more than twenty to become a community—and certainly not in two days. I'm not going to sit here and participate in an inevitable failure."

One of the less "sophisticated" participants pointedly commented, "If you drop out now and we do succeed in becoming a community, you will never know that you were wrong."

"But I'm not wrong," the psychologist responded. "I know what I'm talking about. It's my profession. What you are trying to do is impossible."

So she left that evening. At the end of the next morning the remaining fifty-eight of us became a community.

More surprising is the departure of one or two participants after the group has succeeded in becoming a community. They never say why they are leaving. They just quietly slip away. But the explanation may be that there are a few people who, for one reason or another, just cannot bear that much love. If they cannot, sadly, it may be that community is not possible for them for the time being.

COMMUNITY EXERCISES

Over the years leaders have developed a wide variety of exercises that may assist groups toward greater trust, sensitivity, intimacy, and communication skills. I do not mean to decry them. But in terms of community-building per se, it is my judgment that the experience of achieving community is all the more powerful when it is done without "tricks" or "games" to smooth the process. Consequently the style with which groups in my workshops are led toward community is noteworthy for a certain purity and absence of "gimmicks." Still, there are some things classifiable as "exercises" that may often facilitate the process.

Silence. Silence is the ultimate facilitator of emptiness. After a break in a typical workshop we begin the new session with three minutes of silence. I may ask the group to reflect during these silent periods on what they as individuals may particularly need to empty themselves. Whenever I discern that the group as a whole is having a specific problem with emptiness, I will usually mandate an additional period of silence to deal with the problem. So it was that I ordered the group of Midwestern civic leaders back into silence in order to empty themselves of their well-meaning but pet projects to help their city.

Another group, still in the throes of chaos, was bogged down in focusing on a young man, Larry, whom they perceived—not without reason—as presenting a potential threat. "Something seems wrong to me about this constant focus," I broke in. "I wonder if we're not using Larry as a vehicle to express the distrust we're all feeling toward one another. He's said that he's here because of a whole complex of motives, but no one seems willing to give him the benefit of the doubt. I don't see how we can become a community without giving one another the benefit of any doubts. I'm not talking about total, blind trust. But there's a difference in quality between absolute trust and presuming others to be untrustworthy. Even though we just came out of it twenty minutes ago, I would like us to return to silence now, and during it I want all of us to empty ourselves of whatever there might be in us that would prevent us from giving every other person in the room the benefit of the doubt."

We did so, and the group came out of the silence straight into community.

Stories. The best way to learn is through experience. That is why it is better to let groups struggle toward community without giving them a detailed road map at the beginning which will guide them through the various stages, telling them all the pitfalls to avoid. The next best way to learn is through stories, whose meanings may be particularly useful for leading groups toward community.

The story of the rabbi's gift is so useful that it is told as the prologue to this book. It serves many purposes. One, for instance, is to steer groups away from the kind of vicious confrontation that gave the sensitivity-group movement a bad name. The interaction between Cynthia and Roger was a case in point. Cynthia was a middle-aged chronic schizophrenic who, quite early in the group, began to talk about herself in a manner that was rambling, incoherent, and interminable. I myself was frantically wondering what I might do to put an end to her meanderings, when Roger, an excellent but aggressive therapist as well as a veteran of many sensitivity groups, abruptly spoke up. "Cynthia," he said, "you bore me."

Cynthia looked as if she'd been hit. After a moment of stunned silence I said, "I too was unable to understand much of what Cynthia was trying to tell us. So it is likely, Roger, that others were bored as well as you. But I would like you to remember that Cynthia may be the Messiah."

Roger was duly crestfallen. Being also loving and humble, he was quick to make amends. "I want to apologize to you, Cynthia," he said. "I was feeling bored, but that didn't mean I had to be rude to you. I'm sorry. I hope you'll forgive me."

Cynthia, who perhaps had never been asked for forgiveness before, was now suddenly beaming. "I do tend to ramble," she said. "My daughter's psychiatrist told me that I need limits. So I don't mind it at all if you let me know when I've talked too much, as long as you do it nicely."

"Why don't you sit over here next to me?" Roger said. "If I think you're rambling, all I'll need to do is put my hand on your knee, and you'll know you should stop."

Cynthia tripped over to Roger's side like a young girl on a first date. Several times later that day she became long-winded and incoherent, but she happily stopped in mid-sentence when Roger touched her knee. During the second day of the group Cynthia never said a word. She just sat placidly next to Roger, quite content simply to hold hands with him.

While groups often like to discuss "The Rabbi's Gift" at the beginning, it is remarkable as they proceed how quickly the members tend to forget the story. But when they do, it is an easy matter to bring them back to its message of respect and gentleness. It is a characteristic of true community that it will squarely confront realities. It is also a characteristic that it will do so as gently and respectfully as possible.

Dreams. Dreams may also be very elegantly pointed stories. Only in this case the story is created by or through the unconscious of an individual to meet the needs of the moment. Before an overnight break in the community-building process members of the group are instructed to remember and recount particularly vivid dreams no matter how senseless they might seem on the surface. In almost every group there will be one or more individuals who fill the role of "group dreamer."

One such individual was an elderly lady whose only verbal participation was to recount an exquisite dream each morning. Typical of the early stages of community-building, during this group's first day of work together the members were having difficulty both with my seeming lack of leadership and with acknowledging their own hurts. The next morning the elderly woman was the first to speak. "Scotty told us to pay attention to our dreams," she began. "I don't imagine that it has anything to do with this group, but I'll tell you about mine if you want."

The group signified its interest with silent expectation. "All right," she said. "It probably isn't relevant, but for some reason in my dream I found myself with a friend in the emergency room of a hospital. There had been some dreadful accident or something, and the emergency room was filled with badly wounded people. We kept waiting for the doctor to come. There was nothing we could do in the meantime except wash people's wounds with water and cover them with bandages. Finally, in the company of a paramedic, the doctor arrived, but to our dismay he was totally incompetent. I mean, he was spaced out on drugs or something." (Here the group broke out in laughter at the obvious reference to my leadership.) "But then the strangest thing happened," she went on. "My friend and I were standing over this particularly badly wounded patient. The wounds were just gaping. The paramedic was beside us. He didn't do anything. He simply looked at the patient with love. But when I myself looked down, to my

amazement I saw that all the patient's wounds were healed."
Our group dreamer had pointed the way.

Prayers, Song, and Liturgy.   While I hardly understand the
metaphysics involved, I have repeatedly been impressed by
the apparent power of group prayer, particularly at times of
crisis in the process of community development. Consequently
I often suggest that members pray for the group as a whole.
"Suggest" is the operative word. To mandate it would be a
violation of respect for the religious diversity of the group.
Requiring nonbelievers to pray is inappropriate.

The issue of inappropriateness is also central to the use of
song. To sing "What a Friend I Have in Jesus" would be highly
exclusive of some members in a group containing agnostics,
atheists, Jews, or those of other religions. Usually, however,
having learned respect for diversity, a community can discover
a song that both expresses its spirit at the time and is inclusive,
so that all members feel free to join in enthusiastically. Such
appropriate singing is not merely meaningful; it may be transporting.

The same holds true for ritual. A celebration of the Eucharist may be a transporting way to conclude a community experience for a group composed entirely of Christians but not
for a more diverse one. Yet virtually every short-term community needs some kind of liturgy for its closure. Once a
group has become a community, it then becomes one of its
tasks to develop an inclusive, appropriately tailored ritual to
meet its needs to end itself with both drama and grace.

Confronting Reentry.   Such concluding rituals are one factor in dealing with the problem of reentry. Even in the earliest
days of the sensitivity-group movement, leaders recognized
that it was often painful—sometimes downright traumatic—
for people who have effected a change within themselves to
reenter a society where nothing has changed. For those who
have experienced community it can be very lonely to return to
a society where there is precious little, if any, community. Thus

it is the responsibility of community-building leaders to see to it that people are as well prepared as possible to return from the mountaintop to the narrow valleys still governed and confined by very different rules.

No amount of preparation may completely solve the difficulty. At one massive community-building experience for four hundred Christians over five days the problem of reentry was dealt with thoroughly. First it was raised in the small groups. Then there was a beautiful concluding festival Eucharist. Just before it, our chaplain gave a sermon focusing specifically and eloquently on the issues of reentry. After telling the people how impossible it would be to describe their experience to others unfamiliar with community, he went on to point out: "And those people back home are not only going to misunderstand you; they are not even going to want to hear about it. While you have been here they have been keeping the home together, they have been making the money, they have been minding the children, mowing the lawn, cooking the meals. Instead they are going to want to talk about what they have been doing, the problems that they have had, the sacrifices that they have made. It is important that you be prepared as you leave here to love those people at home."

Five days later I received a letter from a woman who had attended the conference. "It was all very well for the chaplain to tell us to go back and love the people at home," she wrote. "It was enough for me, because I was returning to a good marriage and healthy family. But the two women who drove back with me were returning to unhealthy families and lousy marriages, and they were vomiting all the way."

So the antidote of preparation for the problem of reentry, while necessary, may hardly remove all the pain. The only other antidote is the creation of more community.

CHAPTER VII

Community Maintenance

The tensions between entropic laziness, pulling us back repeatedly into traditional ways of behaving or well-worn defensive patterns, and that part of our nature that stretches toward new, better ways of creating things or relationships are omnipresent in community. Because of this tension, community once attained is never obtained for all time. We naturally fall back. Even the most skilled groups will flow continually in and out of community. Anticommunity divisive factors are always at work. To remain such, therefore, a community must forever attend to its own health. While external service may be its ultimate task, self-scrutiny and the other efforts required for self-maintenance must remain its first priority.

Until now we have focused upon the process of developing genuine community in the first place. No distinction has been made between short-term community (such as might occur in a weekend workshop, where the participants will scatter to the winds on Sunday evening) and long-term community. What happens if community is developed with an existing, relatively stable institution such as a church parish, Hebrew school, or a business corporation? What happens if strangers in a group not only succeed in forming themselves into a community but find the experience so nourishing and important that they decide to continue themselves on an ongoing basis? What are the major problems or issues of community maintenance? How can a community resolve the tension between those forces that work to stultify or disrupt it and those that tend to maintain or enliven it?

Every living organism exists in tension. For there to be life there must be tension. At the level of physiology, the process of this ongoing tension is referred to as homeostasis. Each

136

individual creature, whether it is a cat or a human being, exists in tension between sleeping and waking, rest and exercise, digesting and hunting, hunger and satiety, and so on. For a community to continue to exist, it also must live in ongoing tension. We humans hunger for genuine community and will work hard to maintain it precisely because it is the way to live most fully, most vibrantly. Being the most alive of entities, true communities must consequently pay the price of experiencing even more tension than other organizations.

The parameters over which tension will most frequently be experienced as communities struggle to maintain themselves are:

> Size
> Structure
> Authority
> Inclusivity
> Intensity
> Commitment
> Individuality
> Task definition
> Ritual

To flesh out these parameters, let me describe the vicissitudes over the life span of two long-term communities: the "Order of St. Aloysius" (OSA) and the "Basement Group." Neither actually exists. For the purposes of clarity, completeness, and confidentiality, I have constructed them as composites of similar communities with which I have had actual experience. In relation to the total number of communities that make some effort to maintain themselves, they have done so with marked success.

THE ORDER OF ST. ALOYSIUS (OSA)

Brother Anthony was a man before his time: a sophisticated middle-aged "hippy" in middle America in the days of the

Depression. Born into an Irish Catholic family in Chicago in 1895, he was a diocesan priest by the age of twenty-two. After five years of parish work his inquiring, restless mind led him to request of his diocese further education in psychology. The request was granted, and in 1927 he received his doctorate. Within a short time he was doing some of the very early work in group therapy in this country with groups of priests and monks and nuns. Through this work he experienced a sufficient degree of community to whet his appetite for more. As a consequence, in 1929 he joined a large traditional monastic teaching order. As the years passed, however, he became increasingly dissatisfied with the "active" life of this order. There was too little time for reflection, contemplation, prayer—and too little time to develop or maintain the deep sense of community that he wanted with his brother monks.

A charismatic man, Brother Anthony soon had three followers who yearned with him for a life style of more contemplation and deeper prayer. They petitioned the order to be allowed to establish a branch house with such a life style. The petition was denied. They then explored other more contemplative traditional religious orders—the Benedictines, the Cistercians, the Carmelites. These offered quiet and prayerful life styles, but in each they failed to find the intensity of community they desired. There was too much authority, too much structure. Anthony increasingly came to distrust authority and structure. He petitioned the archdiocese to begin a new order. This petition was also denied.

In 1938 Anthony and his three followers obtained sufficient money from relatives and friends to purchase a small farm in southeastern Illinois and established their own community without the blessing of the Church. The Order of St. Aloysius (OSA) was born. The structure was clear but informal to a degree that was revolutionary in those days. The four brothers would arise at five-thirty in the morning. The first hour of the day was spent together in silent meditation. Mass was celebrated at seven. After breakfast, except for a brief lunch, the day was spent in work until Vespers at five. Supper followed.

From seven to nine each evening the brothers met together in group discussion, not merely of their work and life together but of their individual spiritual journeys. They were very happy. At nine they celebrated Compline, the "tuck you into bed" concluding monastic office of the day, and retired for the night.

From the very beginning the brothers forsook their habits for ordinary work clothes. Initially Brother Anthony's followers wanted to elect him their abbot or superior. He refused adamantly, proclaiming that a genuine community was one in which everyone was a leader. Any authority structure, he said, was destructive to community. It was argued that someone needed to represent the community—to sign checks, tax forms, deeds. Anthony forcefully presented the case that even this would be dangerous and that, despite the inefficiency involved, each brother should sign every check, every legal form. As if that were not enough, he strongly advised that each of them serve in turn as celebrant of the Mass, although Brother Theodore and Brother Arthur were not ordained. "Everyone is a priest," he proclaimed. This too was agreed on, despite the fact that it defied the canons of the Roman Catholic Church. The brothers still thought of themselves as Catholics but had clearly established themselves as renegades.

Initially the work consisted of farming their small acreage, repairing the farmhouse, and begging for money for seed, materials, equipment, and expansion. In short order they turned their attention to converting the smaller barn on their property into a chapel and the larger one into a guesthouse. By early 1940 they were offering hospitality to the homeless tramps passing through the area and to occasional spiritual seekers attracted to the little monastery.

The success of their labors presented them with new joys and new problems. Anthony had made it clear to his brothers that genuine community must be inclusive. Consequently the tramps and other early guests were not only invited to participate in the meals, the farm work, and the services but also to attend the brothers' evening community meetings. Within six months, however, the monks found the presence of tramps drifting in and out of the community meetings so distracting that they were beginning to lose some of their own spirit of community. After much prayer, discussion, and contemplation, even Anthony finally acknowledged that there were limits to inclusivity. The workday was shortened so that the brothers could meet together with their guests for an hour before Vespers to discuss issues of the larger community, restricting the evening for their own nuclear community work. Before long they had to restrict working hours still further. Some of the tramps required social-work services. Moreover, ever more visitors came seeking spiritual direction from the four brothers. Manual labor now ceased with a late lunch.

Two spiritual seekers kept returning, and they asked whether they could join the order. These two then attended the evening meetings and were quickly and smoothly integrated into the nuclear monastic community. In mid-1942 they took the traditional vows of poverty, chastity, and obedience. There were now six monks in OSA. But that year brought another problem. It was not simply that it had become absurd for all six brothers to sign every check; of greater consequence was the war. The brothers were pacifists, but since OSA was not a recognized monastic order of the Catholic Church, they were all potentially draft-eligible. Someone had to represent them to negotiate for the government's recognition of the community as a bona fide monastic order. Brother Anthony refused the position. One of the new brothers, Brother David, a law school graduate who had briefly practiced, was designated to do so. By now the order was totally committed to Anthony's original instincts that all decisions should be made by consensus. It was therefore decided that Brother David should under no circumstances be called abbot, the title signifying special authority. Brother David suggested the title of trustee. It was agreed on. In the months that followed, as the legal trustee of the order he succeeded in negotiating the desired government recognition. He also became its check signer and finance manager.

The war years were quiet ones for the order. There were no more spiritual seekers. The flow of tramps gradually dried up. The community offered hospitality to Jewish and other refugees, but most such refugees moved on to urban communities. The guesthouse was usually empty. Three of the brothers went to work each morning on local farms, where labor was desperately needed. The hour before Vespers was devoted to community prayer for peace. There was time for much study. The community deepened still further, as did the spiritual life of each of the brothers.

It was a gracious respite, because with the end of the war things exploded. The majority of veterans enjoyed their welcome home from overseas as heroes and happily settled into jobs and family life. But there was a minority of young men whose souls had been bruised by the war, by the violence and evil, who turned inward and toward God. Sometimes by word of mouth, sometimes by seeming grace, they were drawn to this small rural Illinois monastic community as if to an invisible magnet. By the beginning of 1947 the guesthouse was full to overflowing with them. Most eventually drifted on, but some asked to stay. These were integrated into the evening community meetings and shortly took vows. An addition was built onto the farmhouse. The chapel was enlarged. By the end of 1949, in the space of a mere three years, the monks of OSA had increased from six to twenty.

But there were also now seeds of chaos in the community. Consensual decision making had become increasingly difficult. Many of the new brothers started to form little alliances and required spiritual direction from the older ones. Several were so scarred by the war that they needed psychiatric treatment outside of the community. Some who had made their vows within a matter of months decided to leave the order. Economically OSA was prospering. More land had been bought, and a highly successful community business had been established developing and marketing hybrid grain seeds. But as a community it was in turmoil and close to chaos.

It was those quiet war years as much as anything that enabled the order to survive. By the end of those years the first six monks had not only become deeply wise and spiritually mature individuals but had also evolved into an extraordinarily cohesive nucleus. Without even functioning as a clique, without even meeting by themselves, they were quietly able to guide the evening meetings to some brutally difficult decisions, painful to themselves as well as to the younger members.

It was decided that new members had been taken in too quickly, without adequate preparation. For this reason a six-month postulancy and a two-year novitiate were established— as in the more traditional monasteries—before vows could be taken. The seriousness of the vows was affirmed. "Pairing" (forming cliques or alliances) was actively discouraged. Several of the more newly vowed members were asked to question the validity of their vocation to monastic life, and the majority of them left. It was established that the remaining vowed monks would constitute a council, meeting one day a month to make the major consensual decisions about the order and that the postulants and novices would be excluded from this decision-making process. While it was determined that the order should still not have an abbot, Brother Anthony, now almost sixty, was prevailed upon to assume the role of novice master, in charge of the preparation of the postulants and novices for their vows and the testing of their vocations. In this way a compromise on the issue of authority was reached for the time being.

By 1956 the number of vowed monks had been reduced to sixteen, but there were four postulants and twelve novices. OSA was functioning very smoothly. It had survived the near chaos. Still, things were not perfect. The older members sensed there was not quite the same depth of joy and community that there had been in the days before and during the war. Moreover, in the nightly community meetings, now thirty-two people strong, half of the novices were voicing complaints about the council. Why should they be exempted from the most important decision making? Was their newness to the order sufficient reason to rank them as second-class citizens? Was not the order supposedly dedicated to genuine community, and was not inclusivity supposedly the sine qua non of community? Furthermore, it was the council that, in secret, made the determination of whether they, as novices, had a genuine vocation to the monastic life. Why should they have to tiptoe about, feeling on trial all the time? Was this true community?

The council took the novices seriously. Again the issues were debated, prayed over, and contemplated in depth and at length, and again effective and innovative compromise was reached. It was decided to retain the postulancy and novitiate as a time of preparation required before vows. The seriousness of both the vows and the issue of vocation was reaffirmed. However, it was decided that the novices were correct in that their exclusion from the council represented a failure to meet the ideals of community. Simultaneously it was realized that the order had become too large. Decisions were made to abolish the council, purchase a new farm, and divide the order into two autonomous houses.

Within six months the new farm had been selected, thirty miles away. And exactly half the vowed monks, postulants, and novices moved there. As in the original house, no one was in charge—no abbot, no superior, no designated head of house; there were only a new legal trustee and a new novice master for each house. It was agreed that on the last Monday of each month the two houses would gather together for any necessary discussion concerning the order as a whole, for a festival Eucharist, and for a party.

With this resolution the fullest spirit of community was restored to the order and to each of its houses. This spirit again served as a magnet. During the 1960s the number of monks and nuns in monastic communities across the country declined dramatically, but not in OSA, which more than doubled in size. By 1969 there were four autonomous houses, with forty-six monks under vows and thirty-eight postulants and novices. While as many young men in the sixties had vocations to monastic life as before, they were no longer willing to tolerate the old, formal authoritarian structures. Indeed, in the 1960s

Vatican II, among other things, vigorously addressed the problem of declining numbers and health within Catholic monasteries and changed the rules in order to gradually allow infinitely more autonomy and less rigidity. But OSA had beaten Vatican II to the punch by thirty years, and thereby exuberantly defied the national norm. From all across the country young people were attracted to the order, and what they found was so fragrant, so beautiful, that many in this time of rampant individualism became willing to commit themselves to it with unswerving dedication.

OSA did not escape, however—nothing could—the issue of individualism. In 1962 several brothers felt called to join the freedom riders in Mississippi. The majority, however, not only were called to maintain its semicontemplative life style but questioned the effect it would have upon the order if any of its members became involved in social activism—if some went one way and others another. After much prayer in the separate houses and at the monthly meetings of the order it was the consensus that it was appropriate for OSA to become involved in this particular social issue and that it could afford to do so without significant disruption of its stability. Eight vowed brothers moved to Mississippi in early 1963. The other brothers daily prayed for their ministry. In 1965 all eight returned to Illinois.

The same type of struggle arose in 1967 when a number of the brothers wanted to participate in marches or in other ways protest the Vietnam War. Once again, after much prayer and contemplation, it was decided to permit this particular kind of social activism. Many brothers marched, and those that stayed home prayed for them.

Not all individual requests were granted, however; several brothers in 1970 petitioned to be allowed a more contemplative life style. One in one house and one in another requested to build a small hermitage on the land and be exempted from the evening meetings. The decision was reached that the primary focus of the order was—and should remain—community and that the nightly community meetings were at least as essential to the order as prayer, liturgy, and contemplation. It was pointed out that if a brother was truly called to a hermetic life style, he could become a member of some other religious order in which this was possible. One of the vowed brothers left OSA to join the Trappists; the other elected to stay without special status.

Another powerful issue that year was women. Throughout the sixties many of the guests visiting the order's houses were women. Some began to want a more permanent association. The brothers were not only aware of the surfacing women's movement but were without exception deeply supportive of it. Grounded in the ethos of inclusivity, they not only found the exclusion of women from certain parts of society repugnant but were moved to examine their own exclusion of women. There were by that time several experimental monastic religious communities containing both men and women and even married couples. Two brothers and a woman friend of the order were commissioned to make a study of these experiments. What they found was not encouraging: a frequent breakdown of celibacy, much turmoil, and little stability or longevity of such communities. A fully integrated life style did not seem advisable. But the brothers were quite desirous of a less exclusive relationship with women religious. Consequently, in 1972 a fifth autonomous house was established just for women. By 1975 it was filled, and the monthly interhouse meetings were more vibrant than ever as a result.

No sooner had it dealt with the issue of women than OSA turned its attention to still another matter. As the monks and nuns became aware of how Vatican II had relaxed Rome's rigid controls over monastic communities, it became clear that it might now be possible for OSA to receive recognition from the Catholic Church. Indeed, aware of OSA's profound success, a representative of the archdiocese had already begun tentatively to sound out the order about a possible reconciliation. Many were quite reluctant at first even to consider the possibility. There was still bitterness over the fact that for more than thirty years they had been forced to be a renegade order, that they had never been helped by the Church—indeed, the Church had stood in their way. Who needs Rome? was the initial, prevailing sentiment. But the tide began to turn when Brother Anthony, now extremely frail but still sharp of mind, stood up at a monthly meeting and said, "The question is not 'Who needs Rome?' We have thus far done perfectly well without her. Instead, the primary question is 'Does Rome need us?' In other words, is the nature of the Roman Catholic Church such that it needs our support as a Eucharistic people?"

This did not put the issue to rest, but it led to an intense examination of the Church, with all of its sins in America and in the world, and whether the brothers, and now sisters of the order as well, desired to reaffirm their identity as Roman Catholics. It was a full year before consensus was reached. The monks and nuns did decide to identify themselves with the Church. But, as they wrote down very clearly, "We of OSA, with our tradition of focus upon the vitality of community, consider ourselves called to exercise ongoing leadership within the Church in regard to what it means to be a people of community."

One final point remained. Even under the relaxed rules of Vatican II, a designated leader was still required for OSA to become recognized by the Church. Despite the order's traditional distrust of leadership positions, it was not a difficult point to resolve. For some time, as the order had continued to grow in size, it had become increasingly clear that OSA did need someone to represent it as a whole—whether in negotiations with Rome or with an insurance company. The position of abbot or abbess was established. But it was made clear that this elected official, who could be either male or female, was empowered only to represent the order and did not have the authority to make any unilateral decisions of consequence. Decision making was to remain consensual, expressed in either the monthly meetings of the order or the daily meetings of its autonomous houses. It was reaffirmed that there would continue to be no "head of house" in the autonomous houses and no authority structure within them.

It is perhaps no accident that one month after OSA became an official religious order Brother Anthony, never a superior, never an abbot, quietly passed away at the age of eighty-one. The order decided to celebrate his death with one of the grandest parties ever thrown by a subdivision of the Church. It required nine months of preparation. No city in Illinois other than Chicago had adequate facilities. People came from all over: a cardinal from the Curia in Rome, three American cardinals, many representatives of the archdiocese, representatives from a hundred other religious orders, delegates from other denominations, politicians, and over a thousand Illinois farmers with their wives and children. The spirit seemed to fill the sterile halls of the hotel where the celebration was held. Even the barmaids and the desk clerks were happy that day.

Today OSA consists of nine autonomous houses, two of women and seven of men, with a hundred and thirty-one monks and nuns under vows and eighty-three postulants and novices. If an official from the Church comes to visit he will be asked if he objects to the Mass being celebrated by the unordained. If he does, one of the ordained brothers or a local priest will be dug up to fit the occasion. Otherwise a slightly modified Mass is daily celebrated in each house by the monks and nuns without regard to ordination, and the Church looks the other way. It would not be correct to say that OSA favors the ordination of women; more accurate is that it is working toward the abolition of ordination. It is no longer a renegade order, but it remains a "radical" one. It is also the most rapidly growing religious monastic order in the nation.

OSA is not an actual order. (I am not sure, for instance, that today the Church would look the other way concerning the unordained celebrating Mass.) It is a composite of features of real orders that have managed to be particularly successful in the late twentieth century. It should be borne in mind that most religious orders are not growing so exuberantly and that most are not as successful in achieving such a degree of community. But it illustrates how ongoing communities must continually construct and reconstruct themselves according to the variety of parameters in order to remain vibrant.

As with any monastic order or other "live in," "intentional community," OSA is a highly *intense* society. The lives of its members are intensely intertwined with one another, with a very high degree of interpersonal interaction. It has deliberately chosen to have a very low degree of *authority* in its organization and leadership and is extremely radical in this regard in comparison to most intense communities of any size. But its insistence on consensual decision making seems to be a key to its success. Remember, however, that the tension of the issue of leadership or authority has been an ongoing one—that there was a period when postulants and novices were excluded from decision making, that the order eventually did have to elect an abbot, and that it must continue to defy the rules of the Church in regard to issues connected with ordination.

As intense large communities go, OSA has only a moderate degree of *structure.* The daily life is highly structured, from the morning meditation period and Mass through work, Vespers, community meeting, and Compline. Politically, on the other hand, it is quite unstructured, with no committees or designated leaders. It can function with this lack of structure only because of the time devoted to community groups, which permits consensual decision making about virtually everything.

OSA decided to deal with the tension of *size* by dividing itself into small autonomous houses. Many religious orders have done likewise. Others, however, have sought to maintain centralization, with a mother house where the superior resides and all postulants and novices are trained. For OSA as a whole the issue of size presents an ongoing tension. Its large monthly meetings have become elaborate, and an abbot did finally have to be elected.

As religious orders go, OSA is highly *inclusive;* but as communities in general are concerned, it is only moderately so. On one hand, postulants and novices are included in the decision making—the order is "co-ed"—and no distinction is made between the ordained and the unordained. On the other hand, the distinction is still drawn between the vowed and those in training, the individual houses are unisexual, and the order has maintained its Catholic identity. Baptists, Jews, Buddhists, and people of other faiths may visit but cannot join. Inclusivity therefore remains an ongoing tension.

As does *individuality*. Individual members have been active in social causes but only with the community's permission. Other individual requests have been denied. Alliances between individuals are highly discouraged, and the traditional vows of individual poverty, chastity, and obedience are maintained.

With regard to vows, like other religious orders, OSA requires of its members a high degree of *commitment*—a degree seldom asked of members of less intense communities. But, as always, there is tension, and it should be remembered that the importance of the vows needed to be reaffirmed early in the community's history.

In terms of *task definition*, OSA would fall into a middle range among communities. Indeed, even among religious orders, it would be defined as "mixed," being neither totally active in the world nor totally contemplative. It defines itself as Roman Catholic but is clearly on the activist fringe of the Church. It has multiple tasks, ranging from its communal work developing hybrid seeds to the conduct of liturgy to individual spiritual growth. In terms of the premium it places on community itself, however, OSA does seem to have a rather unique, primary task.

The amount of *ritual* is great, given the daily Eucharist and offices. In this regard it is rather typical of religious orders, but seldom do nonreligious communities have as much.

There is a fine line between ritual, liturgy, and play. It is no accident that I ended the history of OSA with a joyful celebration. I once asked a wonderful Jewish man to try to tell me the secret of the success of his own very different long-term community, one centering around the development and maintenance of a Hebrew school. He in turn asked his seven-year-old daughter what she thought was best about their community.

She immediately replied, "At the school, Daddy, they laugh a lot." I'm not sure there can be a community that is truly successful when its members do not laugh and celebrate with frequent gusto.

Now that we have seen how an intensive monastic community has dealt with the common tensions of community maintenance, let us examine how these same tensions are met in a very different type of ongoing community.

THE BASEMENT GROUP

At 12:30 P.M. on a Sunday afternoon in late May 1961 the Reverend Peter Sallinger, pastor of the First Methodist Church of Blythwood, New Jersey, was shaking the hands of the last of his parishioners, glad that this generally empty ritual was over. A handsome man of about forty emerged from the shadows at the back of the church. Peter had not noticed him in the congregation. The stranger took Peter's hand. "It was a good sermon," he said, "but that's not why I hung around. I'd like to talk to you sometime at your convenience."

Peter took an instant liking to the man. "How about now?"

The man nodded, and Peter led him back to his office in the parish house. Once seated, Peter asked, "What can I do for you?"

"I'm not sure," the stranger said. "Ralph Henderson is my name. I'm a psychologist and a Christian. That's not a usual combination. I work on the staff of a local psychiatric hospital. There doesn't seem to be any room for religion in our work, and I have kept my Christianity to myself. My wife comes from a fundamentalist background and now hates religion, so I can't talk to her about it either. Going to ordinary church services frankly doesn't do much for me. You seem like a pretty authentic kind of minister. I really don't know what you can do for me. It sounds sort of stupid, but I guess I'm talking to you for no more important reason than that I'm lonely."

There was a moment of silence as they looked at each other. "You're a brave man," Peter said.

"That sounds nice," Ralph responded, "but what leads you to say so?"

"Because it's just about the most vulnerable thing I've ever heard anyone say," Peter answered. "I've been the pastor here for three years now. It's a big church, and I'm considered a good pastor, but my parishioners hardly ever talk to me about anything important, except when someone's dying, and even then they're not very open. I'm sick of their superficiality. You see," Peter concluded, "I'm lonely too."

"So what do we do about it?" Ralph asked.

"There's a thing some Christians talk about—not here much; more down in the Bible Belt if anywhere—called—a Christian support group."

"Go on."

"There's not much more to tell—just a group of people who get together to support one another with their difficult ministries. I have an Episcopal priest friend who's in the same sort of boat as I am—feeling pretty alienated from his congregation. I think he'd be willing to join with us."

"But I don't have a ministry," Ralph said. "I'm not a minister."

"Bull," Peter replied. "Everyone's got a ministry. Yours is in mental health. And you've already told me it's difficult because you're a Christian in an alien profession. As a matter of fact, most of these support groups have been started by business-men. If you want to know what the most difficult Christian ministry of all is, it's in business. That's a really alien world. Anyway, the point is that everyone's a potential minister. Their only choice is whether to be a good minister or a bad one. To be a good one, it helps to be aware that you are, in fact, a minister, and that you do, in fact, have a ministry. I suggest you cultivate that awareness."

Ralph smiled. "Okay, boss."

That is how the Basement Group started: two Protestant clergymen and a Christian psychologist meeting together for two hours one night each week in Ralph's basement den.

Within six months they were joined by a Christian psychiatrist whom Ralph had uncovered, and a Catholic priest who had become known to Peter. It was decided to begin each meeting with three minutes of silence and end with each member saying a brief, heartfelt prayer out loud. Beyond the set time of two hours and the simple liturgy of opening silence and closing prayer there was no structure in the group. A member could speak about whatever he wanted whenever the spirit moved him. The only rule was vulnerability. The members agreed to push themselves to be as vulnerable as possible. They shortly came to realize vulnerability required not only that they speak of intimate matters but also that they listen to one another with openness and a relative emptiness of judgment. They had become a true community.

In the late winter of 1962 the group was joined by a rabbi. There was some discussion that this meant it was no longer specifically a "Christian" support group. The matter did not seem important, however. But the situation was more tricky six months later when Ralph suggested inviting an atheist colleague, a vulnerable man who wanted community but was vociferous in his unbelief. Three successive evenings were required to integrate him. He said he had no trouble with the opening silence but could not participate in the closing prayers. Could he tolerate the rest of the group's praying, he was asked—and listen to its prayers—remaining silent during the ritual? He said he could. This compromise was simple enough. The more basic question was whether an atheist's membership meant the group could no longer be a religious support group. The other members affirmed the centrality of their religious faith to their support and were not willing to park their belief at the door. The atheist committed himself to listening to their belief as long as they were willing to listen to his nonbelief. The believers decided they did not want theirs to be an exclusive faith. The religious tone of the group was maintained, the atheist was included, and the group was defined simply as a support group. This process of inclusion was not easy. By its end, however, the spirit of community was even stronger.

In 1963 the first woman joined—one of the earliest Protestant clergywomen in the state. Given her ground-breaking role, her need for a supportive community was intense. Inclusive in spirit, the group had no difficulty assimilating her. Two businessmen joined the same year.

At the beginning of 1964 Ralph Henderson was offered the chairmanship of a university department of psychology on the West Coast. It was a move he could not refuse to make. Both he and the group grieved over his departure. But in the midst of grief there was much laughter as Ralph's departure stimulated the development of the group's central myth. Until now the group had been meeting each week in the den in Ralph's basement. Finding another place was simple; each member offered his or her own home, church, or synagogue. But in dealing with the matter the group became profoundly aware of how much they all enjoyed meeting specifically in a basement. As they thought about why they should have developed this strange proclivity they came to three conclusions. Ralph, before he left, pointed out that in dreams a basement usually symbolizes the unconscious mind—that which is beneath the surface. Many in the group had become intrigued by the way the spirit or "something" seemed to operate through their unconscious minds to facilitate their work together. Second, they were struck by the analogy between support and a basement. As one member put it, "This group has become so important to me that sometimes it seems like the very *foundation* of my life." Finally the group realized—even its atheist—that they were banded together because they were all ministers or leaders in a world in which they were generally not free to say what they thought or be vulnerable the way they wanted. "It's as if we're sort of *underground*," another member capsulized it. It was only natural, then, that they should want to meet underground.

So it was they came to name themselves the "Basement Group." In the years since then the group has always taken pains to hold its weekly meetings in a basement. Sometimes it has met in elegantly carpeted dens or playrooms. And sometimes it has been crowded into a space next to a furnace and hot-water heater with steam pipes just overhead. But either way, it has now become inconceivable that the group should ever assemble aboveground.

In the beginning some members smoked or drank beer during meetings. Within a short while, however, it was decided that these activities diminished the intensity of interaction. "No smoking, no drinking during group" became an unwritten rule. The issue of parties was also raised during the early days. The members so much enjoyed each other's company, it seemed that they would want to socialize together at other times. One party was held with just the group, and another with spouses. But both were strangely lackluster events, with the usual spirit missing. The group decided it was not called to party, and never has since. But there is no rule that individual members cannot "socialize outside the group." Pairing has never been prohibited. Indeed, over its twenty-five-year life span the group has produced several romantic relationships and one marriage. Any couple pairing has had to talk about their relationship in the group. Another unwritten rule has been "You can't be vulnerable and keep secrets." For the most part, however, group members decided not to relate significantly with each other beyond their two hours a week together. For them the group has been a quiet, hidden lodestone in their more ordinary lives.

Another crucial issue was worked out in the first two years. It was natural for the early members to probe each other and interpret each other's lives. But gradually the group discovered that some degree of chaos was the invariable result. All by itself it came to the wisdom that attempts to heal or convert were generally more destructive than supportive. As it had come to define itself as a group that did not party, so it defined itself quite quickly as "not a therapy group." "We are just, merely and only, a support group," it would tell new members. "It is our purpose to love, not to heal." But as with any genuine community, many members of the Basement Group have experienced great healing through it.

Not all, however. The year 1965 was a difficult one for the group. Ted, the manager of a local country club, joined in February of that year. Charming, witty, and affable, he seemed to fit in well at first. But he arrived at the first session in April magnificently drunk. With inappropriate boisterousness he kept focusing attention on himself, but nothing anyone said to him had any effect. All the group was able to do effectively was make him drink lots of coffee so that he was sober enough to drive home afterward.

The next week Ted was sober and full of remorse. He denied having a drinking problem, said he'd never done anything like that before, and had no idea why it had happened. Group questions about his burdens got nowhere. The following week he arrived intoxicated again. His behavior was so disruptive the group had no choice but to confront him with his alcoholism during the successive session when he was sober once more. Ted proclaimed he was not an alcoholic but this time spoke of his many frustrations in getting the golf course ready and dealing with the complaints of wealthy players. The group hoped this ventilation would be helpful. It was not. Ted was more drunk than ever the following session. Some of the members took him to the emergency room of a local hospital. The hospital would not admit him. During the week several members arranged for a representative from AA to attend the next meeting. With this man's help they continued to confront Ted. Ted denied he was an alcoholic. The group pointed out that anyone who showed up drunk to three out of six meetings was an alcoholic. Ted acknowledged that he might be one but insisted there was no reason for him to attend Alcoholics Anonymous, since he already had a support group. The representative from AA said that Ted had not yet "hit bottom."

The week after that Ted did not appear. The session was spent discussing his case. A member volunteered to get in touch with his wife. The member reported the next week— with Ted present and sober—that Ted's wife was well aware of his alcoholism but felt helpless. The volunteer had recommended that she attend Alanon, and she had seemed grateful for the suggestion. Ted said he resented the group's interference in his private life. The group told him that was tough. The following week Ted showed up in the middle of the group session, once again intoxicated. An emergency meeting was held without him the very next night to discuss how Ted's alcoholism had totally dominated ten consecutive meetings and might well destroy the group. Reluctantly the group came to the conclusion that it had to set limits.

Ted was sober the next session, and the group said to him: "Ted, we cannot compel you to go to AA, although we all agree it would be the best course for you to follow. Nor do we want to kick you out of the group. But for the past ten weeks we haven't been able to do anything except focus on you. Your drinking is preventing the group from fulfilling its function, which is to support *all* of its members. You are welcome to continue in the group, but only sober and only if you stay sober. If you want to drink outside of the group, that's your affair. But if you ever come here intoxicated again, not only will you not be welcome but we will have to refuse to ever allow you back."

The very next meeting Ted showed up drunk and unruly, insisting upon staying. The police were immediately called. No charges were pressed, so the police simply took Ted home. He never showed up at the group again.

Three more sessions were spent largely focusing on Ted as the group dealt with its grief and guilt. Had they failed him? Was there anything more they could have done? Had they done anything they shouldn't have? Could they have been more loving? Ultimately they concluded they had done the best they could, and even if Ted had learned nothing from the experience, they at least had learned something about their limitations. They kept in touch with Ted through his wife for a year until she divorced him and moved to Arkansas to live with her parents. They donated money to help her move. What happened to Ted thereafter no one in the group knows, but his memory is preserved in its traditional wisdom that it cannot solve all problems.

In other instances the group has decided not to set limits. Roger, one of the early businessmen to join the group, shortly received a corporate promotion that required extensive traveling, so that he was able to attend only one out of every three sessions. He offered to "resign," but the group was unanimous in wanting him to continue with them even on a partial basis. This was not a difficult decision, since Roger's commitment to the group was demonstrable and palpable.

More difficult was the problem of the "drifters." These were men and women who, over the years, drifted in and out of the weekly meetings, coming only when they felt like it and lacking any real commitment to the group. Initially they angered the committed members. Why should they be exempted from commitment? Didn't the support, which was the basic purpose of the group, arise out of the commitment of the members to each other? Gradually, however, as the group struggled with the ambiguity of the issue, clarity began to emerge. For one thing, the drifters did not monopolize the group as Ted had done, and their intermittent presence was not sufficiently distracting to destroy the group. They also introduced some new blood and occasional insights. Finally, a few of the drifters ultimately became committed members. Over a period of years, therefore, a policy evolved. It was decided that some people did need to test the waters before arriving at a commitment and that as long as there was a substantial *nucleus* of the committed, the group was able to bear the burden of the uncommitted.

The size of the committed nucleus of the New Jersey Basement Group has varied from three to eleven over the twenty-five years of its existence. Today it is eight. But in some ways the Basement Group is much larger. Ralph and Peter, the two founding members, when they moved away, established new support groups in their new locations. So did three others. Two of these groups eventually disintegrated, but there are now separate Basement Groups in four different cities. They communicate with one another through an annual newsletter, "The Basement Blurb," which reports the events and lessons of each group over the year and publishes contributors' reminiscences about past years as well. It is not only effective networking, it does much to keep the traditions alive and pass them on.

Let us now compare the Order of St. Aloysius and the Basement Group to see the ways in which they have dealt with the issues that all long-term communities must face and how they have aligned themselves similarly or differently along the basic parameters of community maintenance.

Size has never been a problem for the Basement Group as it was for OSA. Because of the mobility of its members—all engaged in separate careers—the nucleus never became larger than eleven, and the group never became so large that it interfered with its task of mutual support.

The Basement Group is a community of low *intensity,* meeting two hours a week. Some true communities have maintained themselves with monthly meetings, but their staying power is generally not great. OSA, on the other hand, with its communal life, routine liturgy, and daily meetings, is a community of high intensity.

The Basement Group is as *inclusive* as a community can be. Anyone interested is welcome; there are no entrance procedures or stages; even drifters are given full membership. Compare this high inclusivity to the much lower inclusivity of OSA, where there are entrance stages, and vows of commitment are eventually required. But note that even the Basement Group could not survive with total inclusivity. Ted's behavior was such that he had to be excluded.

Similarly, the Basement Group has an ultimate degree of room for *individuality.* Only gross antisocial behavior cannot be tolerated. Had its intensity been greater, things might have been different. But 98 percent of the members' lives occur outside of community, so the variety of their life styles in no way interferes with its function. OSA, on the other hand, was unwilling to allow hermits, and, except when they were "on mission" in the civil rights or antiwar movement, all the members were expected to adopt the same life style. Still, it needs to be noted that the Basement Group could survive as a community only because it had a committed *nucleus*. So also was OSA able to survive the tumultuous years after World War II. This is a reflection of an across-the-board rule of community. There must be a high degree of *commitment* to community for a group to become a community in the first place, and there must be a committed nucleus for any community to maintain itself.

The Basement Group has a relatively low degree of *structure*. Each session is held in a basement on a weekly basis, begins on time, and ends on time. But it should be borne in mind that community is not possible with either no structure or total structure. With no structure there is chaos. With total structure there is no room for emptiness. From the end of its opening silence until the beginning of its closing prayers each session of the Basement Group is up for grabs. There is no agenda. No one knows which member will talk first or about what. Vulnerability is the only rule.

There is little authority in the Basement Group. The level of designated leadership and organization is extremely low. All decisions are consensual. In this regard the Basement Group and OSA are similar. Communities can exist with a greater degree of formal leadership, but authoritarian leadership is incompatible with true community, in which everyone's gifts are recognized and everyone leads according to them.

The Basement Group is low along the parameter of *ritual*. There are the opening silence and the closing prayers (which are highly individualized), but there is otherwise no ritual celebration. In part, this lack of ritual is related to the fact that the group falls very high on the parameter of specific *task definition*. OSA has defined its tasks quite clearly, but has many of them: mutual support, religious celebration, the production and marketing of seed, the training of novices, and occasional social action. The Basement Group has been very careful to restrict itself to a single task: mutual support. It does not attempt to celebrate or to heal. Still, there is much laughter during its two-hour sessions, and many have found their membership healing.

The healing effect of community has yet to receive the serious scientific research it deserves. Long-term community, in which the experience is either less intensive (as in the Basement Group) or in which dishes must be washed and money made as an integral part of community life (like OSA), is inevitably a less ecstatic, less dramatic experience than a weekend community workshop. But there is reason to suspect that the healing involved, while more slow and steady, may ultimately be even deeper.

MAINTENANCE OR DEATH?

Since its virtues are so great, the maintenance of genuine community over as long a time as possible is an ideal. However, it is an ideal *on general principle,* which means it is not necessarily virtuous for each and every community to attempt to be immortal. Communities, like individual human beings, are organisms with differing life spans, some of which, as we shall see, are more proper than others.

Alcoholics Anonymous is a community of millions. Organizationally it is an extraordinarily loose, relatively unstructured federation of tens of thousands of small subcommunities, or chapters. New chapters are continually being started, accounting for its phenomenal growth. Yet some chapters fade away and close. This process is not unique to AA. In large monastic orders consisting of dozens of autonomous houses, for example, some of these houses are filled with the spirit and currently growing in size. Some are stable. And some are dying.

The longevity of a community is no more adequate a measure of its success than the length of an individual human life attests to its fulfillment. I have known many beautiful people in their eighties. I have also known some chronically hateful and vicious people of equal age who have lived destructive lives for years. And I have further known saints who died young. Communities have a proper, natural life span that will vary according to the reason(s) for their creation. Some communities seemingly do fail to live out their potential. Others degenerate into institutional senile sterility for a lengthy period after they seem to have outlived their usefulness.

How can a community discern whether it is properly ready to die or whether it is simply in a slump from which it can recover by making a change that will recapture its spirit and help it to maintain itself? There is no formula for discernment that relieves a group, any more than an individual, of the agonizing judgment involved. But there are a few principles that can help. The first is to ask the question. To bear in mind the possibility of death does not hasten one's demise so much as help one live more fully. A long-term community willing to face routinely the frightening prospect of its death is likely either to strive more vigorously for vitality and renewal or get on with the business of dying more efficiently and gracefully.

A second principle is that discernment takes time. I was once a member of a long-term community that initially gathered together with the specific task of creating a new type of social-service organization. We succeeded in this task after a year of weekly meetings but were reluctant to disband at that point, however, for two reasons. One was that we did not want to lose the fellowship of true community that had developed over the year. The other was our uncertainty about whether we had indeed created the best possible organization. So we continued to meet. But the spirit had left. Attendance became poor. The frequency of our meetings was decreased to every other week and then to once a month. Neither the spirit nor the attendance improved. Finally, after two years, we buried the group. Had we been more conscious from the beginning of the group's option to die, I do not think we would have dragged out the process as long as we did. On the other hand, I do think it was proper that we waited for a while at least to discern whether the spirit would bring forth a new task.

In relation to the issue of task, the final guideline of discernment for a community in slump is to ask itself whether it is avoiding a task or whether it no longer has a task. It is not always an easy question to answer. Sometimes a group can be so frightened of its task that it would rather terminate itself than face up to what it is avoiding. But if it can remember to ask itself seriously whether it is avoiding a task, it is not likely to fall into the pit of committing suicide rather than doing the work of remaining vital until the time comes for its natural death.

Questions of community maintenance and community death also revolve around the process called enemy formation. Groups that would not otherwise become a community, we have seen, frequently do so in response to a threat or crisis: a tragedy, a natural disaster, an enemy attack, or war. This is hardly to be decried when the threat is genuine. The problem comes when this instinctive response of cohesiveness to threat is manufactured. The process of enemy formation occurs when a group that has lost the spirit of community attempts to regain it by creating a threat—an enemy—that otherwise would not exist. The example best known is that of Nazi Germany, where the Hitler regime achieved an extraordinary cohesiveness among the majority of Germans by whipping up hatred against a minority, the Jews. But it is a common, widespread phenomenon of which any culture can be guilty. For instance, President Johnson, as best as can be ascertained, whipped up cohesive support in Congress for his policies in Vietnam by manufacturing a fictitious attack against American ships: the Gulf of Tonkin "incident."

The process of enemy formation is perhaps the most devastating form of all human behavior. Individuals engage in it as well as groups. The consequences are the same to both. While initially it may appear to enhance the functioning of a group, it is actually a symptom of community decay and death. In fact, the group has ceased to be a genuine community. It becomes progressively exclusive rather than inclusive. It has become "we against them," and love has been lost. And the imaginary enemy it has created shortly becomes a real one. The Holocaust inevitably spawned militant, military Zionism.

The ultimate result of the Gulf of Tonkin "incident" was to solidify militant communism in Vietnam. Enemy formation is invariably a self-fulfilling prophecy. The nonexistent prophesied threat is called into existence by the prophecy.

To maintain themselves, genuine communities must be ever vigilant not against external forces but internal ones. They must stand for the good rather than against the bad. This is said not to deny the reality of evil in the world but to preserve the good from contamination. If a group previously a community finds itself beginning to indulge in enemy formation, it should seriously consider whether the proper time has not come for its own death—or, at the very least, radical change in itself. The end of once fine traditions is preferable to the nurturing of decay and the forces of hatred and destruction.

Although genuine community is not easily achieved or easily maintained, few would argue with its avowed goals: to seek ways in which to live with ourselves and others in love and peace. Or do we merely pay them lip service as we continue to behave as individuals in ways that do not support those goals? Tragically, such lip service behavior is both reflected and reinforced on a global scale by the behavior of national governments.

A world at peace is the current goal of many national governments. Yet they do not conduct themselves as true communities, which is the only way to achieve it. The true community in dealing with a supposedly evil member must continually agonize over the question of whether the exclusion of that member is justified or is instead a form of scapegoating. Almost as a matter of course, nations accuse each other of being evil. But how accurately is that diagnosis made? To what degree do governments agonize over such a diagnosis? How frequently does scapegoating—or what I have called enemy formation—occur in the course of international relations? The problem of evil is one to be solved by the true community as a whole and not by a single designated leader. To what extent is the problem of evil in international relations met by a community of nations, or to what extent is it met by single nations and their designated leaders?

To achieve genuine community the designated leader must lead and control as little as possible in order to encourage others to lead. In so doing, she or he must often admit weakness and risk the accusation of failing to lead. How willing are our national leaders to risk such accusations? How motivated are they to encourage the development of leadership in and among others? The task-avoidance assumption of dependency is discouraged in order to achieve true community. Do national leaders tend to encourage or generally discourage dependency among the peoples they serve? What are our conceptions of strength and weakness in our designated leaders—national or otherwise—and how well do these conceptions fit reality, particularly in relation to the search for peace?

To be effective in community-making, designated leaders must keep their focus on the groups as a whole. In regard to international relations, do our national leaders generally succeed in maintaining such a global concern? Or do they tend to think first about their own purely national interests or possibly those of their allies? And is not the formation of special friendships or alliances a manifestation of the task-avoidance assumption of pairing, destructive to the development of global community?

Then there are the other task-avoidance assumptions. Do national leaders encourage the body politic to face up to difficult, painful issues or try to steer away from them? And do we, as individuals, prefer to avoid such issues—in part by selecting leaders who promise magically to enable us to flee from them? Is this task-avoidance assumption of flight perhaps not the primary mode of behavior of the body politic? And is the task-avoidance assumption of fight not the prevalent modus operandi in the chaotic arena of international relations? Could it be that national leaders are behaving as if they assumed it their purpose to fight rather than seek consensus or concord, thereby totally losing sight of the task of peacemaking?

Thus, on every front it seems that the rules by which nations behave are generally antithetical to virtually everything we know about the rules of community-making. At a time when war could so easily cause the destruction of the world we continually behave according to rules that seem almost perfectly designed to lead us ever closer to war. We know that the existence of crisis can facilitate the development of community. Yet we seem to be unable to perceive the threat of nuclear holocaust as a crisis of such magnitude and chronicity that we must change the rules.

We know the rules of community; we know the healing effect of community in terms of individual lives. If we could somehow find a way across the bridge of our knowledge, would not these same rules have a healing effect upon our world? We human beings have often been referred to as social animals. But we are not yet community creatures. We are impelled to relate with each other for our survival. But we do not yet relate with the inclusivity, realism, self-awareness, vulnerability, commitment, openness, freedom, equality, and love of genuine community. It is clearly no longer enough to be simply social animals, babbling together at cocktail parties and brawling with each other in business and over boundaries. It is our task—our essential, central, crucial task—to transform ourselves from mere social creatures into community creatures. It is the only way that human evolution will be able to proceed.

PART II
The Bridge

CHAPTER VIII

Human Nature

In examining the phenomenon of community at a relatively local level—a small Quaker school, groups of forty to four hundred who have assembled for two days to two weeks to experiment with communication, the civic leaders of a small city, a single church congregation, a small support group, a convent here, and a monastery there—we have learned some very basic and important principles. We know how to distinguish between genuine community and pseudocommunity. We understand the requirements that must be met before human beings can effectively communicate with one another—before they can enter into community. The dynamics of the community-building process have been elucidated. The challenges of community participation and community maintenance have been discussed. Above all we have learned that, given the right conditions, it is indeed possible for small groups of people to live together routinely with love and in the spirit of peace.

That realization was for me not the end of a search but merely the beginning. For it opened up a new vista of possibilities. If small groups, why not larger ones? If single congregations, why not entire churches? If the civic leaders of a small city, why not all of the citizens of entire towns, cities, and even states? If states, why not the nation? If one nation, why not all of the nations of the world?

It seems difficult to imagine a world in which all differences are transcended, a contemplative world in which realistic decisions are reached by consensus. How could such a world be possible? Ours is a civilization in which racial, cultural, and political differences have driven us apart, a world of action and reaction, of leaders and followers. It is human nature. To take any significant steps in the direction of world community,

169

we presume that human nature would somehow have to change or be changed. Somehow we would all have to become the same. And that too is impossible. Yet in community on a small scale as I experienced it, that presumption proved to be false. Individual differences were accepted and celebrated. Perhaps the first step, then, toward community on a grander scale lies in the acceptance of the fact that we are *not,* nor can we ever be, all the same.

THE PROBLEM OF PLURALISM

Because each of us is unique, inevitably we live in a pluralistic society, and we take pride in the United States as a pluralistic society. More than two hundred million of us manage to live together in relative peace despite being of many races and backgrounds, with very different outlooks, needs, traditions, religions, and economic means. But such pride is often arrogant and provincial. Americans tend to forget the fact that Russian society seems to be able to survive—albeit through different means and styles—at least an equal diversity among its people. And Russians tend to ignore the American success. In any case, pluralism is sometimes celebrated.

Usually, however, pluralism is seen as a problem. For the fact of the matter is that we Americans (or the Russians) live together only in *relative* peace. The relationship in this country between blacks and whites and groups of various ethnic and national origins is generally uneasy at best. The wealthy and the poor are seldom enamored of each other. Special-interest groups deluge Congress with their competing demands. The Christian Church is divided into dozens of denominations. Even within the denominations, Christians squabble with each other as the debate between Lutheran synods, pre- and post-Vatican II Catholics, liberal and conservative Southern Baptists often becomes acrimonious.

Pluralism also characterizes the nations of the world, and if their squabbles do not become actual war, the weapons deemed necessary for their defense directly cost the people of the world well over a trillion dollars a year. The indirect costs are incalculable, and such is the destructive power of these weapons that entire populations suffer constant uncertainty as to their survival. Thus the so-called "deterrence" of the arms race seems merely to aggravate the problem of pluralism. There is only one decent solution to the problem, whether it is within a church, within a nation, or within the world as a whole: community.

Remember that community is a state of being together in which people, instead of hiding behind their defenses, learn to lower them, in which instead of attempting to obliterate their differences, people learn not only to accept them but rejoice in them. It is not a place for "rugged" individualism. As a place for "soft" individualism, however, it actually encourages pluralism. Through community the problem of pluralism ceases to be a problem. Community is a true alchemical process that transforms the dross of our differences into golden harmony.

To understand more deeply how this happens, we must also understand at the most radical level just why we human beings are so different and, at the very same time, just what it is that we all have in common. We must answer the question What is human nature?

THE ILLUSION OF HUMAN NATURE

To most people a myth is a tall tale, a story that is not true or real. Increasingly, however, psychologists are coming to realize that myths are myths precisely because they are true. Myths are found in one form or another in culture after culture, age after age. The reason for their permanence and universality is precisely that they are embodiments of great truths.

Dragons are creatures of myth. Long before the fire-breathing fantasies of today's comic books and television cartoons, Christian monks throughout Europe were illuminating manuscripts with painstaking illustrations of dragons. So were

Taoist monks in China. And Buddhist monks in Japan. And Hindus in India. And Muslims in Arabia. Why? Why dragons? Why should these mythical beasts be so extraordinarily ecumenical and international?

The reason is that dragons are symbols of human beings. And as mythical symbols, they say something very important about the basic truths of human nature. We are snakes with wings, worms that can fly. Reptilelike, we slink close to the ground and are mired in the mud of our animal nature and the muck of our cultural prejudices. Yet, like birds, we are also of the spirit, capable of soaring in the heavens, transcending, at least for moments, our narrow-mindedness and sinful proclivities. So it is that I sometimes tell my patients that part of their task is to come to terms with their dragonhood, to decide whether they want most to exercise the more slothful or more spiritual aspects of their nature.

As a mythic symbol—and all myths are about human nature, one way or another—dragons are relatively simple. But as in dreams, many meanings can be condensed into a single myth. Take the wonderful story of Adam and Eve, the Garden, the apple, and the snake (dragons have slipped in, even here). Is it a story of our fall from grace and alienation from our environment? Or is it a story of our evolution into self-consciousness (and hence that shyness that is so essentially human)? Or both? It is also a story of human greed and fear and arrogance and laziness and disobedience in response to the call to be the best we can be. And it tells us that we can no longer go back to that unself-conscious state of oneness with the world (the way is blocked by a flaming sword) but can find our salvation only by going forward through the rigors of the desert into ever deeper levels of consciousness.

Even the simplest of myths is multifaceted, because, like dragons, we are multifaceted beings. Indeed, this is the very reason for myths. Our nature is so multifaceted and paradoxical that it cannot be captured in words that represent single, simple categories. Myths are required to contain and embrace the richness of human nature.

Because it is multifaceted and complex, simplistic definitions of human nature not only fail to do its richness justice, they are extremely dangerous. Any falsity is dangerous, and the misapprehension of human nature particularly so, since such misapprehension is one of the foundations of war. The primary false notion—the illusion—of human nature is that people are the same. You have all heard this illusion in one of its many forms: "People are pretty much alike the world over"; "Under the skin all men are brothers"; "They have a different kind of government, but the Russian people are basically just like us."

This illusion is the basis for the "evil ruler" theory. Growing up during World War II, I was deeply indoctrinated with this theory. Many of us had German friends and relatives who seemed as humane as we. Since we believed that the Germans were "just like us," the only way we could account for their atrocious behavior was to assume that somehow they had been enslaved by the madman Hitler, the evil ruler. Erich Fromm's seminal work, *Escape from Freedom*, was so important precisely because it exposed this illusion.* In it, Fromm compellingly demonstrated that insofar as they had become enslaved, it was because the German people had sold out to Hitler. He elucidated profound and unique forces in German history, culture, and society which encouraged their sellout. Hitler did not so much wrest their freedom from them as they willingly escaped from it. They mostly colluded with Hitler.

Despite this insight of almost fifty years ago, we continue to perpetuate the simplistic notion that people are all alike by believing that the Russian people are "just like us" and using the "evil ruler" theory to explain their behavior as a nation. So we believe that the Russian people are thirsting for democracy, "just like us," but that it is only their "evil rulers in the Kremlin" who keep them from achieving it. I do not mean to equate the governments of Nazi Germany and Soviet Russia. They are quite different. Yet we have responded to each with

*Erich Fromm, *Escape from Freedom* (New York: Rinehart, 1941).

"the evil ruler" theory, as if both governments had the same kind of ruler and as if the Russians have nothing to do with their government. Hedrick Smith, Moscow bureau chief for *The New York Times* during the Watergate period, discovered that the Russian people—"the man in the street"—simply could not understand what all the fuss was about or why the Americans would even consider deposing a strong ruler such as Nixon over such a minor, ordinary affair.* So much for crediting the Russians with a simple thirst for democracy "just like us."

Would that things were so simple! But while it is true that governments do not entirely enslave their people, it is also simplistic to assume that governments—totalitarian and otherwise—do not influence and in some way blind their citizens. Here in America the leaders we elect to office tend to perpetuate that blindness, just as the totalitarian government of Russia in its own way tends to perpetuate the blindness of its citizens.

Yet it would still be simplistic to think that the interaction between the government and the people obeys the same dynamics in Russia and in the United States or in any other country. The relationship between government and governed is a kind of ongoing dance of culture. Since cultures, like their people, are not all the same but profoundly different, these dances of culture are no more similar than fox-trots, waltzes, polkas, and horas.

Even so, to state that the human beings of a different culture share absolutely *no* similarities is yet another oversimplification. The previously mentioned article, "Education as Transformation: Becoming a Healer Among the !Kung and the Fijians," describes the lifelong process of training (largely self-training) that the healers of these two "primitive" cultures underwent.† Although the languages and concepts of both

* Hedrick Smith, *The Russians* (New York: Ballantine Books, 1977), pp. 320–324.
† Richard Katz, "Education and Transformation: Becoming a Healer Among the !Kung and Fijians," *Harvard Educational Review*, Vol. 51, No. 1 (1981).

"medicine" and healing in specific or religion in general were utterly different in the two cultures, the dynamics of the process of transformation of these healers over the years were remarkably similar. In fact, the transformational journey of healers in these two "primitive" non-Christian cultures is much the same as that undertaken by many Christian monks and nuns and other spiritual seekers in our own culture. I submit that the dynamics of the spiritual journey are the same the world over. They are a given of human nature and are one of the complex features we all have in common.

The dynamics of spiritual development provide another example of the simultaneous uniqueness and similarity of human beings. Men and women are uniquely different. While anatomic differences are obvious, over the years I have come to be equally aware of the nonanatomic differences—of not only our different sexes but also our different sexualities, our different styles. The argument is endless regarding the degree to which psychological femininity and masculinity are genetically or culturally determined. But while the nature/nurture debate rages on, no one—least of all myself—can doubt the profound difference between the spirit of maleness and the spirit of femaleness. Yet in the course of twenty years of practicing psychotherapy, I have been impressed by the reality that men and women must come to terms with the very same psychospiritual issues and climb over the same hurdles on their way to maturity. Male or female, they need to learn how to individuate themselves from their parents, their spouses, and their children; how to develop a full sense of responsibility and autonomy, and, once this is done, how to develop a capacity for surrender; how to deal with physical aging and struggle with the mystery of their own death. Subjectively and objectively, I, a man, am dramatically different from you, a woman. Yet simultaneously we are both equally human.

Subjectively and objectively, being an American is very different from being a Russian. There are many ways in which we do not think alike. But we also must face the same mortality and struggle with the same issues of what it means to be hu-

man. Male and female, Russian and American, with this gene
or that, from a stable home or a broken home, we are each one
of us both body and spirit. It is to that reality that the myth of
dragons speaks. We are all dragons.

Thus the answer to that all-important question "What is
human nature?" must be a paradoxical one. Human beings
are profoundly different and profoundly similar. But perhaps
because it would be a much simpler world if we were all alike,
it is the tendency of human beings in all cultures to err dreadfully on the side of severely underestimating our differences.
That our cultural differences are, in fact, enormous was con-
clusively demonstrated in Ruth Benedict's *Patterns of Culture,**
in which she described three cultures wherein the prevailing
styles, tastes, sexual roles, values, expectations, and world views
were not only dramatically different but sometimes diametri-
cally opposed. Further, what is considered "normal" in one
culture could be judged distinctly abnormal in another, and
even conceptions of good and evil are to a considerable extent
culturally determined.

To cite another example of this cultural determinism, most
of the supposed evils that we Americans ascribe to Russian
communism actually have very little to do with communism.
The Russian tradition of exiling political dissidents to Siberia
is an ancient one, extending back several centuries before Karl
Marx was born or Lenin came to power. It is no more communist than czarist. We criticize communist leaders for restricting the travel of foreigners or offering them pretentious
displays that unrealistically show off the "wonders" of Soviet
society. Yet it was the custom for the czars to build fake villages
filled with happy peasants (who would at night return to their
real hovels) for the benefit of eighteenth- and nineteenth-
century tourists. Soviet society is indeed totalitarian, but the
communist revolution replaced one totalitarian government
with another. The majority of Russians for hundreds of years
have demonstrated a tendency to submit themselves to pow-

* Ruth Benedict, *Patterns of Culture* (Boston: Houghton Mifflin, 1961).

erful leaders. Over and over again our own leaders tell us that it is necessary to deal realistically with the Russians. It is difficult, however, to understand how we can be realistic when we have not even learned how to distinguish between our political differences and our far deeper cultural ones.

That is not to say that all cultural differences are immutable, as I once learned to my chagrin. During my tour of duty on Okinawa I decided I wanted to visit the psychiatric hospitals there. A number of Americans were similarly interested, so the interpreter for our hospital, a sophisticated Japanese woman, organized a daylong tour for us. Having noted that the patients in one hospital slept on nothing but a tatami mat to separate them from the cement floor, another American exclaimed, "It's terrible the way the patients are treated here. I didn't imagine that their hospitals would be this bad. You'd think that they'd at least give their patients beds to sleep on."

Since the place seemed more neat and orderly than many of the state hospitals I had visited in America, I was quick to chide him. "You shouldn't assume this to be a bad hospital," I pontificated. "In Japanese culture it is normal to sleep on tatami mats. The patients would probably be frightened by beds. They wouldn't know what to do with them. Coming from a different culture, they prefer sleeping this way."

At this point our interpreter chided *me*. "It is true that this is not necessarily a bad hospital," she said. "It is also true that if you put a Japanese peasant in a hotel room with a bed, he would be likely to unroll his tatami mat the first few nights. However, once a Japanese adult has had a chance to sleep on a bed, it is seldom that she or he will sleep on a tatami mat again, given the choice."

Among those who recognize that some cultural differences, at least, are capable of change, it is almost always assumed that it is their culture, their reality, that is both good and superior and that it is the people of *other* cultures who must change. But that again is an expression of the illusion of human nature carried to an even more dangerous extreme. Not only does it postulate that all human beings are essentially alike, it assumes that they *should* be. And those who cannot, will not, or do not want to change—to be "just like us"—are marked as enemies, whether the peoples of another nation or culture or the neighbors whose life style is different from ours.

The reality of human nature is that we are—and always will be—profoundly different, for the most salient feature of human nature lies in its capacity to be molded by culture and experience in extremely variable ways. Human nature is flexible; it is indeed capable of change. But such a phrase fails to do justice to the glory of human nature. Far better is the phrase "the capacity for transformation." It is the capacity for transformation that is the most essential characteristic of human nature. And again paradoxically, this capacity is both the basic cause of war and the basic cure for war.

THE CAPACITY FOR TRANSFORMATION

Since human nature is so subtle and many-faceted, it cannot be captured in a single definition. Still, we need handles. So when I am asked "Dr. Peck, what is human nature?" my first answer is likely to be "Human nature is to go to the bathroom in your pants."

That, after all, is the way you and I and all of us started out: doing what came naturally, letting go whenever we felt like it. But what then happened to each of us, at about the age of two, is that our mothers (or fathers) began telling us, "You're really a nice kid and I like you a lot, but I'd sort of appreciate it if you'd clean up your act." Now, this request initially makes no sense whatsoever to the child. What makes sense is to let go when the urge hits, and the results are always interesting. To the child, keeping a tight fanny and somehow getting to the toilet just in time to see this interesting stuff flushed away seems profoundly unnatural.

But if there is a good relationship between the child and its mother, and if the mother is not impatient or overcontrolling (unfortunately these favorable conditions are often not met, which is the major reason that we psychiatrists are so interested in toilet training), then something quite wonderful happens. The child says to itself: "You know, Mommy's a nice old gal, and she's been awfully good to me these last couple of years. I'd like to pay her back in some kind of way, give her a present of some kind. But I'm just a puny, helpless little child. What present could I possibly be able to give her that she might want—except this one crazy thing?"

So what happens is that as a gift of love to its mother the child begins to do the profoundly unnatural: to hold that fanny tight and make it to the toilet on time. Yet by the time that same child is four or five, it has come to feel profoundly natural about going to the bathroom in the toilet. When, on the other hand, in a moment of stress or fatigue, it forgets and has an "accident," it feels very unnatural about the whole messy business. What has occurred, in the space of two short years, is that out of love the child has succeeded in *changing its nature*.

This capacity we have been given to change—to transform—ourselves is so extraordinary that at other times when asked "What is human nature?" I facetiously (because it is only one side of the paradox) respond that there is no such thing. For what distinguishes us humans most from other creatures is not our opposing thumb or our magnificent larynx or our huge cerebral cortex, it is our dramatic relative lack of instincts—inherited, performed patterns of behavior that give other creatures a much more fixed and predetermined nature than we have as humans.

I live in Connecticut on the shore of a large lake. To this lake every March when the ice melts there comes a flock of gulls, and every December when it freezes they depart, presumably for parts south. I do not know where they go, but acquaintances have recently suggested it's Florence, Alabama. (My ornithologist friends tell me that there is no such thing as migratory gulls, but they just haven't met my gulls.) Anyway, scientists who have studied migratory birds have come to realize that with their little bird brains they are actually able to navigate by the stars so as to hit Florence, Alabama, right on the dot every time. The only trouble with this is that they have relatively little freedom. It's either Florence, Alabama, or not at all. They cannot say, "Well, this time I think I'll winter in Waco, Texas, or Bermuda." But because of our relative lack of instincts, what most distinguishes us human beings is our enormous freedom. We have the freedom (if we have the financial wherewithal) to choose to winter in Alabama or Bermuda or Barbados, or to stay home or to do something totally unnatural and turn around and go in the opposite direction up to northern Vermont to slide down icy hills on awkward slats of wood or fiberglass.

There are those who believe that our freedom, our ability to exercise control over our behavior and our environment are gifts of God. Others believe that they are the end result of eons of human evolution. Perhaps they are both. And nowhere is our capacity for transformation more evident than through the successive stages of psychological growth from infancy, through adolescence, to adulthood. Thereafter, however, our willingness, if not our capacity, to change is far less evident as we become older and more set in our ways, more convinced of the rightness of our own opinions, less interested in new things, more rigid. Indeed, when I was young I thought this was the way it had to be. As I watched the adults in my life move into their fifties and sixties and seventies, they all seemed to become more fixed in their "nature."

But then, at the age of twenty, I spent the summer with John P. Marquand, the celebrated author, who was then sixty-five years old. That summer "blew my mind." Marquand was interested in everything, including me—and no important sixty-five-year-old had ever before been truly interested in unimportant twenty-year-old me. Three or four times a week he and I used to argue late into the night, and I could actually win some of these arguments. I could *change his mind.* In fact, I saw him change his mind as a result of one thing or another several times a week. So it was that by the end of summer I came to the extraordinary awareness that this man had not grown old mentally. In fact, if anything, he had grown younger, more flexible, developing more rapidly from a psychological stand-point than most adolescents. And for the first time in my life I realized that we do not have to grow old mentally. Physically, yes, we must age and become decrepit. But mentally, spiritu-ally, no.

We come now to still another interesting paradox: it is the most psychologically and spiritually mature among us who are the least likely to grow old mentally. Conversely, much (not all—there are biological factors involved) of what we call se-nility is a fatal end-stage form of psychological and spiritual immaturity. We have a common expression for the senile: they have entered their "second childhood." They become whiny and demanding and manipulative and self-centered. But usu-ally this is not because they have entered their second child-hood; usually it is because they have never left their first. It is just that the veneer of adulthood has worn thin.

So it is that psychotherapists, who are in the business of "adult-making," know that many people who look like adults are really emotional children in adult clothing. That is not because their patients are necessarily more immature than the average person. To the contrary, those who genuinely assume the humble but honorable role of patient do so precisely be-cause they are the ones who are being called out of immatu-rity, who are no longer willing to tolerate being stuck, even though they may not yet see the way out, who are called to transformation.

A mentor of mine, an Irish Jesuit, once said to me in his marvelous brogue, "Ah, Scotty, an adult is a marvelous thing!" He meant, of course, that an adult is a creation to marvel at; there are so relatively few of them. This relative paucity of adults, however, is not a cause for despair. Evidence points to the fact that the number of those who are being called into adulthood has been rapidly increasing over the past two gen-erations. In any case, true adults are those of us who have learned to continually develop and exercise their capacity for transformation. Because of this exercise, progress along the journey of growth often becomes faster and faster the further we proceed on it. For the more we grow, the greater becomes our capacity to be *empty*—to empty ourselves of the old so that the new may enter and we may thereby be transformed.

So it is our capacity for transformation that makes us, in part, such different people. Lacking a fixed, set nature, possessing the freedom to do the new, the different, the unnatural, it is inevitable that we humans should be molded into or choose multiple paths. What most characterizes the human species, therefore, is its variability. By virtue of different genes, different childhoods, different cultures, and different life experiences (and, perhaps above all, by different choices), we have become transformed or have transformed ourselves in different ways. And it is these profound differences of temperament, character, and culture that make it so difficult for us to live together harmoniously. Yet by exercising this same capacity for transformation, it is possible for us to transcend our own childhoods, our cultures, and our past experience, and hence, without obliterating them, to transcend our differences. Thus what was originally the cause of war can eventually become its cure.

REALISM, IDEALISM, AND ROMANTICISM

Those who believe that a world at peace is an impossibility—the so-called hawks—generally refer to themselves as realists. It is a strangely spurious self-designation whose primary rationale is the assumption that it is human nature to be warlike. Throughout all of recorded history, the hawks would maintain, human beings of all cultures and at all times have been at war. Actually this is not totally accurate. Sweden and Switzerland, for instance, have not been at war for more than several hundred years. But it is sufficiently close to being correct for the hawks to say that the making of war seems to be a reality of human nature and hold that we should be "realistic" by adjusting to this reality and being warlike ourselves.

These same hawks will often refer to doves as idealists, or

more frequently as "empty-headed idealists" or "fuzzy-headed idealists." And they are right—not, I hope, about the empty- or fuzzy-headedness—because we are indeed idealists. For I would define the idealist as one who believes in the capacity for transformation of human nature. If, indeed, human nature is warlike (although I am very unclear as to what extent aggression is an innate rather than an acquired pattern of behavior), we still possess the potential to change that behavior.

For whatever the other characteristics of human nature, it is precisely this capacity for transformation that is its most salient feature—the characteristic above all others that is responsible for the evolution and survival of the human species. It is the hawks, or so-called realists, who are out of touch with the essence of what it means to be human, the idealistic doves whose thinking is more in accord with the reality of human nature. It is the idealists who are the realistic ones.

There is one way, however, in which idealistic doves may be out of touch with reality. When I give disarmament workshops and the participants become all enthused, some of their faces fall when I tell them I expect it will take us a dozen years (which is about all the time we have left) to achieve disarmament. They thought it might take a mere six months. That is because they are romantics. I would define romantic as one who not only believes in the capacity for transformation of human nature but also believes it is easy. It isn't easy. But it is possible.

There are profound reasons why it isn't easy. What we call personality can best be defined as a consistent pattern of organization of psychic elements. Consistency is the key word in this definition. There is a consistency to the personality of individuals—and to the "personality" of cultures or nations as well—a consistency that has both its dark side and its light side, its good and its bad.

Let me cite an example from my own practice. When new patients came to see me they would usually find me dressed in an open-collared shirt and comfortable sweater and perhaps even slippers. If they came back to see me a second time and found me in a tie and business suit, ready to leave for a speaking trip, that would probably be all right. If they came back a third time, however, and found me in a long flowing robe, wearing elaborate jewelry, chances are they wouldn't come back to see me a fourth time. One of the reasons that many patients kept returning for my services was that I was pretty much the same old Scotty every time they came. There was a consistency to my personality that allowed them to know where they stood. It gave them something to "hang their hats on." We need a certain amount of consistency in our personalities so that we may function effectively in the world as trustworthy human beings.

The dark side of that consistency, however, is what we psychotherapists call resistance. The personality—whether that of an individual or a nation—inherently resists change. Patients come to psychotherapy, one way or another, asking to change. But from the moment therapy begins, they start acting as if change was the last thing they wanted and often will fight it tooth and nail. Psychotherapy, designed to liberate, shines the light of truth upon ourselves. The truth will set you free—but first it will make you damn mad—is an adage that reflects this resistance.

So it is not easy for us to change. But it is possible. And it is our glory as human beings. The perception of this glory was the foundation of what once might properly have been called American idealism. The Declaration of Independence, the Constitution, the Bill of Rights—the documents on which this country was founded—were based on quite profound ideals. Their basic function was to create a society that would maximize people's freedom to change—change their religions, change their dwelling places, change their life styles, change their minds through the free flow of information, change their governors.

It is notable that two hundred years ago this new nation spent virtually no money and no energy attempting to control the behavior of the other nations of the world. Yet one by one, almost ten by ten, the peoples of these nations followed our spiritual and political example to seek the same freedoms for themselves. It is hard to escape the conclusion that in the years since, our political and spiritual leadership has declined in inverse proportion to the increasing amounts of money and effort we have expended to manipulate other countries. The subtleties of the virtues and vices of "isolationism" aside, it seems we are in real danger of forsaking our idealism in our role as international "superpower." We might for the moment want to remember that Alcoholics Anonymous—without doubt the single most effective agency of human transformation in our society—has a well-known saying: "The only person you can change is yourself." We might also remember that attempts to convert others tend toward chaos and away from community. I wonder, if we in the United States were to concentrate—as our overwhelmingly major priority—on making ourselves the best possible society we can be, whether the nations of the world might once again, without any pressure except the influence of example, begin to emulate us. But that would require us to be willing, at some risk, to recapture the idealism that once made this nation so great.

CHAPTER IX

Patterns of Transformation

The key to community is the acceptance—in fact, the celebration—of our individual and cultural differences. Such acceptance and celebration—which resolves the problem of
pluralism and which can occur only after we learn how to
become empty—is also the key to world peace. This does not
mean, however, that as we struggle toward world community
we need to consider all individuals or all cultures and societies
equally good or mature. To do so would be to fall prey once
again to a complex variation of the "illusion of human nature,"
a variation that says "We are all different but all the same or
equal in our differences." It simply is not true. The reality is
that just as some individuals have become much more mature
than others, some cultures are more or less flawed than others.

Thus we need labor under no compulsion to feel the same
degree of attraction to each and everyone—or the same degree of taste for every culture. So Gale Webbe wrote in his
classic work on the deeper aspects of spiritual growth that the
further one grows spiritually, the more and more people one
loves and the fewer and fewer people one likes.* This is because when we have become sufficiently adept at recognizing
our own flaws so as to cure them, we naturally become adept
at recognizing the flaws in others. We may not like people
because of these flaws or immaturities, but the further we
ourselves grow, the more we become able to accept—to love—
them, flaws and all. Christ's commandment is not to like one
another; it is to *love* one another.

Like community itself, that love is not easy to muster. It is a
part of the journey of the spirit. If that journey is not under-

* Gale D. Webbe, *The Night and Nothing* (San Francisco: Harper & Row, 1983),
p. 60.

stood it can be a major factor in driving us human beings even further apart. The knowledge of its principles, however, can do much to bring us together in peace.

THE STAGES OF SPIRITUAL GROWTH

Just as there are discernible stages in human physical and psychological growth, so there are stages in human spiritual development. The most widely read scholar of the subject today is James Fowler of Emory University.* But I first came to an awareness of these stages through my own personal experience.

The first of these experiences occurred when I was fourteen and began attending Christian churches in the area. I was mainly interested in checking out the girls but also in checking out what this Christianity business seemed to be about. I chose one particular church because it was only a few blocks down the street and because the most famous preacher of the day was preaching there. It was in the days before the "electronic church," but this man's every sermon was broadcast over almost every radio frequency across the country. At fourteen I had no trouble spotting him as a fraud. On the other hand, up the street in the opposite direction was another church with a well-known minister—not nearly as famous as the first but still probably among the top thirty in the Who's Who of preachers of the day—a Presbyterian named George Buttrick. And at age fourteen I had no trouble spotting George Buttrick as a holy man, a true man of God. What was I to think of this with my young brain? Here was the best known Christian preacher

* James W. Fowler, *Stages of Faith: The Psychology of Human Development and the Quest for Meaning* (San Francisco: Harper & Row, 1982). See also James Fowler and Sam Keen, *Life Maps: Conversations on the Journey of Faith*, ed. Jerome Berryman, (Waco, Tex: Word Books, 1978). See also the work of Jean Piaget, Erik Erikson, and Lawrence Kohlberg, who, roughly in sequence, provided some of the intellectual underpinnings in this century for Fowler's work. Fowler offers us six stages. I have restricted myself to four. Our different systems quite clearly overlap, however, and in no way contradict each other.

of the day, and as far as I could discern at age fourteen, I was well ahead of him. Yet in the same Christian religion was George Buttrick, who was obviously light years ahead of me. It just didn't compute. So I concluded that this Christianity business didn't make any sense, and I turned my back on it for the next generation.

Another significant noncomputing experience occurred more gradually. Over the course of a decade of practicing psychotherapy a strange pattern began to emerge. If people who were religious came to me in pain and trouble, and if they became engaged in the therapeutic process so as to go the whole route, they frequently left therapy as atheists, agnostics, or at least skeptics. On the other hand, if atheists, agnostics, or skeptics came to me in pain or difficulty and became fully engaged, they frequently left therapy as deepy religious people. Same therapy, same therapist, successful but utterly different outcomes from a religious point of view. Again it didn't compute—until I realized that *we are not all in the same place spiritually*.

With that realization came another: there is a pattern of progression through identifiable stages in human spiritual life. I myself have passed through them in my own spiritual journey. But here I will talk about those stages only in general, for individuals are unique and do not always fit neatly into any psychological or spiritual pigeonhole.

With that caveat, let me list my own understanding of these stages and the names I have chosen to give them:

STAGE I: Chaotic, antisocial
STAGE II: Formal, institutional
STAGE III: Skeptic, individual
STAGE IV: Mystic, communal

Most all young children and perhaps one in five adults fall into Stage I. It is essentially a stage of undeveloped spirituality. I call it antisocial because those adults who are in it (and those I have dared to call "People of the Lie" are at its bottom) seem generally incapable of loving others. Although they may pretend to be loving (and think of themselves that way), their relationships with their fellow human beings are all essentially manipulative and self-serving. They really don't give a hoot about anyone else. I call the stage chaotic because these people are basically unprincipled. Being unprincipled, there is nothing that governs them except their own will. And since the will from moment to moment can go this way or that, there is a lack of integrity to their being. They often end up, therefore, in jails or find themselves in another form of social difficulty. Some, however, may be quite disciplined in the service of expediency and their own ambition and so may rise to positions of considerable prestige and power, even to become presidents or influential preachers.

From time to time people in this stage get in touch with the chaos of their own being, and when they do, I think it is the most painful experience a human can have. Usually they just ride it out unchanged. A few, I suspect, may kill themselves, unable to envision change. And some, occasionally, convert to Stage II.

Such conversions are usually sudden and dramatic and, I believe, God-given. It is as if God had reached down and grabbed that soul and yanked it up a quantum leap. The process also seems to be an unconscious one. It just seems to happen. But if it could be made conscious, it might be as if the person said to himself, "Anything, anything is preferable to this chaos. I am willing to do anything to liberate myself from this chaos, even to submit myself to an institution for my governance."

For some the institution may be a prison. Most people who have worked in prisons know of a certain type of "model prisoner"—cooperative, obedient, well disciplined, favored by both the inmates and the administrative population. Because he is a model prisoner, he may soon be paroled, and three days later he has robbed seven banks and committed seventeen other felonies, so that he lands right back in jail and, with the walls of the institution to govern him, he once again becomes a "model prisoner."

For others the institution may be the military, where the chaos of their lives is regulated by the rather gentle paternalistic—and even maternalistic—structure of military society. For still others it might be a corporation or some other tightly structured organization. But for most, the institution to which they submit themselves for governance is the Church.

There are several things that characterize the behavior of men and women in Stage II of their spiritual development, which is the stage of the majority of churchgoers and believers (as well as that of most emotionally healthy "latency"-period children). One is their attachment to the forms (as opposed to the essence) of their religion, which is why I call this stage "formal" as well as "institutional." They are in fact sometimes so attached to the canons and the liturgy that they become very upset if changes are made in the words or the music or in the traditional order of things. It is for this reason that there has been so much turmoil concerning the adoption of the new Book of Common Prayer by the Episcopal Church or the changes brought about by Vatican II in the Catholic Church. Similar turmoil occurs for similar reasons in the other denominations and religions. Since it is precisely these forms that are responsible for their liberation from chaos, it is no wonder that people at this stage of their spiritual development become so threatened when someone seems to be playing footloose and fancy-free with the rules.

Another thing characterizing the religious behavior of Stage II people is that their vision of God is almost entirely that of an external, transcendent Being. They have very little understanding of the immanent, indwelling God—the God of the Holy Spirit, or what Quakers call the Inner Light. And although they often consider Him loving, they also generally feel He possesses—and will use—punitive power. But once again, it is no accident that their vision of God is that of a giant benevolent Cop in the Sky, because that is precisely the kind of God they need—just as they need a legalistic religion for their governance.

Let us suppose now that two adults firmly rooted in Stage II marry and have children. They will likely raise their children in a stable home, because stability is a principal value for people in this stage. They will treat their children with dignity as important beings, because the Church tells them that children are important and should be treated with dignity. Although their love may be a bit legalistic and unimaginative at times, they will still generally treat them lovingly, because the Church tells them to be loving and teaches something about how to be loving. What happens to children raised in such a stable, loving home, treated with importance and dignity (and taken to Sunday school as well) is that they absorb the principles of Christianity as if with their mother's milk—or the principles of Buddhism if raised in a Buddhist home, or of Islam if raised in a Muslim home, and so on. The principles of their parents' religion are literally engraved on their hearts, or come to be what psychotherapists call "internalized."

But once these principles become internalized, such children, now usually late-adolescents, have become self-governing human beings. As such they are no longer dependent on an institution for their governance. Consequently they begin to say to themselves, "Who needs this fuddy-duddy old Church with its silly superstitions?" At this point they begin to convert to Stage III—skeptic, individual. And to their parents' great but unnecessary chagrin, they often become atheists or agnostics.

Although frequently "nonbelievers," people in Stage III are generally more spiritually developed than many content to remain in Stage II. Although individualistic, they are not the least bit antisocial. To the contrary, they are often deeply involved in and committed to social causes. They make up their own minds about things and are no more likely to believe everything they read in the papers than to believe it is necessary for someone to acknowledge Jesus as Lord and Savior (as opposed to Buddha or Mao or Socrates) in order to be saved. They make loving, intensely dedicated parents. As skeptics they are often scientists, and as such they are again highly submitted to principle. Indeed, what we call the scientific method is a collection of conventions and procedures that have been designed to combat our extraordinary capacity to deceive ourselves in the interest of submission to something higher than our own immediate emotional or intellectual comfort—namely, truth. Advanced Stage III men and women are active truth seekers.

"Seek and you shall find," it has been said. If people in Stage III seek truth deeply and widely enough, they find what they are looking for—enough pieces to begin to be able to fit them together but never enough to complete the whole puzzle. In fact, the more pieces they find, the larger and more magnificent the puzzle becomes. Yet they are able to get glimpses of the "big picture" and to see that it is very beautiful indeed—and that it strangely resembles those "primitive myths and superstitions" their Stage II parents or grandparents believe in. At that point they begin their conversion to Stage IV, which is the mystic communal stage of spiritual development.

"Mysticism," a much-maligned word, is not an easy one to define. It takes many forms. Yet through the ages, mystics of every shade of religious belief have spoken of unity, of an underlying connectedness between things: between men and women, between us and the other creatures and even inanimate matter as well, a fitting together according to an ordinarily invisible fabric underlying the cosmos. Remember the experience when, during community, I suddenly saw my previously hated neighbor as myself. Smelling his dead cigar butts and hearing his guttural snoring, I was filled with utter distaste for him until that strange mystical moment when I saw myself sitting in his chair and realized he was the sleeping part of me and I the waking part of him. We were suddenly connected. More than connected, we were integral parts of the same unity.

Mysticism also obviously has to do with *mystery*. Mystics acknowledge the enormity of the unknown, but rather than being frightened by it, they seek to penetrate ever deeper into it that they may understand more—even with the realization that the more they understand, the greater the mystery will become. They love mystery, in dramatic contrast to those in Stage II, who need simple, clear-cut dogmatic structures and have little taste for the unknown and unknowable. While Stage IV men and women will enter religion in order to approach mystery, people in Stage II, to a considerable extent, enter religion in order to escape from it. Thus there is the confusion of people entering not only into religion but into the same religion—and sometimes the same denomination—not only for different motives but for totally opposite motives. It makes no sense until we come to understand the roots of religious pluralism in terms of developmental stages.

Finally, mystics throughout the ages have not only spoken of emptiness but extolled its virtues. I have labeled Stage IV communal as well as mystical not because all mystics or even a majority of them live in communes but because among human beings they are the ones most aware that the whole world *is* a community and realize that what divides us into warring camps is precisely the *lack* of this awareness. Having become practiced at emptying themselves of preconceived notions and prejudices and able to perceive the invisible underlying fabric that connects everything, they do not think in terms of factions or blocs or even national boundaries; they *know* this to be one world.

There are of course many gradations within and between the four stages of spiritual development. We actually have a name for the person between Stage I and II: the backslider. This is the kind of man (we will use men for our example for the sake of simplicity; women also fall in between but tend to have slightly more subtle styles of doing so) who drinks, gambles, and leads a generally dissolute existence until some good Stage II folk come along and have a chat with him and he is saved. For the next two years he leads a sober and righteous and God-fearing life until one day he is found back in a bar, a brothel, or at the racetrack. He is saved a second time, but once again he backslides, and continues bouncing back and forth between Stage I and Stage II.

Similarly, people bounce back and forth between Stage II

and Stage III. There is the kind of man, for example, who says to himself: "It isn't that I don't believe in God anymore. The trees, the flowers, the clouds are so beautiful that obviously no human intelligence could have created them; some divine intelligence must have set it all in motion billions of years ago. But it's just as beautiful out on the golf course on Sunday morning as it is in church, and I can worship my God just as well there." Which he does for a few years until his business undergoes a mild reversal, and in panic he says to himself, "Oh, my God, I haven't been praying." So back to church he goes for a couple of more years until there is an upturn in the economy (for all I know because he's been praying so hard), and gradually he begins to slip back out onto his Stage III golf course again.

Similarly, we see people bouncing back and forth between Stage III and Stage IV. A neighbor of mine was one such person. By day Michael expressed his highly analytic mind with brilliant accuracy and precision, and he was just about the dullest human being I have ever had to listen to. Occasionally in the evening, however, after he had drunk a bit of whiskey or smoked a little marijuana, Michael would begin to talk of life and death and meaning and glory and become "spirit-filled," and I would sit listening at his feet enthralled.* But the next day he would exclaim apologetically, "God, I don't know what got into me last night; I was saying the stupidest things. I've got to stop smoking grass and drinking." I do not mean to bless the use of drugs for such purposes but simply to state the reality that in his case they loosened him up enough to flow in the direction he was being called, from which in the cold light of day he retreated back in terror to the "rational" safety of Stage III.

Perhaps predictably, there exists a sense of threat among people in the different stages of religious development.

* See the early "Don Juan" books by Carlos Castenada (Simon and Schuster) for a description of the role of psychoactive drugs in his Stage III to Stage IV conversion. The first of these was *The Teachings of Don Juan: A Yaqui Way of Knowledge*, 1973.

Mostly we are threatened by people in the stages above us. Although they often adopt the pretense of being "cool cats" who have it "all together," underneath their exteriors Stage I people are threatened by just about everything and everyone. Stage II people are not threatened by Stage I people, the "sinners." They are commanded to love sinners. But they are very threatened by the individualists and skeptics of Stage III, and even more by the mystics of Stage IV, who seem to believe in the same sorts of things they do but believe in them with a freedom they find absolutely terrifying. Stage III people, on the other hand, are neither threatened by Stage I people nor by Stage II people (whom they simply regard as superstitious) but are cowed by Stage IV people, who seem to be scientific-minded like themselves and know how to write good footnotes, yet somehow still believe in this crazy God business.

It is extremely important for teachers, healers, and ministers (and we are all of us teachers, healers, and ministers whether we like it or not; our only choice is whether to be good teachers, healers, and ministers or bad ones) to be cognizant of this sense of threat between people in the different stages of spiritual growth. Much of the art of being a good teacher, healer, or minister consists largely in staying just one step ahead of your patients, clients, or pupils. If you are not ahead, it is unlikely that you will be able to lead them anywhere. But if you are two steps ahead, it is likely that you will lose them. If people are one step ahead of us, we usually admire them. If they are two steps ahead of us, we usually think they are evil. That's why Socrates and Jesus were killed; they were thought to be evil.

Similarly, it is very difficult to reach down two or more steps. For this reason a Stage IV person, even though advanced himself or herself, will not be the best therapist for many. Generally speaking, Stage II people and programs offer the best therapy for Stage I people. Psychiatrists and psychologists in this country—primarily a Stage III group—have generally served their culture well as guides for those making the journey out of a dependent Stage II mentality. Stage IV therapists do best leading highly independent people toward a recognition of the mystical interdependence of this world. Most all of us are pulling someone up with one hand while we ourselves are being pulled up by the other.

An understanding of the stages of spiritual development is important for building community. A group of only Stage IV people or only Stage III people or only Stage II people is, of course, not so much a community as a clique. A true community will likely include people of all stages. With this understanding, it is possible for people in different stages to transcend the sense of threat that divides them and to become a true community.

In my experience the most dramatic example of this possibility occurred in a relatively small community-building group I led several years ago. To this two-day group of twenty-five there came ten fundamentalist Stage II Christians, five Stage III atheists with their own guru—a brilliant, highly rational trial lawyer—and ten Stage IV mystical Christians. There were moments I despaired that we would ever make it into community. The fundamentalists were furious that I, their supposed leader, smoked and drank and vigorously attempted to heal me of my hypocrisy and addiction. The mystics equally vigorously challenged the fundamentalists' sexism, intolerance, and other forms of rigidity. Both of course were utterly dedicated to converting the atheists. The atheists in turn sneered at the arrogance of us Christians in even daring to think that we had gotten hold of some kind of truth. Nonetheless, after approximately twelve hours of the most intense struggle together to empty ourselves of our intolerances, we became able to let one another be, each in his or her own stage. And we became a community. But we could not have done so without the cognitive awareness of the different stages of spiritual development and the realization that we were not all "in the same place," and that that was literally all right.

My experience suggests that this progression of spiritual development holds true in all cultures and for all religions.

Indeed, one of the things that seems to characterize all the great religions—Christianity, Buddhism, Taoism, Islam, Judaism, Hinduism—is their capacity to speak to people in both Stage II and Stage IV. In fact, I suspect this is why they are great religions. It is as if the words of each had two different translations. Let us take a Christian example: "Jesus is my savior." At Stage II this is often translated into a Jesus who is a kind of fairy godmother who will rescue me whenever I get in trouble as long as I remember to call upon his name. And that's true. He will do just that. At Stage IV "Jesus is my savior" is translated as "Jesus, through his life and death, taught me the way I must follow for my salvation." Which is also true. Two totally different translations, two totally different meanings, but both of them true.

Again in my experience, the four stages of spiritual development also represent a paradigm for healthy psychological development. We tend to be born Stage I creatures. If the home into which we are born is stable and secure, by midchildhood we have become law-abiding, rule-following people. If the home at all supports and encourages our uniqueness and independence, in adolescence we routinely question the laws, the rules, and the myths as budding skeptics. And if the natural forces of growth that lead us to question are not excessively resisted by threats of damnation from church or parents, after a while, in adulthood we slowly begin to understand the meaning and spirit that underlie the letter of the myth and the letter of the law. There may, however, be destructive forces in the home environment which cause people to become "fixated" in one stage or another. Conversely, there are rare, difficult-to-explain cases of people who develop further and faster than would be expected. The wonderful and probably accurate book *Mister God, This Is Anna*, for instance, described a seven-year-old girl already well into Stage IV, despite a presumably chaotic early childhood.*

It is also important to remember that no matter how far we

* Fynn, *Mister God, This Is Anna*. (New York: Ballantine Books, 1976).

develop spiritually, we retain in ourselves vestiges of the previous stages through which we have come, just as we retain our
vestigial appendix. I don't suppose I could be writing this were
I not basically a kind of Stage IV person. But I can assure you
that there exists a Stage I Scott Peck, who at the first sign of
any significant stress is quite tempted to lie and cheat and steal.
I keep him well encaged, I hope, in a rather comfortable cell,
so that he won't be let loose upon the world. (And I am able to
do this only because I acknowledge his existence, which is what
Jungian psychologists mean by the "integration of the
Shadow." Indeed, I do not attempt to kill him if for no other
reason than that I need to go down into the dungeon from
time to time and consult him, safely ensconced behind the
bars, when I am in need of a particular kind of "street smarts.")
Similarly, there is a Stage II Scott Peck, who in moments of
stress and fatigue would very much like to have a Big Brother
or Big Daddy around who would give him some clear-cut,
black-and-white answers to life's difficult, ambiguous dilem-
mas and some formulas to tell him how to behave, relieving
him of the responsibility of figuring it all out for himself. And
there is a Stage III Scott Peck, who if invited to address a
prestigious scientific assembly, under the stress of such an occasion would want to regress to thinking, Well, I better just
talk to them about carefully controlled, measurable studies
and not mention any of this God business.

The development of the individual through these spiritual
or religious stages is that process to which we most properly
give the name conversion. I have mentioned that conversions
from Stage I to Stage II are usually sudden and dramatic.
Conversions from Stage III to Stage IV are generally gradual.
The first time I ever spoke of these stages was at a symposium
in conjunction with the psychologist Paul Vitz, author of *Psychology as Religion.** During the question-and-answer period
Paul was asked when he had become a Christian. He scratched
his head for a moment and said bemusedly, "Let's see; it was

---

* Paul C. Vitz, *Psychology as Religion: the Cult of Self-Worship* (Grand Rapids, Mich.:
Eerdmans, 1977).

somewhere between 1972 and 1976." Compare this with the more familiar image of the man who will tell you: "It was at eight-thirty in the evening of the seventeenth of August!"

It is during the process of conversion from Stage III to Stage IV that people generally first become conscious that there is such a thing as spiritual growth. There is a potential pitfall in this consciousness, however, and that is the notion some have at this point that they themselves can *direct* the process. "If I take a bit of Sufi dancing here," they tell themselves, "and visit a Trappist monastery there, and do a bit of Zen meditation as well, along with some est, I will reach nirvana." But that's not how it operates, as the myth of Icarus tells us. Icarus wanted to reach the sun (which symbolizes God). So out of feathers and wax he built himself a pair of wings. But as soon as he even began to get close to the sun, its heat melted his man-made wings and he plummeted to his destruction. One meaning of this myth, I believe, is that we cannot get to God under our own steam. We must allow God to do the directing.

In any case, whether sudden or gradual, no matter how different in other respects, Stages I to II and Stages III to IV conversions do have one thing in common: a sense on the part of the persons converted that their own conversions were not something they themselves achieved but rather gifts from God. Certainly I can say of my own gradual Stages III to IV conversion that I was not smart enough to find my way alone.

As a part of the process of spiritual growth, the transition from Stage II to Stage III is also a conversion. We can be converted to atheism or agnosticism or, at least, skepticism! Indeed, I have every reason to believe that God has a hand in this part of the conversion process as well. One of the greatest challenges, in fact, facing the Church is how to facilitate the conversion of its members from Stage II to Stage IV without them having to spend a whole adult lifetime in Stage III. It is a challenge that the Church has historically avoided rather than begun to face. As far as I am concerned, one of the two greatest sins of our sinful Christian Church has been its discouragement, through the ages, of doubt. In so doing, it has consistently driven growing people out of its potential community, often fixating them thereby in a perpetual resistance to spiritual insights. Conversely, the Church is not going to meet this challenge until doubt is properly considered a Christian virtue—indeed, a Christian responsibility. We neither can nor should skip over questioning in our development.

In fact, it is only through the process of questioning that we begin to become even dimly aware that the whole point of life is the development of souls. As I said, the notion that we can totally direct this development is a pitfall of such awareness. But the beauty of the consciousness that we are all on an ongoing spiritual journey and that there is no end to our conversion far outshines that one pitfall. For once we become aware that we are on a journey—that we are all pilgrims—for the first time we can actually begin to cooperate consciously with God in the process. This is why Paul Vitz, at the symposium I mentioned, correctly told the audience: "I think Scott's stages have a good deal of validity, and I suspect that I shall be using them in my practice, but I want you to remember that what Scotty calls Stage IV is the beginning."

TRANSCENDING CULTURE

The process of spiritual development I have described is highly analogous to the development of community. Stage I people are frequently pretenders; they pretend they are loving and pious, covering up their lack of principles. The first, primitive stage of group formation—pseudocommunity—is similarly characterized by pretense. The group tries to look like a community without doing any of the work involved.

Stage II people have begun the work of submitting themselves to principle—the law. But they do not yet understand the spirit of the law. Consequently they are legalistic, parochial, and dogmatic. They are threatened by anyone who thinks differently from them, and so regard it as their responsibility to convert or save the other 90 or 99 percent of humanity who are not "true believers." It is this same style of functioning that characterizes the second stage of the community process in which the group members, rather than accepting one another try vehemently to fix one another. The chaos that results is not unlike that existing among the various feuding denominations or sects within or between the world's different religions.

Stage III, a phase of questioning, is analogous to the crucial stage of emptiness in community formation. In reaching for community the members of a group must question themselves. "Is my particular theology so certain—so true and complete— as to justify my conclusion that these other people are not saved?" they may ask. Or "I wonder to what extent my feelings about homosexuals represent a prejudice bearing little relation to the reality?" Or "Could I have swallowed the party line in thinking that all religious people are fanatics?" Indeed, such questioning is the required beginning of the emptying process. We cannot succeed in emptying ourselves of preconceptions, prejudices, needs to control or convert, and so forth, without first becoming skeptical of them and without doubting their necessity. Conversely, individuals remain stuck in Stage III precisely because they do not doubt deeply enough. To enter Stage IV they must begin to empty themselves of some of the dogmas of skepticism such as Anything that can't be measured scientifically can't be known and isn't worth studying. They must begin to doubt even their own doubt.

Does this mean, then, that a true community is a group of all Stage IV people? Paradoxically the answer is yes and no. It is no because the individual members are hardly capable of growing so rapidly as to totally discard their customary styles of thinking when they return from the group to their usual worlds. But it is yes because in community the members have learned how to behave in a Stage IV manner in relation to one another. Among themselves they all practice the kind of emptiness, acceptance, and inclusiveness that have characterized the behavior of mystics throughout the ages. They retain their basic identity as Stage I, II, III, or IV individuals. Indeed, knowledge of these stages is in part so important because it facilitates the acceptance of one another as being in different stages—different places spiritually. Such acceptance is a prerequisite for community. But, wonderfully, once such acceptance is achieved—and it can be achieved only through emptiness—Stage I, II, and III men and women routinely possess the capacity to act toward one another as if they were Stage IV people. In other words, out of love and commitment to the whole, virtually all of us are capable of transcending our backgrounds and limitations. So it is that genuine community is so much more than the sum of its parts. It is, in truth, a mystical body.

The individual journey through the stages of spiritual development is also a journey into and out of culture. Erich Fromm once defined socialization as the process of "learning to like to do what we have to do."* It is what happens when we learn to feel natural about going to the bathroom in the toilet. The conversion from Stage I to Stage II is essentially a leap of socialization or enculturation. It is that point at which we first adopt the values of our tribal, cultural religion and begin to make them our own. Just as Stage II people tend to be threatened, however, by any questioning of their religious dogma, so they are also "culture-bound"—utterly convinced that the way things are done in their culture is the right and only way. And just as people entering Stage III begin to question the religious doctrines with which they were raised, so they also begin to question all the cultural values of the society into which they were born. Finally, as they begin to reach for Stage IV, they also begin to reach toward the notion of world community and the possibility of either transcending culture or—depending on which way you want to use the words—belonging to a planetary culture.

Aldous Huxley labeled mysticism "the perennial philosophy"† because the mystical way of thinking and being

---

* Erich Fromm, *The Sane Society* (New York: Fawcett Premier Books, 1977), p. 77.
† Aldous Huxley, *The Perennial Philosophy* (New York: Harper & Row, 1970).

has existed in all cultures and all times since the dawn of recorded history. Although a small minority, mystics of all religions the world over have demonstrated an amazing commonality, unity. Unique though they might be in their individual personhood, they have largely escaped free from—transcended—those human differences that are cultural.

The journey out of what we know as culture can be frightening at times. Mine began at fifteen when I left a New England prep school in opposition to my parents' hopes for me. In so doing I was blindly taking my first giant step out of the WASP culture that seemed to predominate in America, with all its emphasis on materialistic success, conformity, "tastefulness," and "the good life." What was to become of me? I could not become an Irish, Italian, or Polish Catholic. Nor a southern good old boy. Nor a New York Jew. I was not black. Where on earth was I to go? I was terrified—so terrified that I actually welcomed the sanctuary that a psychiatric hospital then briefly provided me. It gave me a place to be. I had no idea at the time that it is a common practice for women and men to seek psychotherapy in anxiety precisely because they have already begun the journey out of culture.

I continue today no longer to belong anywhere in terms of what is usually thought of as culture. But I am far from being alone. Slowly I have found a person here and a person there in the same predicament. And ours was not a miserable affair, like the poor "man without a country" who was doomed forever to roam the seas in a narrow sailing vessel. To the contrary, we were far more free than most to move through the nations of the world, no longer bound by cultural conventions. There were times when it was lonely, but in recent years men and women without a culture have been joining me by the tens of thousands. None of us would go back, even if we could, but we do from time to time experience a certain poignant sadness that, as perpetual pilgrims, we "can't go home again." Like my dear colleague, patient, and friend Ralph.

Ralph has made the whole journey. Born into poverty in Appalachia, he underwent a Stage I to Stage II conversion in his late adolescence and became a southern fundamentalist preacher. In response to the civil-rights and anti-Vietnam War movements of the sixties he began the laborious process of questioning each and every one of his values. Grace stayed with him as he grew in love and sophistication. Now a man of great spiritual power and holiness, he recently had the opportunity to return to his roots in Appalachia. A niece was elected one of six homecoming queens for a large local pageant involving a number of regional high schools. At a high moment in this pageantry each homecoming queen was supposed to be presented with a rose by her father. Having lost her father in a farming accident, she asked her uncle Ralph if he would fill in. Happy to do so, he flew back to Appalachia for the ceremonies.

When I next saw him Ralph described these ceremonies in exquisite detail. With the unerring eye of a cultural anthropologist he recounted that each of the six homecoming queens wore dresses of the same style but different colors for the central moment of the ritual. This came at half time, when the queens were driven four times around the football field, each in a Chevrolet Impala convertible to match the color of her dress. There were other ceremonies. Indeed, each queen required four changes of dress during the afternoon and evening. Ralph told how a matron supervised these changes from a dressing room in the football stadium with Teutonic efficiency and lists of details prepared months in advance. As he described these liturgical matters I sat enthralled by the humor and pathos and richness of it all.

But when he finally came to the end of the tale of his weekend Ralph switched gears and announced: "For some reason, though, I've been feeling depressed ever since I got back. I even started feeling that way in the airplane."

"Sadness and depression are very close to each other," I commented, "but I sense that you are more sad."

"You're right," Ralph exclaimed. "It is sadness that I'm feeling. But I don't know why. I don't have any reason to be sad."

"Yes, you do," I countered.

"I do? Why should I feel sad?"

"Because you've lost your home."

Ralph looked puzzled. "I'm not sure I understand."

"You've just finished describing an elaborate ritual of Appalachian culture with all the objectivity of the greatest anthropologist," I explained. "There is no way you could do this if you were still a part of that culture. You have become separated from it, from your roots. That's what I mean when I say you've lost your home. I suspect this trip back made you aware of the light years you have traveled beyond it."

A tear trickled down Ralph's cheek. "You've hit the nail on the head," he acknowledged. "The funny thing about it is that there's a certain joy along with the sadness. I'm glad to be back here with my wife and you and my patients. I had no desire to stay down there. I belong now right where I am. But it's not the simple, unconscious kind of belonging that those people have down there. I sort of regret that lost simplicity, that innocence. But I know it isn't a holy innocence down there; it's just innocence. They have more than their share of pain and worries worse than mine. But they don't have to worry about the whole world."*

Nowhere in all of literature is there a better description of someone who had transcended culture than in the Gospels. Before and since Jesus, from time to time there have been saints who have transcended their culture and also had "no place to lay their heads." But they were one in ten thousand, if that. Today it is different. Because of a multiplicity of factors—most particularly instant, mass communication that brings foreign cultures to our door, and the availability of psychotherapy that leads us to question the programs, cultural and otherwise, within which we were raised—the number of people entering the mystical stage of development and transcending ordinary culture seems to have increased a thousandfold in the course of a mere generation or two. They remain a minority—currently no more than one in twenty.

* This story was told in a briefer version in the introduction to the 1985 hardcover gift edition of M. Scott Peck, *The Road Less Traveled* (New York: Simon and Schuster).

Still, one wonders if the explosion in their numbers might represent a giant leap forward in the evolution of the human race, a leap toward not only mystical but global consciousness and world community.*

ISRAEL

There are some who worry that categorizing people in stages of spiritual growth may have a fragmentizing effect—that the designation of different kinds of believers may be destructive to community in general and the "community of the faithful" in particular. While I understand the concern about hierarchies and their potential for elitism, I do not feel the worry is justified. The supposed "community" of the faithful has been noted in history for excluding, punishing, and frequently even murdering the doubter, the skeptic, and others who did not fit the mold. And my own repeated personal experience with the knowledge that we are at different stages of spiritual development facilitates rather than hampers the formation and maintenance of true communities. Still, it is good for us to bear in mind that the relatively undeveloped are quite capable of community and that the most developed of us still retain vestiges of the earlier stages. As Edward Martin put it in his poem "My Name Is Legion":†

> Within my earthly temple there's a crowd;
> There's one of us that's humble, one that's proud,
> There's one that's broken-hearted for his sins,
> There's one that unrepentent sits and grins;
> There's one that loves his neighbor as himself,
> And one that cares for naught but fame and pelf.
> From much corroding care I should be free
> If I could once determine which is me.

* Perhaps the greatest prophet of this leap was Teilhard de Chardin.
† Edward Sanford Martin, "My Name Is Legion," *Masterpieces of Religious Verse,* ed. James Dalton Morrison (New York: Harper & Row, 1948), p. 274.

It may also help to remember the basic meaning of the word
"Israel." The Old Testament quite early in the drama tells us
of Jacob. He was clearly a Stage I sort of chap—a liar, thief,
and manipulator who had cheated his brother out of his in-
heritance. As this part of the story or myth opens, typical of
many Stage I people, Jacob is in trouble. On the lam from his
brother, wandering through the desert, one evening Jacob left
his family to sleep alone. In the middle of the night, however,
he was accosted by a strongly built stranger. They did battle
with each other in the darkness. It was a desperate struggle,
lasting hour after hour, as they wrestled together. But finally,
just as the first glimmer of dawn came to the horizon, Jacob
felt himself beginning to get the upper hand. Exulting, he
threw all his resources into vanquishing this being who had
assaulted him for no apparent reason. Something extraordinary then happened. The being reached out and lightly
touched Jacob's thigh, and the thigh was instantly, effortlessly
pulled out of joint and broken. Crippled, Jacob then clung
onto the stranger. He did this not to continue an obviously lost
battle—he was an utterly defeated, broken man—but because
he knew now he was in the presence of divinity. So in that first
faint light of dawn he pleaded with his adversary not to leave
before giving him a blessing. The stranger agreed and not
only blessed Jacob but told him, "Henceforth you will be called
Israel, meaning he who has struggled with God."* And Jacob
limped off into the future.

There are today three meanings to the word "Israel." One
refers to a rather small area of the earth's surface on the
eastern coast of the Mediterranean, currently a nation-state
with a brief, already tortured history. The second refers to the
Jewish people dispersed the world over, with a long and tortured history. But the most basic meaning refers to the people
who have struggled with God. As such it includes all the Stage
I people, who have just begun the struggle, who do not yet

* Genesis 32:22–32. I am indebted to Frederick Buechner for bringing the meaning of this story home to me in his superb book of sermons appropriately named
after this great myth: *The Magnificent Defeat* (New York: Seabury, 1968).

know by whom they have been assaulted, who are still in the midst of total darkness before even seeing their first dawn, before even receiving their first breaking and their first blessing. Israel also includes those people once broken and once blest, the Stage II Hindus and Muslims and Jews and Christians and Buddhists the world over. Israel also includes those twice broken and twice blest, the atheists and agnostics and skeptics, whether in Russia or England or Argentina or in this country, who question and thereby continue on with the great struggle. And finally it includes the thrice broken and thrice blest mystics from all the cultures of the earth who have even come to seek future breakings for the blessings they now know will follow.

Israel includes the entirety of our struggling infant humanity. It is the whole potential community on the planet. We are all Israel.

CHAPTER X

Emptiness

The sacrificial stage of emptiness is the bridge between chaos and community. Yet precisely because it is emptiness, the stage often feels more like jumping into a void than stepping onto a bridge. Nonetheless, the degree to which we can develop world community and thereby save our skins is going to depend primarily on the degree to which we human beings can learn to empty ourselves.

Our responsibility as individuals to empty ourselves in order to achieve peace was stated clearly by the Hindu mystic Krishnamurti twenty years ago in his book *Freedom from the Known:*

> We are each one of us responsible for every war because of the aggressiveness of our own lives, because of our nationalism, our selfishness, our gods, our prejudices, our ideals, all of which divide us. And only when we realize, not intellectually but actually, as actually as we would recognize that we are hungry or in pain, that you and I are responsible for all this existing *chaos,* for all the misery throughout the entire world, because we have contributed to it in our daily lives, and are a part of this monstrous society with its wars, divisions, its ugliness, brutality and greed—only then will we act.*

In describing our usual primitive group behavior, Krishnamurti also uses the word "chaos." But there is an alternative. In a group that moved out of chaos into emptiness

* J. Krishnamurti, *Freedom from the Known* (New York: Harper & Row, 1969), p. 14.

during the night and into community the following morning, a member reported:

> I had a dream last night where I was in a store. The salespeople offered me three things. One was an unusually elegant car. Another was a diamond necklace. The third was a blank sheet of paper. Something told me to choose the blank piece of paper. Money did not seem to be the issue. I could equally well have chosen the car or the necklace. But as I left the store I felt strangely right about my choice. That was all there was to the dream. When I awoke and remembered it this morning I was puzzled as to why I'd been so silly as to choose the blank piece of paper. But now, when I see how we have become a community, I realize I did indeed make the right choice.

How strange, in the world's terms, to choose a blank piece of paper! Yet throughout the ages mystics have extolled not only the virtues of emptiness but also of meditation. Meditation can probably best be defined as the process by which we can empty our minds. Indeed, perhaps the most sophisticated variety of meditation is what Zen Buddhists call "No Mind." Its goal is to make the mind like a blank page.

But why? Why make the mind blank? It is important for people who find the concept of emptiness frightening to remember that meditation—emptiness—is not an end in itself but the means to an end. It is said that nature abhors a vacuum. So it is that the moment we become empty something comes into our emptiness. The virtue of meditation is that whatever comes into emptiness is beyond our control. It is the unforeseen, the unexpected, the new. And it is only from the unforeseen, the unexpected, the new that we learn.

Throughout the ages mystics have also been known as "contemplatives." Contemplation and meditation are intimately related. Contemplation is a process by which we think about—mull over and reflect upon—the unexpected things that happen to us in our moments of meditation and emptiness. True contemplation, therefore, requires meditation. It requires that we stop thinking before we are truly able to think with any originality.

There is a narrow and a broad definition of contemplation. The narrow definition merely refers to the reflection on the experiences of our life. The broader definition includes prayer and meditation as well as reflection upon the unexpected experiences that occur in life and in our relationship to life. These three should not be rigidly or arbitrarily separated; in reality they blend into each other. However, I use the word "contemplative" in the broader sense to refer to a life style rich in reflection, meditation, and prayer. *It is a life style dedicated to maximum awareness.*

Although religious professionals are often the greatest experts on contemplation, it is hardly necessary to be a monk or a nun to practice a contemplative life style. In fact, it is not even necessary to believe in God. Prayer, for instance, has been defined by one theologian as nothing more—and nothing less—than a radical response to life and its mysteries.* For God, should you so choose, substitute the word "life." If you continually ask questions of life and are continually willing to be open and empty enough to hear life's answer and to ponder the meaning, you will be a contemplative.

True communities are invariably contemplative; they are self-aware. It is one of the primary characteristics of community. Again, I do not mean to imply that communities must be religious in the usual sense of the word. But a collection of individuals cannot become a community unless, as individuals, they are willing to become, at least to some degree, empty and contemplative. And they cannot maintain themselves as a community unless they continually contemplate themselves as an organism. To survive, a community must repetitively stop whatever it is

* Matthew Fox, *On Becoming a Musical Mystical Bear: Spirituality American Style* (Ramsey, N.J.; Paulist Press, 1976).

doing to ask *how* it is doing, to think about where it, the community, needs to go, and to be empty to hear the answers.

The ultimate purpose of emptiness, then, is to make room. Room for what? Room for God, the religious would say. But since God means so many things to different people, including nothing at all, I prefer generally to say that emptiness makes room for the Other. What is the Other? It can be virtually anything: a tale from a strange culture, the different, the unexpected, the new, the better. Most important, for community, the Other is the Stranger, the other person. We cannot even let the other person into our hearts or minds unless we empty ourselves. We can truly listen to him or truly hear her only out of emptiness. Sam Keen, speaking of the emptying required for listening, wrote: "This discipline of bracketing, compensating, or silencing requires sophisticated self-knowledge and courageous honesty. Yet without this discipline each present moment is only the repetition of something already seen or experienced. In order for genuine novelty to emerge, for the unique presence of things, persons, or events to take root in me, I must undergo a decentralization of the ego."*

Keen also speaks of "silencing the familiar and welcoming the strange." Thus whether it is achieved by "bracketing," "compensating," or "a decentralization of the ego," silence is the most essential ingredient of emptiness. It is no accident, therefore, that we routinely use silence in community-building groups to lead them into emptiness. Christian mystics will sometimes speak of how "Before the Word there was silence." Indeed we can say that the Word came out of silence. It had to. Recently one of my hosts, a famous opera singer, not even knowing of my interest in the topic, spontaneously informed me that "more than one half of Beethoven is silence." Without silence there is no music; there is only noise.

Since peacemaking is our end, let me give an example of cross-cultural misunderstanding that was caused by mental fullness, clutter, and noise but was finally clarified out of si-

* Sam Keen, *To a Dancing God* (New York: Harper & Row, 1970), p. 28.

lence and emptiness. The situation occurred at an international symposium of theologians from all corners of the globe. When we assembled after one of the plenary sessions for discussion in our assigned small group, a man from Ghana who was a practitioner and teacher of what is known as African traditional religion began by saying he didn't understand all the stuff that had been said in the preceding lecture about a "suffering God." "It's the most ridiculous thing I ever heard," he exclaimed. "God doesn't suffer."

"Of course He suffers," almost everyone in the group affirmed, quoting Dietrich Bonhoeffer or this authority or that. But with each rebuttal the African just dug in his heels deeper, maintaining ever more vehemently, "I've never heard anything so silly in my life." The more he stuck to his guns, however, the more adamant the group became in its attempt to change his mind. The clamor escalated until our little group of adults became as noisy as a third-grade classroom after the teacher had been absent for an hour.

"Stop," I cried suddenly. "The average IQ in this room is probably around a hundred and sixty. Surely we can communicate better than this. Let's just stop and be silent for three minutes and see what happens."

The group obeyed. After the silence one of the Americans began talking about how much he loved his children. In fact, he said, he missed them right then, and that hurt him. He felt hurt when they were sick or injured. Their trials and tribulations pained him. He worried over their future, and that too was a kind of suffering. His children were the most important aspect of his life, he told us, and he would hardly have it different, but in certain ways his love for them made his existence much more painful than it might be otherwise.

"Ah, now I understand," the African exulted with obvious pleasure. "Of course there is pain with love, and of course God loves, so He hurts over us the way we hurt over our own children. The problem, you see, is that in our language the word 'suffer' refers solely to bodily suffering, to physical pain. And we do not believe that God has a body. He is pure spirit.

So to talk of Him experiencing bodily pain seemed absurd to me. But does God hurt? Oh, yes, of course God hurts."

One wonders how many thousands—how many millions—of times each day such misunderstandings arise among people of different cultures, even among people of the same culture, because we fail to bracket, to "silence the familiar," to empty ourselves of our semantics and traditional images. I am reminded of the time when Soviet Premier Nikita Khrushchev came to the United States and, at the start of one of his speeches, clasped his hands above his head and bounced up and down. Americans were furious. Had he not already said that Russia would bury us, and here he was bouncing up and down like a cocky prizefighter who had just triumphed in a boxing match! Yet some years later a man familiar with the culture told me that this was a traditional Russian gesture meaning "hands clasped in friendship across the sea."

Unless we empty ourselves of such preconceived cultural or intellectual images and expectations, we not only cannot understand the Other, we cannot even listen. Indeed, we cannot even feel empathy. So in a recent article, "Toward Empathy: The Uses of Wonder," the psychiatrist Alfred Margulies writes of bracketing and emptiness when he says:

> Regarding empathy, Freud wrote that it "plays the largest part in our understanding of what is inherently foreign to our ego."
>
> ... In a now famous letter to his brothers, Keats wrote that Shakespeare possessed the quality of a *"Negative Capability,* that is when man is capable of being in uncertainties, Mysteries, doubts, without any irritable reaching after fact and reason." How accurately he captured the therapist's and poet's dilemma! This "irritable reaching" is what Husserl and Freud were warning against; the ability to maintain an evenly hovering attention, to suspend the world, requires a negative capability, the capacity to go against the grain of needing to know.

... The negation of what is known, the negative
capability, topples the familiar and, in this sense, is an
act of will and even aggression. . . . This negation of
the self by the therapist involves a kind of self-
aggression: to submerge oneself, to submit to not
knowing, and to put oneself aside. Perhaps it is one
component of the sometimes exhausting nature of
therapeutic work—the therapist not only bears intense
effects, but also denies the self in the pursuit of the
other.*

The process of entering emptiness—exercising what Keats
called the "negative capability"—is necessarily an ongoing one.
Jesus possessed that capability and used it to overcome prejudice in healing empathy and love transcending culture. Let
me take the liberty of imagining an internal dialogue in Jesus'
mind during one of the stranger of the many strange incidents
recounted in the Gospels.†

Jesus was camped with his disciples near Tyre and Sidon.
He was "between engagements," tired and in need of self-
replenishment. As the disciples were busying themselves with
the chores—they knew enough to leave him alone at such
times—Jesus was sitting in the sun, enjoying its warmth penetrating his blood, relishing the quiet and solitude, in relation
to God as always but blissfully relaxed. Suddenly, from around
a little hill, a woman came trotting up to him. He could see by
her dress that she was no Israelite but a foreigner, a filthy,
untouchable Canaanite. Jesus recoiled in disgust. She began to
babble in an atrocious accent. Waves of fury filled Jesus. What
right did she have to interrupt one of his few precious moments of peace? He was tempted no longer to recoil but to
jump forward and slap her, kick her, drive her away in his
rage. But the habit of excercising emptiness won. He turned
inward. I'm confused, he thought. I'm feeling overwhelmed. I

* Alfred Margulies, "Toward Empathy: The Uses of Wonder," *American Journal of
Psychiatry*, Vol. 141, No. 9 (Sept. 1984), pp. 1025–30.
† Matthew 15:21–28.

don't know what I'm doing. I need to get away and be quiet and empty.

Jesus turned and ran from the woman into the tent. He huddled in the far corner. "Why won't they leave me alone, God?" he asked. "Surely You don't want me to have anything to do with her, do You? But now I have asked You a question, haven't I, Abba? So let me be empty. Let me listen."

But Jesus could not hear God. All he could hear was the woman continuing to babble to his disciples right outside the tent. He wished they would send her away. He listened to them trying to do that, but she refused to go. Finally two of the disciples came into the tent. "We can't get rid of her, Master, just by telling her you're busy. But if you tell us to, we'll take care of her one way or another."

Jesus looked up at them, spontaneously saying, "I was sent here just to minister to the lost sheep of the house of Israel." Immediately, however, the habit took over. "Is that true, Abba? That is why You sent me, isn't it? There goes another question. Listen. Be empty."

"So you do want to get rid of her?" the disciple queried.

"Am I sent here just to minister to Israelites, Abba? Be empty. Oh, no, God, do You really want me to minister to everyone? To anyone and everyone? Be empty. Listen."

"Well?" The disciples pushed for an answer in the silence.

But the silence continued as Jesus stayed empty. Spasms of agony passed across his face like the shadows from windy clouds. Finally he said, "Send her in."

The disciples looked astonished, standing there dumbly. Irritably Jesus repeated, "I told you to send her in." Then he thought, All right, now I've done it. I've engaged myself. Do it decently. Be empty. Listen. Despite her accent, listen. Be empty. Hear what she has to say.

The flap of the tent was pulled open and the untouchable creature came in. But even as he felt like recoiling again, Jesus reminded himself, Be empty.

"Master," said the woman, falling to her knees, "my daughter is grievously vexed with a demon. Please heal her, please."

Oh, God, another case of possession, Jesus thought. I don't have the energy. I'm so tired, Abba. And now you give me a Canaanite demon to boot. But be empty. It's a child, after all. The poor child. Still, it's a Canaanite child. I can't be responsible for the whole world.

"It is not right," Jesus said to the woman, laying upon her the full strength of the negative side of his ambivalence, "to take the food meant for the children and cast it to dogs." But even as he finished speaking, the habit took over and he again turned inward. That was not necessarily fair, and hardly kind, he thought. Be empty. Listen to the woman. Forget her clothes. Penetrate her accent. Be open and empty and listen.

"True, Master," the woman said, "but even the dogs are fit to eat the crumbs that fall from the children's table."

Tears filled Jesus' eyes. The humility, he thought, my God, the humility. I could never deny myself to anyone so humble. Would that the Israelites could generally be so humble. You've taught me again, Abba. You used this woman to do it, didn't you? I am meant for the whole world.

The tears still in his eyes, the love poured out of Jesus. "Oh, woman," he exclaimed with joy, "great is your faith. Be it unto you this moment as you will."

Emptiness requires work. It is an exercise of discipline and is always the most difficult part of the process that a group must undergo if it is to become a community. Like any discipline, it can become easier if we make it a habit, as I have suggested Jesus did. But even if habitual, it is still painful. For emptiness always requires a negation of the self and the need to know, a sacrifice.

There is a sweet Hasidic story of a rabbi in a small Russian town at the turn of the century who accomplished this "submission to not knowing," who learned to live in emptiness. For years he had pondered the mysteries of the universe and the deepest religious questions. Finally he concluded that when one got down to the very root of things, one just did not know. Then one morning, shortly after reaching this conclusion, he was walking across the town square when a Cossack, the town

policeman, accosted him. The Cossack was in a bad mood and
thought he would take it out on the rabbi. "Hey, Rabbi," he
demanded, "where do you think you're going?"

"I don't know," the rabbi answered.

This reply now truly infuriated the Cossack. "What do you
mean, you don't know?" he yelled. "Every morning at eleven
o'clock for the past twenty years you've crossed this square on
your way to the synagogue to pray. Here it is eleven in the
morning, you're headed in the direction of the synagogue,
and you tell me you don't know where you're going. You're
trying to make a fool out of me, that's what you're doing, and
I'll teach you not to do that."

So the Cossack grabbed the rabbi and dragged him off to
the local jail. Just as he was about to push him into the cell the
rabbi turned to him and said, "You see, you just don't know."

There are few among us who do not have great difficulty
tolerating the emptiness of not knowing. After all, knowledge
of the past, the present, and even the future—and above all
self-knowledge—are touted as the ultimate goals of the human
experience. That is why the question I am most often asked is
"Tell us, Dr. Peck, how we can *know* that we are doing the right
thing."

I must reply that there is no such formula, and I speak once
again of Jesus, who, like all of us (albeit in different proportions, apparently) had two parts to his mind: a divine part and
a human part. In his divine part he seemed to know not only
that he would be crucified (and anyone with a little political
savvy could have figured that one out) but also that he would
be resurrected on the third day, that a church would be built
on Peter, his Rock, and that it would all turn out to be comedy
rather than tragedy in the end. But in the human part of his
mind he did not seem to know this at all. This is the Jesus who
sweated blood in the Garden of Gethsemane. That was the
moment of decision—and he just didn't know. Had he known
beyond any shadow of a doubt, with one hundred-percent
certainty, that he would be resurrected on the third day and
that a church would be built on Peter, his Rock, and that

hundreds of millions of us would worship today in his name, going to the cross would simply have been a smart investment. Three, six hours of agony would be a small price for all that one hundred-percent guaranteed glory. But it was precisely because he didn't know, because he threw himself into the Cloud of Unknowing and cast his being into the arms of the even to him unknowable God, that his sacrifice lay.

And so it is also for all of us. Our love, our sacrifices, are made manifest, more than in any other way through our willingness not to know. Consider an everyday example: child raising. Let's say that a sixteen-year-old girl comes to her parents and asks, "Mommy, Daddy, can I stay out until two o'clock this Saturday night?" There are three ways in which the parents may respond to such an ordinary request. One is to say, "No, of course you can't; you know darn well your curfew is ten." At the other extreme are parents who say, "Of course, dear, whatever you want." What characterizes these two responses—both of which may be said to stem from absolute certainty—is the ease with which they are made. They are reflexive, shoot-from-the-hip, immediately formulistic reactions that require no thought or effort from such mothers or fathers.

What good parents do, on the other hand, is to take that question seriously. "Should she or shouldn't she?" they ask themselves. "We don't know. It's true that her curfew is ten, but we established that when she was fourteen, and it's probably no longer realistic. On the other hand, there's going to be drinking at the party she's going to, and that's worrisome. But she's doing well at school and handles her homework responsibly, and maybe we should express our appreciation for and faith in her sense of responsibility. On the other hand, the boy she's going out with seems pretty immature. What should we do? Should we compromise? What would the best compromise be? We don't know. Should it be midnight? One o'clock? Eleven o'clock. We don't know. Which should we decide on?"

Ultimately it probably doesn't matter much what such parents decide, because whatever it is, their decision will be a thoughtful one. And while their daugher may not be perfectly happy with it, she will know that her question—and hence she herself—has been taken seriously. She will know that she is important and valuable enough for her parents to agonize over in the emptiness of their not-knowing. She will know that she is loved.

So, having said that there is no formula in answer to that inevitable question, I can only say further, "The unconscious is always one step ahead of the conscious mind, and it is therefore impossible ever to *know* that you are doing the right thing (since knowing is a function of consciousness). However, if your will is steadfastly to the good, and if you are willing to suffer *fully* when the good is ambiguous, your unconscious will always be one step ahead of your conscious mind in the right direction." In other words, you will do the right thing even though you will not have the consolation of knowing at the time that it is the right thing.

Those who seek certainty, or who claim certainty in their knowledge, cannot tolerate ambiguity. The word "ambiguous" means "uncertain" or "doubtful," or "capable of being understood in more than one way." And because that means not knowing—perhaps not ever being able to know—we have great trouble with ambiguity in our culture. It is not until we move into Stage IV of our spiritual growth that we even begin to become comfortable with ambiguity. We start to realize that not everything is "black or white," that there are multiple dimensions to things, often with contradictory meanings. So it is that mystics of all cultures and religions speak in terms of paradox—not in terms of "either/or" but in terms of "both/and." The capacity to accept ambiguity and to think paradoxically is both one of the qualities of emptiness and one of the requirements for peacemaking.

Perhaps the best known and most telling of all Christian paradoxes was Jesus' statement: "He that saves his life shall lose it; and he that loses his life, for my sake, shall find it."* By

* Matthew 10:39.

this Jesus did not mean that each and every one of us is called to be victim to bodily murder as he was. He did mean, however, that death of the psychological self is required for salvation. This same sacrifice of self is required for emptiness. Such sacrifice usually does not mean actual physical death. But it always means some kind of death—the death of an idea or ideology, or a traditionally held cultural view, or even at the very least simply an entrenched pattern of "black or white" or "either/or" thinking.

Elisabeth Kübler-Ross was the first person to have the courage to talk with people who were dying and ask them how they felt. Out of her work she wrote the classic *On Death and Dying,* in which she elucidated the five successive stages people go through as they face their impending death: denial, anger, bargaining, depression, and acceptance.* First, people tend simply to *deny* the reality of the situation. "They must have gotten my lab test mixed up with someone else's," they will think or say. Then, as they realize this is not the case, they get angry—angry at the doctors, the nurses, the hospital, angry at their families, angry at God. Then they bargain: "Maybe if I go back to church and start praying, my cancer will go away" or "Maybe if I start being nicer to my children, my kidney disease will stop progressing," they tell themselves. But when they realize that there really is no way out—that the jig is up— they become depressed. If they are able to do what we therapists call "work through" their depression, however, they can reach the fifth stage, in which they truly accept their death. It is a surprisingly beautiful stage of peace, tranquillity, spiritual light—almost like a resurrection of sorts.

But most people who are dying do not go through all these stages. The majority die still denying, still angry, still bargaining, or still depressed, because when they hit the stage of depression it is so painful that they retreat into denial, anger, or bargaining. They are unable to "work through" their depression.

* Elisabeth Kübler-Ross, *On Death and Dying* (New York: Macmillian, 1969).

The most exciting thing about Kübler-Ross's work is not merely what it tells us about the psychological process accompanying physical death; it is that we go through exactly these same stages, in the same order, whenever we make any significant spiritual change or step in our psychological growth. In other words, all change is a kind of death, and all growth requires that we go through depression.

Let us say, for example, that there is a flaw in my personality, and my friends start criticizing me for its manifestations. My first reaction is one of *denial:* She just got out of the wrong side of the bed this morning, I think, or He's really just angry at his wife. Through such things I tell myself that their criticisms really don't have anything to do with me. But if my friends keep it up, then I get *angry* at them. What gives them the right to stick their noses into my business? They don't know what it's like to be in my shoes. Why don't they keep their noses in their own darn business?, I think, or perhaps even tell them. If they love me enough to keep after me, however, then I *bargain:* Actually I haven't given them many pats on the back lately or told them what a good job they're doing. And I go around smiling at my friends and being of good cheer, hoping that will shut them up. But if it doesn't work—if they still insist on criticizing me—I finally begin to contemplate the possibility: Maybe there really *is* something wrong with me. And that's *depressing.* But if I can hang in there with that depressing notion, contemplate it, stay with it, analyze it, I can not only discern the nature of the flaw in my personality but begin the work of isolating and naming it and ultimately eradicating it, killing it, *emptying* myself of it. And should I succeed at this work of assisting a part of me to die, I will emerge from the other end of my depression a new and better and, in some sense, resurrected person.

Kübler-Ross's stages of dying are also highly analogous to the stages of individual spiritual growth and to the stages of community development. For in every case we are talking about *change.* Emptiness, depression, and death are analogous because they are the concomitants of the bedrock we must reach if we are to effect change. These stages are basic to human nature and the patterns and rules of human change, whether as individuals or as groups—and not only of small group change but also large group change.

Take the behavior of the United States between 1964 and 1974 in relation to Vietnam, for instance. As evidence began to accumulate that our policies were not working there, the first response of the U.S. was to *deny* that evidence. The policies were fine, we thought, we simply need a few more military advisers and a few more dollars to implement them. When our policies continued to fail we became *angry*. We'll show them, we thought. We'll turn the country into a parking lot if we have to. Regular troops were sent in by the division. We bombed "the hell out of them." The rage was palpable. The time of the body count had begun. Enemy corpses were dragged behind personnel carriers. It was the time of My Lai and other atrocities. And our policies continued to fail.

So then we began to *bargain*. It took five years, as we attempted to obtain "peace with honor," which meant an end to the war without having to acknowledge that we were in any way at fault. In objective fact, that bargaining also failed. The fact is that we lost the war. The most "powerful" country in the world was brought down by one of the "least." We withdrew our hundreds of thousands, and our "enemy" took over. Yet in our collective mind—whose capacity to deceive itself is as great as that of the individual mind—we somehow managed to believe we had succeeded in our bargaining. We had not lost a major war that we had instigated, had we? We had never actually surrendered, had we? No, we had "extricated" ourselves from a "situation."

The greatest tragedy of the Vietnam War, to my mind, is that this nation was never willing to suffer a true and full psychological *depression* over it. We have failed to acknowledge collectively our national sin. We have never publicly apologized. We have never fully admitted that we were *wrong*. Having been unwilling to do the work of depression, we have been unable as a nation to grow from our failure, to learn how to be different. So, by and large, our policies toward communism and Third World nations have not changed as a consequence of their failure. We have not changed. Much of the time Americans act as if Vietnam had never happened.

So there is the equation between emptiness, depression, and psychological death. They are the bridge between chaos and community, between the decadent and the revitalized, between sin and reformation. It is for this reason that the participants in a disarmament workshop I once led quite properly decided to focus the last part of their time together on the issue of how to do the work of depression.

The essence of the emptying process—the work of depression and the agony of sacrifice—is the willingness to give up, to surrender. It is rare during the process of community-building that I address myself to an individual's problems. Occasionally, however, when a member is having particular difficulties in giving up something, emptying herself or himself of some past outdated attachment or resentment—when someone says something such as: "I just can't forgive my father for having molested me when I was a child" or "I just can't get over my anger at the way the Church treated me when I got divorced," I may tell the following Zen Buddhist story.*

Two monks, Busho and Tanko, were traveling from one monastery to another on a rainy day. Halfway in their journey they came to a crossroad that had become a gigantic mud puddle. A young woman in a lovely kimono was standing at one corner looking forlorn. Busho went up to her and asked if she needed help getting across the road. She said she did. "Well, then," Busho exclaimed, "jump up on my back." She jumped on his back, and Busho waded across the road and gently put her down on the other side. Then he and Tanko continued their journey through the mud and rain.

They arrived at their destination just before nightfall, tired and hungry. They washed and then were fed a good meal by the other monks. After dinner Tanko said, "Busho, how could

* I was introduced to this story, "The Monk and the Woman," in Anthony de Melo, S.J., *The Song Bird* (Chicago, Loyola Univ. Press, 1983), p. 138.

you? How could you have carried that woman? You know that we monks are not supposed to have anything to do with women. Yet you invited one to actually jump on you, and not only that, but a young and beautiful one. What might people have said if they had seen you? You disgraced your vows and our order. How could you?"

Busho looked at him. "Tanko, are you still carrying around that young woman?" he asked. "Why, I put her down over five hours ago."

As I have said, the purpose of emptying ourselves is to make room for the new. The only reason to give up something is to gain something better. Peace is undeniably better than war. Thus we must ask, "Of what do we have to empty ourselves in order to gain peace?" What traditional attitudes and styles of behavior must we lay aside? What outmoded viewpoints, policies, understandings, and resentments are we still carrying around? To what hidden opportunities must we be open and empty?

CHAPTER XI

Vulnerability

We defined "emptiness" as "openness to the Other"—whether it is a strange idea, a stranger, or God. But what happens if the Other is dangerous? What happens if the new idea is wrong, if the stranger is a murderer, if the voice of the Other is that of the Evil One? May we not be wounded?

Indeed, yes. Openness requires of us vulnerability—the ability, even the willingness, to be wounded. But it is not a simple, black-or-white matter. For one thing, the word "wounded" is itself ambiguous. It can mean either "to be damaged" or simply "to be hurt." I sometimes draw the distinction by asking if anyone in my audience is vulnerable enough to volunteer for an unknown but painful experiment. Some brave soul always is, and what I then do is pinch his upper arm quite sharply. "Did that hurt?" I ask, and my victim, rubbing his arm, somewhat grievously replies that it did. "Did it damage you?" I then inquire. After thinking for a few seconds my victim responds: "It certainly did hurt, but no, I cannot say that it actually damaged me." The point is that if you were deliberately to put your arm into a grinding piece of machinery, you would be an utter idiot. You would be damaged for naught. But if you attempt to live your life without ever being hurt, you won't be able to live at all, except perhaps in a very softly padded cell.

The word "vulnerability" is also ambiguous because it does not distinguish between physical and emotional wounding. It is not just that as children we will not be able to climb trees without risking scraped knees; it is more a matter of emotional pain. There is no way that we can live a rich life unless we are willing to suffer repeatedly, experiencing depression and despair, fear and anxiety, grief and sadness, anger and the agony of forgiving, confusion and doubt, criticism and rejection. A life lacking these emotional upheavals will not only be useless to ourselves, it will be useless to others. We cannot heal without being willing to be hurt.

Before one of the exorcisms in which I was involved I had the task of discerning whether a certain interested man should be a member of the treatment team. I was sufficiently ambivalent to leave the decision up to him. "You are welcome to join the team," I finally told him, "as long as you come in love. By love I mean that if there is a conflict between the patient's healing and your self-protection, your self-protection has to go." He decided, I suspect wisely, not to participate.

If Jesus, the healer, taught us anything, he taught us that the way to salvation lies through vulnerability. So it is that when he was alive he walked vulnerably among Romans and tax collectors and other unfitting characters (which included women in his sexist culture), among outcasts and foreigners, Canaanites and Samaritans, among the diseased, the demoniacs, and lepers, and infectious. And when the time came that he should die, he vulnerably submitted himself to the killing wounds of the entrenched Establishment of his day, which is why the theologian Dorothee Sölle has referred to Jesus as God's unilateral disarmament.*

Good theology makes good psychology. If theology is good, it is good because it is true; and if it is true, it generally works in the long if not the short run. So what happens when we make ourselves vulnerable to another person? What happens when I say, "I wrote a book all about discipline, and I don't even have the self-discipline to stop smoking. Sometimes I think I'm a hypocrite, a real phony. Sometimes I think I'm not even on the right road myself. Sometimes I feel I don't know where I am. I feel lost and scared. And tired. Although I am only fifty, sometimes I'm so very tired. And lonely. Will you help me?" The effect on others of that kind of vulnerability is almost invariably *disarming*. They are most likely to respond,

---

* Dorothee Sölle, *Of War and Love* (Maryknoll, New York: Orbis Books, 1984), p. 97.

"You seem like an authentic person. I'm tired and scared and lonely too. Of course I'll help you in any way I can."

But what happens when we behave invulnerably, when we gird ourselves with psychological defenses and pretend that we are cool cats who have got it all together, rugged individualists who seem to be in complete control of our lives? What happens is that other people gird themselves with *their* psychological defenses and pretend that they too are cool cats who have got it all together, and our human, personal relationships become nothing more than that of two empty tanks bumping against each other in the night.

So it is also with the relationships between nations. It is our international policy to be as invulnerable as possible. Of course it is the policy of all other nations also to be invulnerable. But these are policies of hopelessness. They offer no possibility of peaceful relationships, much less world community. They offer only greater and greater threats of death and destruction. Without unilateral initiatives of vulnerability there is no way out.

I do not mean my words to be taken simplistically. I am not talking about a foolish vulnerability. I am not suggesting that if you live in the inner city of our nation's capital (as Lily and I did for several years) you take all the locks off your doors, because if you do you're going to be ripped off—and you're not going to be ripped off tomorrow, you're going to be ripped off tonight. I am speaking of a willingness to become vulnerable. I am told that this nation possesses enough nuclear weaponry to blow up every person on the planet ten times over. If we on our own initiative disposed of half of that weaponry, what a dramatic gesture of vulnerability and peacemaking that would be! And we would still have enough to blow everyone up five times over!

The laying down of physical weapons is not the only way that we humans, individually or collectively, can make ourselves vulnerable. When we lecture together on these matters, Keith Miller will say: "I'm not sure I agree with Scotty that the best thing to do is to get rid of half of our nuclear weapons.

What I think we should do is to apologize to the Russians. We should tell them that we have not behaved as Christians toward them. We have not loved them with our whole hearts. We have not wished the best for them. We have not rejoiced in their successes. We have not loved them as ourselves. We should say that we are sorry and humbly ask them to forgive us." Vulnerability in whatever form always requires at least a small step of faith, and for some it might even be easier to relinquish half our weapons than acknowledge imperfection.

I have never been able to make any progress discussing even partial disarmament with a hawk. The reason is that such people labor under what I call a "control mentality" or "what if?" psychology. They feel that it is both necessary and possible to live in a world in which all contingencies can be controlled, a world in which there are no risks. Thus to my proposal that we unilaterally cut our nuclear arsenal in half, or to Keith's that we ought to apologize to Russia—or to any other such proposal— they invariably respond: "Yes, but *what if* the Russians, instead of realizing it to be a vulnerable gesture of peacemaking, interpret it as a sign of weakness? And then take advantage of it?"

The problem is that there are always "what ifs." Although the so-called hawks very much like to think of themselves as realists, they do not like to face this reality. Theirs is a psychology of fear and distrust, and their resultant behavior, typical of that motivated fear, is rigid and one-dimensional. Sometimes almost humorously so. Such people have even said to me, "Dr. Peck, if you can show me a way we can be vulnerable without risk, why then I'll be happy to be vulnerable."

Risk is the central issue of vulnerability. But again we must learn to think in more paradoxical terms and on more than one level at once. As the Muslim Sufi Nagshband commented: "When people say 'weep,' they do not mean 'weep always.' When they say 'Do not cry,' they do not mean you to be a permanent buffoon."* So it is not a matter of total invulnerability versus absolute pacifism any more than we should con-

* Idries Shah, *The Way of the Sufi* (New York: Dutton paperback, 1970), p. 150.

clude either that the Russians "are just like us" or that they are utterly alien or evil. It is incumbent upon us to exercise our wits to discern toward just whom we should behave vulnerably and toward whom not, and when and how and to what degree.

Jesus, with great cunning, avoided many traps that were set for him and delayed his crucifixion as long as he could do so with integrity. So it is that we are not called upon to be utterly defenseless. On the other hand, anyone who takes Christianity with full seriousness will realize that crucifixion is not just something that happened to that one, solitary man 1950-odd years ago. They will also realize that to live life to its fullest, they must be willing to share themselves with and for others. And that there is no such thing as vulnerability without risk—either of total rejection or of having others take advantage of their vulnerability. That risk is always there.

Of all variants of vulnerability the one most difficult is the revealing of some imperfection, problem, neurosis, sin, or failure—all of which tend to be subsumed under the heading of "weakness" in our culture of rugged individualism. It is a ridiculous cultural attitude, because the reality is that, as individuals or nations, we are all weak. We all have problems, imperfections, neuroses, sins, failures. And to attempt to hide them is a lie.

Our cultural attitude is particularly ridiculous for those who call themselves Christians. He whom they call "Lord" not only lived and died vulnerably but was a failure according to our usual measurements. We worship a man whose life was ended by his execution as a petty, provincial political prisoner between two even more ordinary criminals, spat upon by his executioners, betrayed by his followers, and largely deserted by his friends—a total loser in the world's terms. Perhaps the best motto for Christianity is "In weakness, strength."* Certainly the most compelling prerequisite for membership in the true Church is that one has to know oneself to be a sinner. It is quite properly a Church of Weaklings, worshiping a God who in par-

* See II Corinthians 12:9.

adoxical weakness rules the world. But this is strange doctrine for most who are far more dedicated to a world of "principalities and powers" (by which Paul meant a world that operates according to the devil's rules).* As G. K. Chesterton stated so well: "The Christian ideal, it is said, has not been tried and found wanting; it has been found difficult and left untried."†

Vulnerability, then, is not only the ability to risk being wounded but is most often made manifest by revealing our woundedness: our brokenness, our crippledness, our weaknesses, our failures and inadequacies. I do not think that Jesus walked vulnerably among the outcasts and crippled of the world purely as a sacrificial act. To the contrary, I suspect he did so because he preferred their company. It is only among the overtly imperfect that we can find community and only among the overtly imperfect nations of the world that we can find peace. Our imperfections are among the few things we human beings all have in common.

I sometimes refer to psychotherapy as the honesty game. People who come to therapy suffer from lies—either lies they have been told by their parents, their siblings, their teachers, the media, or lies they have told themselves. These lies can be corrected only in an atmosphere of honesty as nearly complete as two human beings can possibly create between each other. So it is that psychotherapists should be willing, when appropriate, to be honest and perfectly "up front" about their own brokenness. Indeed, only honest people can play a healing role in the world. It is no accident that one of the classics of our time is entitled *The Wounded Healer*.‡ As someone once said in a community-building workshop: "The greatest gift we can give each other is our own woundedness." The genuine healer has to be wounded. Only the wounded can heal.

It is the policy of the United States, Russia, and virtually all other nation-states to appear to be as invulnerable as possible,

* Ephesians 6:12.
† G. K. Chesterton, *What's Wrong with the World?* Pt. I, chap. 5, 1910, in Bartlett's *Familiar Quotations* (Boston: Little, Brown, 1980), p. 742.
‡ Henri Nouwen, *The Wounded Healer* (Garden City, N.Y.: Doubleday, 1972).

not only in terms of weaponry but in every aspect of the political process. As a nation we attempt to act as if we had no weaknesses. The doctrine of infallibility is hardly restricted to the papacy. The United States no more than Russia admits mistakes or sin. Our politicians have trapped themselves in a false image of invulnerability and infallibility. It will be only when we are willing to discard such primitive images of strength that we will become weak and yet strong enough to lead the nations toward global community.

Weak and yet strong enough? Again we are faced with paradox. For it is one of the unavoidable paradoxes of this life that beyond a certain point, as either individuals or nations, the more invulnerable we attempt to become, the greater becomes our jeopardy. As a nation the United States has long since passed that point. The spiral of piling weapon system upon weapon system, threat upon counterthreat, only becomes ever more deadly, and there is absolutely no way out except through genuine unilateral initiatives of weakness and vulnerability.

We have heard this word "initiative" many times. How many times has our government proclaimed through media that it has taken a "bold, new initiative" in attempting to "halt the arms race?" And then we wonder why the Russians don't respond, and we take that as further proof of their evil intentions. Somehow Russian "initiatives" don't seem to get anywhere either. But our use of the word is dishonest. If used genuinely, "initiative" implies both risk and a willingness to act unilaterally. Our initiatives never involve either. We simply say, "We'll get rid of this if you'll get rid of that." The proposal is always bilaterally phrased and represents no risk whatever. Our so-called "initiatives" are merely ploys and are inevitably met with counterploys, and vice versa. The problem is symbolized by the subtitle of a recent (and otherwise excellent) American book, *Negotiating Agreement Without Giving In.** Similarly, we generally misuse the word "negotiation."

* Roger Fisher and William Ury, *Getting to Yes: Negotiating Agreement Without Giving In* (New York: Penguin Books), 1981.

In building community, some brave soul always has to start. There must, in truth, be initiatives. One by one people genuinely risk rejection or other injury as they escalate (or "de-escalate") the group into ever deeper levels of vulnerability and honesty. It is always individual, always unilateral, and always risky. That's the reality of it.

I do not argue for a policy of appeasement. That would be simplistic, as the world has clearly learned on a number of occasions over the past sixty years. Yet our policy of deterrence by military might alone is equally simplistic. The safety of peace cannot be cheaply bought, our leaders tell us. I agree. Paradoxically, it can be obtained only through dangerous risk. It is bizarre, however, that currently war seems to be the sole risk we are willing to take. The central problem of the arms race is not that we are risking too much but rather far too little on behalf of peace. Our strategy needs to be far more complex and multidimensional than "peace through strength." Specifically, we need to pursue additionally, with at least equal vigor, the "peace through weakness" strategies that build community. Otherwise there is no hope. For the reality is that there can be no vulnerability without risk; and there can be no community without vulnerability; and there can be no peace— ultimately no life—without community.

CHAPTER XII

Integration and Integrity

Community is integrative. It includes people of different sexes, ages, religions, cultures, viewpoints, life styles, and stages of development by integrating them into a whole that is greater—better—than the sum of its parts. Integration is not a melting process; it does not result in a bland average. Rather, it has been compared to the creation of a salad in which the identity of the individual ingredients is preserved yet simultaneously transcended. Community does not solve the problem of pluralism by obliterating diversity. Instead it seeks out diversity, welcomes other points of view, embraces opposites, desires to see the other side of every issue. It is "wholistic." It integrates us human beings into a functioning mystical body.

The word "integrity" comes from the verb "to integrate." Genuine community is always characterized by integrity. It is no accident that Erik Erikson also labeled the final stage of individual psychosocial development "Integrity." Just as it characterizes the highest mystical, wholistic form of individual functioning, so the integrity of community characterizes the highest form of group functioning. Conversely, the lowest—the most evil and destructive—forms of both individual and group behavior are characterized by their lack of integrity.

We psychologists use a verb that is the opposite of the verb "to integrate": "to compartmentalize." By it we refer to the remarkable capacity we human beings have to take matters that are properly related to each other and put them in separate, airtight mental compartments where they don't rub up against each other and cause us any pain. An example would be that of the businessman who goes to church on Sunday mornings, believes that he loves God and God's creation and his fellow human beings, and then on Monday morning has no trouble with his company's policy of dumping toxic wastes in a nearby stream. He has put his religion in one compartment and his business in another and is what we call a "Sunday morning Christian." It may be a very comfortable way to operate, but integrity it is not.

Integrity is never painless. It requires that we let matters rub up against each other, that we fully experience the tension of conflicting needs, demands, and interests, that we even be emotionally torn apart by them. Take, for example, the fact that this country, on whose coinage is written the words "In God We Trust," is also the leading manufacturer and seller of weapons in the world. What are we to do with this? Should we be perfectly comfortable about it? Should we keep these matters in separate compartments? Or should we wonder if there is a conflict between them and agonize over the tension of trying to resolve that conflict? Should we consider, for instance, with integrity, changing the inscription on our coinage to read "In Weapons We Trust" or "In God We Partially Trust?"

Since integrity is never painless, so community is never painless. It also requires itself to be fully open, vulnerable, to the tension of conflicting needs, demands, and interests of its members and of the community as a whole. It does not seek to avoid conflict but to reconcile it. And the essence of reconciliation is that painful, sacrificial process of emptying. Community always pushes its members to empty themselves sufficiently to make room for the other point of view, the new and different understanding. Community continually urges both itself and its individual members painfully, yet joyously, into ever deeper levels of integrity.

To follow the drum of community-making and peace is to march to vibrations very different from those of the drum of war-making. It is vitally important, therefore, that we become skilled at recognizing these different vibrations. Perhaps the essence of that skill is the capacity to discern between the sound of integrity and the sound of its absence.

WHAT IS MISSING?

Difficult though integrity may be to achieve, the test for it is deceptively simple. If you wish to discern either the presence or absence of integrity, you need to ask only one question. What is missing? Has anything been left out?

I first learned to apply this test at the age of fifteen when I began to follow the events of the Korean War in the newspapers. Each morning I avidly read the latest statistics in *The New York Times:* "Thirty-one MIGs shot down; all American planes returned unharmed." The next day: "Thirty-four MIGs shot down; one American plane slightly damaged." Next day: "Twenty-nine MIGs shot down; one American plane and pilot lost." Clearly, as the articles and editorials informed me, our planes were technologically far superior to the MIGs and our pilots not only better trained but smarter than the North Koreans or Chinese. The next day: "Thirty-seven MIGs shot down; all American planes returned unharmed." And so it went, day after day, week after week, month after month. Initially I was filled with patriotic pride at my nation's triumphs. But then a gradual uneasiness crept in. The problem was that the same paper informed me that North Korea, China, and Russia were industrially underdeveloped countries. Granted their planes were of shoddy manufacture and their pilots untrained, but I slowly began to wonder how these underdeveloped nations could keep turning out all these thousands of planes just to get shot down by the dozens every day. The pieces didn't fit together. Either one or more of the pieces was deformed—a lie—or one or more of the pieces was *missing*. That was when I stopped believing everything I read in the newspapers. Nothing in the years since has caused me to begin again.

Approximately a decade later I read a massive and engaging novel by Ayn Rand, *Atlas Shrugged*.* In it she made a seem-

* Ayn Rand, *Atlas Shrugged* (New York: Random House, 1957).

ingly compelling case for her philosophy of rugged individualism and unrestrained free enterprise. Something about that philosophy, however, bothered me—something I couldn't quite put my finger on. It kept gnawing at me until one day I finally realized that there were essentially no children in the book, which was a panoramic novel of around a thousand pages recounting the sweep of society and the drama of many lives. But there were virtually no children. It was as if children did not exist in her society; they were missing. And of course that is exactly one of the social situations in which rugged individualism and unrestrained capitalism fall short: where there are children and others who, like children, need to be cared for.

Five years later still, early in my psychiatry training, I was taught: "What the patient does not say is more important than what he or she does say." It is an excellent rule. The most healthy patients, for instance, during the course of a few psychotherapeutic sessions, will talk of their present, past, and future in a well-integrated fashion. Should a patient speak only of the present and future, never mentioning childhood, you can be sure that there is at least one unintegrated, unresolved, and important issue in childhood that must be brought to light for full healing. If the patient speaks only of her childhood and her future, the therapist can tell that she has some major difficulty dealing with "the here and now"—often a difficulty connected with intimacy and risk. And should the patient never make mention of his future, one might properly be led to suspect that he may have a problem with fantasy and hope.

Now let me jump ahead several decades to 1985, thirty-one years after the Supreme Court desegregation decision. I had the opportunity to give a lecture in Little Rock, Arkansas. It was open to the public, and nine hundred people attended. Not one was black. I do not use this example to fault that particular city; the same scenario has been repeated only slightly less dramatically in many others. I use it to make the point, once again, that a lack of integrity always reflects a lack of integration and the reality that something is being left out. In this instance, as I looked around at my audience, the incomplete integrity of our society was visually obvious. What was missing was black faces. Relative to our own history and other societies, we have made clear progress in the area of racial integration. But clearly we have a long way to go.

There is another test for integrity, which may not be quite so easy to comprehend. If no pieces of reality are missing from the picture, if all the dimensions are integrated and colored in, then in all probability you will be looking at a paradox. At the root of things, virtually all truth is paradoxical. Buddhist literature is generally more penetrating in this regard than Christian writing. Zen Buddhism in particular is the ideal training school for paradox. My favorite light-bulb joke is "How many Zen Buddhists does it take to change a light bulb?" The answer: "Two: one to change the light bulb and one to *not* change the light bulb."

Lest this seem silly rather than profound to the Western one-dimensional mind, let me say that I do not consider that this is simply "my" book. I have written it only because other people have *not* written it: publishers, editors, booksellers, farmers, carpenters, and others—all of whose labor was required to enable me to perform this particular labor. Since their labor has allowed me to specialize in book writing, I am not against specialization on general principles. But when specialization leads to a compartmentalized kind of thinking that concludes: This is my book, or This is my country, we have lost sight of the whole picture. And our thinking falls into error.

If a concept *is* paradoxical, that itself should suggest that it smacks of integrity, that it gives off the ring of truth. Conversely, if a concept is not in the least paradoxical, you should be suspicious of it and suspect that it has failed to integrate some aspect of the whole. Take, for example again, the ethic of rugged individualism. There is nothing paradoxical about it. It runs with only one side of the truth: that we are called to individuation, wholeness, and self-sufficiency. Its fallacy is that it ignores the other side of that same truth: that we are also called to recognize our inadequacy, our brokenness, and our interdependence. And being fallacious, it fosters a dangerous self-centeredness. For the reality is that we do not exist either by or for ourselves. Indeed, Buddhism teaches that the very notion of the self as an isolated entity is an illusion. It is an illusion that many fall prey to because they do not or will not think with integrity.

If I think with any integrity at all, I immediately realize that my life is utterly nurtured not only by the earth and the rain and the sun but also by those farmers, publishers, booksellers, as well as by my patients, my children, my wife, and other teachers—indeed by the entire fabric of family, society, and creation. Obviously, then, I cannot consider myself of greater importance than my family, my society, or my ecology—compartmentalize myself—with any righteousness whatsoever. As soon as we think with integrity we will realize that we are all properly stewards and that we cannot with integrity deny our responsibility for stewardship of every part of the whole.

Indeed, the more I strive toward integrity, the less I find myself using the word "my." "My" wife is not my possession. The identity of "my" children is only very slightly of my own making. In one sense the money I have earned is mine, but on a more profound level it has been a gift to me from all manner of good fortune, including parents, fine teachers, and fine universities, a public that reads what I have written, and a few personal talents I didn't even have the wisdom to ask for. The law may say that the property I own in Connecticut is "my" land, but it has been farmed by many generations of white and red people before me and I hope will continue to be farmed by generations of strangers to come. The flowers in the garden are not "my" flowers. I do not know how to create a flower; I can merely steward or nurture one.

As stewards we cannot be isolationists. We should no more say that "this group isn't for me" than we should say "Nicaragua has nothing to do with me" or "The people starving in

Ethiopia are not my concern." Nor can we say with integrity that "what we do in Nicaragua or Ethiopia is solely the concern of government leaders; they, the politicians, are the specialists in such matters; it is their job, not mine." It was such an attitude toward our own governors that allowed them to plunge ever deeper into the morass of Vietnam which they themselves largely created.

The reality that integrity dictates against isolationism has unfortunately been used, however, by our government as justification for its misdirected attempts to be a global dictator. Thus we have regarded it as our right to be the "world's policeman," a position that is as arrogant, unintegrated, and self-centered as that of isolationism. And since every other nation-state would also like to be the world's policeman, it is a position obviously unworkable even in theory, as well as in its actual results: the escalating arms race and frantic international meddling. Once again we are brought face-to-face with the dangers of our simplistic, black-or-white, either-or, one-dimensional, primitive thinking, which would hold that we have to be either isolationists or global manipulators. Once again we are faced with the necessity for a more paradoxical, multidimensional, intellectually demanding, world view.

World views are religions, and all wars are "holy wars." If we are to move away from war, therefore, we must begin to develop intellectual standards that distinguish between true religions and false religions, true prophets and false prophets, between integrated and unintegrated world views. Otherwise the only standards will be those that can win out over the others on a bloody battlefield. While community must and can integrate a diversity of viewpoints or religions, this does not mean that all religious thought and practice is equally mature or valid. What are the criteria for discerning religious integrity? Truth in religion is characterized by inclusivity and paradox. Falsity in religion can be detected by its one-sidedness and failure to integrate the whole. To illustrate this further, let us examine that body of religious thought that is closest to home for most Americans: Christian doctrine.

PARADOX AND HERESY

False thinking or doctrinal expression in the name of faith is labeled heresy.

Until six years ago I didn't have the foggiest idea of what heresy was, and I couldn't have cared less. In fact, the very concept smacked to me of the Inquisition and seemed inherently dangerous and properly relegated to the Middle or Dark Ages. But then I became involved with a case of possession. The patient was both suicidal and homicidal at the time and required continuous hospitalization. A month before the exorcism, as part of the preparatory investigation, I said to her, "Tell me about Jesus."

She picked up a piece of paper and drew the cross. "There are three Jesuses up here, two on the left, two on the right, and three down here on the bottom part."

"Cut out that stuff," I said, trying to penetrate the craziness. "How did he die?"

"He was crucified."

Something propelled me to ask: "Did it hurt?"

"Oh, no," she responded.

"No?" I asked in amazement.

"No. You see, he was so highly developed in his Christ consciousness that he was able to project himself into his astral body and just take off from there."

That seemed to be a wacky sort of "new age" answer, but I didn't make anything more of it until that evening, when I spoke with an experienced Catholic priest who was serving as a consultant in the case. The woman's response had been bizarre enough for me to mention it in the course of our conversation. "Oh," he immediately commented, "that's Docetism."

"What on earth is Docetism?" I asked.

"Docetism was one of the very early Church heresies," he responded. "The Docetists were a group of early Christians who believed that Jesus was totally divine, and his humanity was just an appearance."

Such was my introduction to heresy. It turned out that the patient in question was a walking textbook of Christian heresies. Christian heresy is something of which only people who call themselves Christians can be guilty, I came to learn. If you call yourself a Hindu or Muslim or agnostic, you can believe anything you want and Christian thinkers will usually not concern themselves with the veracity of your beliefs. Christian heresy, however, is something put forth in the name of Christianity but which seriously distorts, undermines, or dilutes the truth of Christian doctrine.

In the case of Docetism the destructive nature of heresy is quite readily apparent. If Jesus were totally divine and his humanity just an appearance, then, as my patient believed, his suffering on the cross was simply a divine charade, and his sacrifice (which is the core of what Christianity is all about) was an illusion, a celestial sham. Docetism strikes viciously at the very heart of Christian doctrine.

But note that the opposite of Docetism—a belief that Jesus was totally human—also utterly undermines Christian doctrine. If Jesus was totally human, then God did not come down "to live and die as one of us," and there was no divine love or sacrifice manifest either. Nor would Jesus have been *the* Messiah. If Jesus were totally human, then it is possible for anyone, whether James Jones or the Reverend Moon, to be a messiah.

At the heart of Christian doctrine, therefore, resides paradox. Jesus is neither simply totally divine nor totally human but both. Paradoxically, he who was the Son of Man was also the Son of God. And not simply 50 percent one and 50 percent the other. Paradox does not divide into categories but transcends categories through a mystery that may never be fully comprehensible and yet is often more real than the purely logical.

Most heresy, Christian or otherwise, arises when we fail to embrace both sides of the paradox. As a Christian, for instance, I can say the whole reality is that God, paradoxically, resides both inside of us in Her "still small voice" and simultaneously outside of us in all His transcendent and magnificent Otherness. Whenever people focus primarily on just one side of that paradox, they get into trouble. When they belong totally to the school of "immanence," in which they give credence only to the god within, each and every one of their own little narcissistic thoughts can assume the status of revelation. When they belong totally to the school of "transcendence," which focuses only on the external god, they are highly likely to fall prey to what I call the "heresy of orthodoxy." For if God is entirely outside of us, then how can He/She communicate with us mere mortals? The answer the transcendists have come up with is that God somehow, magically, communicates with His rare chosen prophets, such as Moses, Christ, or Saint Paul. Then it is up to a priestly class to interpret these prophets to the poor lay people who cannot themselves be in touch with God. Thus not only is orthodox doctrine born but it may also be forced down people's throats by the keepers of the doctrine—through murder and torture if necessary. So it was that by denying the indwelling divinity of their victims the Inquisitors were far worse heretics than anyone they put to death in the name of heresy.

Still another example: Fifteen centuries ago a hard-working Irish monk, Pelagius, preached that salvation is achieved only by the doing of good works. The problem with this teaching is that it can encourage an utterly unrealistic pride in one's achievements, and it has quite properly come to be known therefore as the heresy of Pelagianism. Three centuries ago, on the other hand, there was a group of Christians who believed salvation is the result of grace alone. Because, in accord with their belief, they passively sat around quietly waiting for grace to happen, they became known as Quietists. It is hardly a doctrine to encourage the social action—feeding the poor, clothing the naked, healing the sick, and ministering to those in prison—which Jesus called us to do. So it is that Quietism is also a heresy. Because the reality is that salvation is the effect of both grace and good works in a paradoxical mixture that is sufficiently mysterious to defy any mathematical formulation.

A number of points need to be borne in mind. First, all of the old Christian heresies are alive and well. They are also getting people into trouble—either as individuals, like my Docetist patient, or as groups. Inquisitions, for instance, are heresies at work on a societal level.

Second, heresy is not a specifically Christian matter. All religions can have their own, and some heresies are shared between religions. Muslims, for instance, have probably had as much difficulty in coming to terms with the paradox that salvation is a result of both grace and good works as have Christians.

Third, heresy in its broadest definition—a basic half-truth—is not even specifically religious. The ethic of rugged individualism, running as it does with only one side of the paradox, is as much a heresy for the secular as for the religious. And it is as destructive as any designated doctrinal one.

Fourth, all heresy has spiritual implications. The notion that, as individuals or nations, we can be invulnerable is another heresy that is neither specifically secular nor religious. Yet it arises out of a failure of spirit, compounds that failure, and is recognized as a heresy by the deepest thinkers of every religion.

Fifth, being a distortion of reality, all heresy is potentially destructive. In relation to the issue of vulnerability, Mohammed said: "Trust in God, but tie your camel first." Being a "both-sided," paradoxical proclamation, it is a true statement. But there are people and nations that direct all their energies into only tying their camels, making knot after knot in the reins, just as we add weapons system to weapons system and then think that maybe with yet another weapons system we can make ourselves finally, irrevocably, and totally secure. But we forget God in this, failing to remember that there must be some vulnerability, some risk, some reliance upon His/Her grace. Or we attempt to avoid the paradox through specialization, saying to our clergy, "You people pray for peace but leave the knot-tying up to us politicians." The problem is, however, that our camel's tether now has thirty-seven knots in it, and it is going to take a lot of untying—the dismantling of one weapons system after another—as well as faith and risk before we can be free and workable again.

Finally, heresy is destructive only when it dictates behavior. As an idea alone it has no importance. Behavior is the key. There are atheists who behave like Christian saints and properly professing Christians who behave like criminals— who are criminals. No one knew this any better than Jesus, who instructed us: "By their fruits you shall know them." Or "Handsome is as handsome does," which proclaims the same reality.

A consequence of this reality is that, while all forms of thinking should be tolerated, some forms of behavior should not be. Ted had to be kicked out of the Basement Group not because of his ideology but because of his behavior. In community I have met with many bizarre ideologies. Yet I have never seen anyone committed to community-building undermine community development simply by the expression of heretical ideas. To the contrary, because it integrates diversity, in community partial ideas tend to become whole ideas, and the initially simplistic thinking of community members tends to become increasingly complex, paradoxical, flexible, and sane. Consequently there is no such thing as a belief or theology— no matter how false, incomplete, or heretical—that cannot be accepted in the inclusiveness of true community. Conversely, the attempt to exclude individuals because of their beliefs, however silly or primitive, is always destructive to community. There is yet another paradox: *the persecution of heresy is itself heresy.*

BLASPHEMY AND HOPE

So in the end it is behavior that counts. Heretical (unreal) thinking is dangerous only because it tends to lead to unrealistic, and hence dangerous behavior. Conversely, a true or right religious belief that does not lead toward right or righteous behavior does not even deserve the name "religious."

We must assume that *genuine* religious belief is radical. Religious questions and issues are life's most basic, fundamental concerns of creation and destruction, nature and purpose, good and evil—of ultimate meaning. If a so-called religious belief is not radical, we must suspect that it is mere superstition, no deeper than the belief that a black cat means bad luck. On the other hand, if economic and political behavior is unrelated to a supposedly deep faith, such behavior is unrooted, ungrounded. It is unintegrated. It lacks integrity. To put it yet another way, the profession of a religious belief is a lie if it does not significantly determine one's economic, political, and social behavior.

This raises two profound issues. One is the problem of the separation of Church and State. Our heritage of religious freedom is one of the greatest blessings of this nation. The requirement for government to restrain itself from imposing a particular religious-belief system on its citizens is both a cornerstone of democracy and an evolutionary step in the history of civilization. Yet if this restriction also obliges citizens to refrain totally from seeking to express their religious views within political and economic spheres, it will inevitably lead to utterly "privatized" and superficial religious practice. It would require us to be "Sunday morning Christians" (or one of the other religious equivalents). It would secure only the freedom of a meaningless religion.

That is why I referred to the issue of separation of Church and State as a problem. No separation means the demise of religious freedom. Total separation means the demise of genuine religion. Obviously the solution to the problem requires a middle path—a delicate and often paradoxical balance that must be struck and restruck between the competing needs of religious freedom and religious expression. It should be equally obvious that simplistic thinking about the issue will only obscure matters.* Conversely, the capacity to discern between thinking on the matter that is well integrated and thinking that lacks integrity will be most helpful.

The other issue raised by the need to integrate religious belief with behavior is the problem of blasphemy. The numbering of the Ten Commandments is no accident. While the violation of the first and second (idolatry) is perhaps at the root of all sin, the violation of the third is the sin of sins.

The violation of the third commandment—"Thou shalt not take the name of the Lord, thy God, in vain"—we call blasphemy. It is even less understood than idolatry, and doubly wicked. I am amazed, as I go about the country, at the common misunderstanding of the nature of blasphemy. Most people think of it as swearing or the use of bawdy language. To

* For this reason any further analysis of the problem of the separation of Church and State is deserving of an entire book in itself. It might be pointed out, however, that tangential issues are also obscured by simplistic thinking. The manner in which the abortion debate is currently being conducted is a case in point. There are no simple solutions. Anyone who thinks with integrity on the subject will feel torn apart. On the one hand, there is no question that abortion is murder of a sort and that a policy of abortion on demand does tend to diminish what Albert Schweitzer called "reverence for life." On the other hand, there is no question as to the magnitude of the suffering that would result for both parents *and* children if abortion of the misbegotten were not an option. With integrity we must be left with the tension.

To legally say "Thou shalt not abort" is simplistic. Something is *missing*, left out. We cannot with integrity take responsibility away from individuals as to what they will do with their lives and pregnancies and then put it nowhere. *The responsibility has to go somewhere.* We cannot with integrity say "Thou shalt not abort" unless we are talking about *our* children, unless we, as a *community*, are willing to assume great responsibility for the financial and psychological health of the individual parents and child to be.

Of course at present we do not even begin to have sufficient genuine community in this country to either foot the bill or fit the bill. Consequently legislation against abortion that puts responsibility nowhere would merely be atavistic. All it would do would be to return us to where we were thirty years ago, with coat hangers for the poor and trips abroad or other loopholes for the rich. I look forward to the day when there may be sufficient community in this country for us to say with compassion and integrity, "Thou shalt not abort." But until that day arrives we need to continue to live with the full tension of the issue as we work—as rapidly as possible, we hope—toward a better future, where genuine community is the norm rather than the exception.

say "God damn" when you hit your finger with a hammer or "Oh Christ" when you realize you have made a mistake is what they would consider blasphemy. But that is not what the Third Commandment is about at all.

I certainly imagine that God would prefer us to adore Him rather than to be angry at Him. Yet, also in my imagination, He is quite tolerant of us even when we are cursing Him or blaming Him for our misfortunes. While such anger may be ignorant or immature, we are still in relationship with Him. I doubt He expects us to feel unceasingly beatific about Him, any more than we might expect a wife to be unfailingly joyous over her husband's behavior, or vice versa. Any deep relationship will involve—indeed, require—turmoil, and I suspect God is big enough not to be terribly bothered if we damn Him now and then (and swearing is seldom that significant). What really infuriates Him, however, is to be *used*. And that is what is meant by blasphemy: the using of the Name of God when you are not in relationship with Him for the purpose of pretending that you are.

Two quite different experiences come to mind. I once had the opportunity to attend a conference at which the great Muslim (Sufi) teacher Idries Shah lectured on both Saturday and Sunday. Toward the end of Sunday he commented: "I have been speaking to you for four hours now, and you may have noticed that I have not yet used the words 'love' or 'God.' We Sufis do not use these words lightly. They are . . . they are *sacred*."

The other experience concerned a couple with whom, by accident, I had to spend a weekend (and who, incidentally, took pains to criticize my "bad" language). They seemed very religious. Every other sentence they spoke began with "The Lord did this" or "The Lord did that." And virtually every sentence in between was about who was having an affair with whom, who was getting a divorce, who was not attending church regularly, or whose children were coming to grief. I made no comment about their use of language, but when I finally escaped from them at the end of the weekend I felt that if I had to hear "The Lord did this" one more time I would have puked.

That couple's blatant overuse of religious language is what the Second Commandment means by "taking the name of the Lord in vain." It simultaneously trivialized God while sugar-coating their own meanness—although I cannot imagine it served effectively to disguise their pettiness from anyone other than themselves.

As blasphemy goes, I do not think that couple's was terribly serious. For all I know, they were guilty of no greater sin than habitual gossiping. The more serious forms of blasphemy are more subtle and hence, simultaneously, more difficult to spot or describe and therefore more effective. But whatever its degree, blasphemy is the lie of lies. It is the use of the sacred to hide the profane, of apparent purity to cloak guilt, of the noble to disguise the ignoble, of beauty to cover up ugliness, of the holy to bless depravity. It is both the pretense of piety and the willful use of piety as a pretense. While all lying is a man-ifestation of a lack of integrity, blasphemy represents the most vicious failure of integrity. Its most basic mechanism is that psychological trick we have called compartmentalization.

There is something truly diabolic about blasphemy. The very word "diabolic" comes from the Greek verb *diabolein*, which means "to throw or cast apart." The opposite in Greek would be *sym-bolein:* "to throw or cast together." In a very real way "symbolic" refers to integration and "diabolic" refers to compartmentalization. And it is important to remember that blasphemy always requires behavior. A person who has occa-sional profane thoughts but does not act upon them is not a blasphemous individual. Rather it is the person who mouths holy thoughts but behaves profanely who is the blasphemer. Blasphemy is the form of compartmentalization that allows some routinely to profess the truth while routinely acting the lie.

So we have come full circle. Any form of behavior that stems from a lack of integration, that represents compartmentaliza-tion, is blasphemy. The "businessman who goes to church on

Sunday mornings, believes that he loves God and God's creation and his fellow human beings, and then on Monday morning has no trouble with his company's policy of dumping toxic wastes in a nearby stream"—who is "a Sunday morning Christian"—is guilty of blasphemy. Regardless of its intensity, regardless of the degree of consciousness or deliberateness involved, such compartmentalization of religion is invariably blasphemous. And "the fact that this country, on whose coinage is written the words 'In God We Trust,' is the leading manufacturer and seller of weapons in the world" means that we are a largely blasphemous nation.

The degree of compartmentalization in American life is such that blasphemous behavior is the norm rather than the exception. When something is normal we are usually so close to it that we cannot see it in perspective. We are, for instance, so accustomed to our coinage that we don't even think about what is engraved on it. It is difficult, therefore, to perceive evil in the customary, in what is considered normal. Our newspapers bombard us with nuclear megatonnage statistics on a daily basis to the point that our sensitivities become so numbed we don't realize that the "normal" behavior those statistics represent is in fact insane. We must not allow such closeness to blind us to the habitual blasphemy of our churches and society. I want you to be upset by it.

But I do not want you to be discouraged by it. For the fact of the matter is that there are many encouraging signs that Americans are becoming increasingly intolerant of blasphemy in their government and churches.

At first the wide acceptance of my work, integrating science and religion, was surprising to me. People were excited by it, as if I were saying something dramatically *new.* Yet I was quite aware that my writing was deeply rooted in the understanding of authorities who were speaking before I was even born. What was so different? Gradually, however, I came to realize that what was new were not my words but the people reading them. People were different! And then, as I contemplated this change, I saw that there was much more at stake than even the integration of science and religion. What was really happening, I realized, is that humanity is fortunately moving out of an age of excessive specialization into an age of integration.

I say "fortunately" for several reasons. Evil is inherent in excessive specialization. During the Vietnam War days I used to wander around the halls of the Pentagon talking to officials about the war. "Oh, yes, Dr. Peck, we understand your concerns, yes, we do," they would say. "But you see, we're just the Ordnance Branch. We are responsible for seeing to it that the napalm is manufactured and shipped to Vietnam, but we're not responsible for the war. That's policy. You want to talk to the people in the Policy Branch down the hall." So I would go down the hall to hear again, "Oh, yes, Dr. Peck, we understand your concerns, yes, we do, but you see, here in the Policy Branch we just execute policy. Policy is made in the White House. You need to talk to the people in the White House." So it was that in 1971 the entire Pentagon acted as if it didn't *really* have anything to do with the war. This phenomenon occurs in all large institutions with specialized departments and subdepartments—including business corporations, universities, and even churches—where there is a tendency for the group conscience to become so compartmentalized, fragmented, and diluted as to be nonexistent.

The movement out of an age of excessive specialization into an age of integration is not visible just in the integration of religion and science; it can be seen in all quarters: Alcoholics Anonymous, the holistic medicine movement, the ecology movement. These are all movements of integration. Just as encouraging is the increasing integration of religion with politics and religion with economics. The Pastoral Letter of the National Conference of Catholic Bishops on the nuclear arms race is no historical accident. Its critics spoke out of the old age of specialization, screaming, "You bishops should not be talking about such matters. The arms race is not your specialty. You are violating the separation of Church and State. You should stay in your cathedrals where you belong. The arms race is the specialty of the politicians and should be left up to them."

But fortunately these old specialties are breaking down. For the movement out of an age of excessive specialization into an age of integration is a movement toward integrity. A dramatically increasing number of people who are transcending traditional culture "don't buy it anymore." They have learned how to spot blasphemy for what it is, and they are insisting upon integrity with all the power at their disposal.

In thinking about power, we must face the possibility that as the forces of integrity increase, the forces of anti-integrity will fight back with increased viciousness. The battle may soon heat up. Until now, for instance, the disarmament movement has not been sufficiently powerful to be a significant threat to the entrenched establishments that benefit from, use, control, and manipulate the arms race. But things are changing. As the disarmament movement continues to grow in strength— and it will grow—there is the dreadful possibility that some may actually try to start a war with the specific purpose of attempting to discredit the movement. The people of peace are indeed going to have to be "as wise as serpents and innocent as doves."

Be that as it may, the movement is growing. Many in the movement who do not get to travel as I do feel isolated and are amazed at the tales I bring back from across the land. There is no place, no county in these United States, where the standards are not rising in relation to integrity. Rapidly. It is a grass-roots phenomenon. The entire Christian Church—virtually every denomination—is almost explosively awakening to its ethical responsibilities for peacemaking. The specialized separation between clergy and laity is breaking down as all Christians are being called to be ministers. We are beginning to be suspicious of the media, which are so largely controlled by big business and big government. We are developing a keener and keener nose for propaganda. We are more and more able to spot compartmentalization. Increasingly our guts are becoming sensitive not only to the pap of politicians but particularly to that brand of lack of integrity that is blasphemy. There is great reason for hope. We are moving out of the age

of excessive specialization into the age of integration. We are
moving.

PART III
The Solution

CHAPTER XIII

Community and Communication

Communication takes many forms: written and oral or verbal and nonverbal. Similarly, there are many standards by which we can judge the effectiveness of communication. Is it clear or unclear, verbose or precise, thorough or limited, prosaic or poetic? These are just a few of the parameters for such judgment. There is one standard, however, that takes precedence over all others: does communication lead to greater or lesser understanding among human beings? If communication improves the quality of the relationship between two or more people, we must judge it from an overall standpoint to be effective. On the other hand, if it creates confusion, misunderstanding, distortions, suspicion, or antipathy in human relations, we must conclude it to be ineffective—even in those instances in which the communicator is evil, deliberately desires to sow seeds of mistrust and hostility, and may achieve that end.

The overall purpose of human communication is—or should be—reconciliation. It should ultimately serve to lower or remove the walls and barriers of misunderstanding that unduly separate us human beings one from another. The word "ultimately" is important. Confrontive, even angry communication is sometimes necessary to bring into focus the clear reality of those barriers before they can be knocked down. In the process of community-building, for instance, individual differences must first be allowed to surface and be fought over so that the group can ultimately learn to accept, celebrate, and thereby transcend them.

But the principal purpose of effective communication needs to be borne in mind. If it is not, the communication becomes task-avoiding. When people confronting each other with their differences lose sight of reconciliation, they begin to act as if their purpose in being "together" is merely to fight with each other. The reality, however, is that the proper task of communication is to create love and harmony among us. It is peacemaking.

The rules of community-making are the rules for effective communication. The essence of what occurs in a community-building workshop, for instance, is that the participants learn these rules. Since communication is the bedrock of all human relationships, the principles of community have profound application to any situation in which two or more people are gathered together. Peacemaking and reconciliation—community-making—is not just a global matter; it is a matter of concern within any business, any church, any neighborhood, any family.

Not only are there basic equations between community, communication, and peace but also between them and the concepts of integration and integrity. The movement out of an age of excessive specialization into an age of integration is basically synonymous with the community movement. And this movement is currently being reflected at every stratum of human relationships.

When I was a child, for instance, the dictum that "children should be seen and not heard" was no joke. Children and parents were separated—specialized—into very separate castes, with all the attendant barriers to communication involved in a caste system. So also were husbands and wives. I can remember my mother explaining why she could not take an expensive but longed-for trip to a health spa: "I cannot spend your father's money for something he doesn't approve of." But this division of the family into first-, second-, and third-class citizens is breaking down. Husbands and wives are no longer necessarily or totally specialized into breadwinners and child raisers. And authorities are largely in agreement that healthy families actually encourage children to "talk back" to parents in certain ways. We are moving.

But of course nothing is ever simple. Young children should not talk back when they are instructed to refrain from running into the street. Parents should exercise authority over their children when properly required for their protection. Commitment of late adolescents to the family as community should not be total; it is generally their task to learn to strike out on their own. And there remain some marriages in which role specialization of husbands and wives is not only efficient but healthy. The principles of community should not be applied in the same way to both a family with small children and a community-building weekend workshop composed entirely of adults. But this hardly means that these principles do not apply at all. To the contrary, the whole thrust of modern psychology is to move the family more in the direction of community. The average family still has a long way to go in that direction. But we are moving.

Similarly, excessive specialization in business is beginning to break down. In 1968 a top-level manager consulted me on how to motivate his middle managers. "I've done this to them and that to them," he said, "and still they're unproductive. What should I do?" "It seems to me that they probably hold the key to the solution of your problem," I responded. "Have you thought of asking *them* how they might become more motivated and productive?" He not only had not thought of it, he then refused seriously to consider it. Today it is unlikely that he would be so stupid as to avoid cooperating with his employees on a mutual problem simply to preserve rigidly an authority system that is a barrier to human communication. For the old rigid divisions between labor and management are beginning to be set aside as we learn that there are many ways in which the application of community principles can increase business productivity.

Again, nothing is simple. A community is a group of all leaders. Yet a business must have an authority structure. I am a member of the board of directors of a foundation to promote community. Community-building begins at home, and we work hard to promote community among and between our board and staff. At the same time the Foundation is a complex business, and we could not function without a clear-cut chain of command from the chairman of the board to the president to the headquarters administrator to the administrative assistant. It is not a matter of either/or, but of both/and.

While business is beginning to incorporate some of the principles of community, it is only just beginning. Even the service businesses such as health care and education seldom operate in anything but the old mode. Psychiatrists, for instance, know intellectually the benefits of a "therapeutic community." Yet almost never do psychiatric treatment units fulfill their potential in this regard. Neither physicians nor nurses desire to make themselves vulnerable to each other, much less to the patients. So the necessary authority system is also a specialized caste system in which the patients—supposedly the ones being served and most in need of self-esteem—are a kind of untouchables at the bottom of the heap. Similarly, when I speak to college students about community, the one refrain I hear repeatedly is "The teachers not only hang together; they don't respect us." Nonetheless, in a college here or a hospital there, occasional experiments are being conducted in the active recognition of common humanity. We are moving.

So it is that popular books about communication in marriage, family, and business, almost nonexistent forty years ago, now flood the market. And while their quality often leaves something to be desired, it seems to be improving. Important as community is in these spheres—and peacemaking without question begins at home—it is even more urgent in our quest for global peace. But those institutions that can tip the balance between war and peace have barely been touched by the concept of community. Within and among these institutions there is a notable lack of communication and a perpetuation of rules that are in fact antithetical to community. They are the institutions of the arms race, the Christian Church, and the United States government. Yet there is hope. For as President Eisenhower put it, "People want peace so much that governments had better get out of the way and let them have it."*

---

* Dwight D. Eisenhower, *London Sunday Times*, 1960. Quoted in *Treasury of Presidential Quotations* (Chicago: Follett Publishing Co., 1964), p. 209.

CHAPTER XIV

Dimensions of the Arms Race

THE ARMS RACE AS INSTITUTION

It might seem strange that I have labeled the arms race an institution. Ordinarily we think of an institution as a building, such as a bank, or a collection of buildings, such as a university. The word "institution" implies a stable organization—sometimes even a stultified one—with rules and traditions, staff and budget, bricks and mortar. The term "arms race," on the other hand, sounds more like a process of change and instability.

Unfortunately, the arms race is very much an institution. It has buildings, bricks and mortar, and real estate aplenty. When I was in the army, one of its basic training centers, Fort Leonard Wood, was the fourth-largest city in Missouri. Speaking recently on the northern Gulf Coast of Florida, I saw a region that looked more like an overgrown military base than a diocese or other civilian center of population. As for budget, the arms race has the largest in the world—over a trillion dollars annually, to which the citizens of the United States contribute approximately a third. It is not only big business, it is the biggest business, employing tens of millions of men and women. While tribes or nations have temporarily gathered stockpiles of weapons since the dawn of history, only in the last fifty years has the arms race become a self-perpetuating institution. And it is thriving in terms of size. Any other institution would envy its growth. There is no instability associated with this growth, however. The arms race is extraordinarily stable, unchanging, immovable, and seemingly set in stone.

Recently I had the opportunity to reread a book written in 1961 by the political scientist Mulford Sibley, *Unilateral Initiatives and Disarmament.** We speak of "future shock" and "megatrends" and bemoan the rapidity of social change. Yet every word of Sibley's book is as appropriate to the situation today as it was when written. As far as the arms race is concerned, *nothing has changed*. There is something about this lack of change that not only smacks of institutionalization but also inherently smells foul, even malicious. As the early Christian theologian Origen said, "The Spirit stands for progress, and evil, then, by definition is that which refuses progress." Certainly, whatever the reasons, we have made absolutely no progress in deinstitutionalizing the arms race.

It is a quality of institutions that they tend to perpetuate themselves regardless of their appropriateness. They generally continue long after they have outlived their usefulness. It is a matter of sheer inertia. And the larger the institution—the more employees, the more bricks and mortar—the greater the inertia and forces of self-perpetuation. One does not get rid of the fourth-largest city in Missouri or the weapons industry without resistance. Being in many dimensions the largest of all institutions, the arms race will, as a result of weight alone, continue until the end of civilization unless something is done about it. If all the reasons for its existence were to vanish, it would (and does) create new ones to preserve its being. The arms race is not just going to go away. If it is ever going to end, it is going to do so only by being *actively torn down*.

Peacemaking, therefore, requires a call to action. It may require certain moments of substrategies of quiet resistance, but only within the framework of a large plan of forceful action. Conversely, the major obstacle to peacemaking is passivity. The arms race is maintained, despite its insanity, not only by the inertia and resistance of those within the institu-

* Mulford Sibley, *Unilateral Initiatives and Disarmament,* in "The Beyond Deterrence Series" (American Friends Service Committee, 1961).

tion—its direct or indirect employees—but also by the passivity of those outside the institution.

In fact, it is this institutional quality of the arms race that is the major determinant of such passivity. It all seems so huge, so impregnable, so beyond our capacity as individuals to do anything about it. "You can't fight city hall," as the saying goes, and the arms race is so much larger than city hall. Certainly anyone who is "realistic" would not attempt to take it on. And those who are "idealistic" enough to take it on are likely to be squashed, are they not? It seems hopeless. Yet if there is any one thing more than any other that perpetuates the arms race, it is this sense of individual hopelessness or helplessness.

The omnipresent threat of nuclear holocaust is not some accidental unpleasant state of affairs resulting from forces beyond our control. To the contrary, it is the direct result of our failure to embrace such community-making principles as emptiness, integrity, and vulnerability. But these failures can be rectified. We are not stuck with them. There is more than enough room in our institutions for the creative changes that would reverse our failure. Ultimately all that is required for peace is that we overcome our lethargy and resistance to change. To do that, however, we must encounter our first enemy: this sense of helplessness.

THE PSYCHOLOGY OF HELPLESSNESS

The strongest and most insidious root of the arms race is the extraordinary lack of concern about it. This apathy in response to gross insanity is itself multirooted, but perhaps the most significant factor involved is the general sense of helplessness among us. One might expect such a feeling among the uneducated, impoverished, and disenfranchised. So it is all the more remarkable among the educated, sophisticated, and ordinarily curious.

In the summer of 1984 I was the speaker at a five-day conference on the subject "spirituality and community." The three hundred and fifty attendees were highly educated, spiritual seekers. To prepare them for their work in small groups I gave my first morning lecture on the subject of vulnerability and alluded to some implications for disarmament. During the question-and-answer period I was asked if I planned to say anything more about the arms race. I said I intended to give a whole talk on the subject several days hence. In the small groups that followed, many complained about this. That evening I put aside my planned speech and told the three hundred and fifty that I had been informed of their objections and that, clearly, we already had a large community problem to face. I asked all who did not want me to talk about the arms race to raise their hands.

Approximately 25 percent—ninety people—raised their hands.

"You represent such a substantial minority," I said, "that if you continue to feel this way, I will refrain from speaking about it. First, however, I want to deal with you about the problem. To begin, how many of you do not want me to talk about the arms race because you already know what I will say?"

No one raised a hand.

"How many of you, then," I asked, "do not want me to talk about the arms race for any one or more of the following reasons: It doesn't have anything to do with spirituality. You're sick of hearing about the subject. You've made up your mind and you don't need any more information. Or you feel it's all hopeless and there isn't anything you can do about it anyway?"

All ninety raised their hands.

I spoke to them briefly of integrity, of how spirituality should not be compartmentalized, of how Christianity needs to be integrated with economic and political behavior, of how Dag Hammarskjöld taught us: "In our era, the road to holiness necessarily passes through the world of action."* Then I opened up the issue for general discussion. In the end the

---

* Dag Hammarskjöld, *Markings* (New York: Knopf, 1974), p. 122.

community decided unanimously to allow me to talk about the arms race.

This was not an isolated instance—except that having a relatively captive audience, I was able to sway its mind. The attendance at most of my disarmament lectures in any given city averages less than half the size of my other audiences. People are apathetic about the topic. About their own spiritual journey they feel they can do something; about the arms race they feel impotent.

Nowhere, to my knowledge, has the general feeling of apathy and helplessness toward the arms race been more eloquently described than by Dr. Nicholas Humphrey when he gave the third Bronowski Memorial Lecture, "Four Minutes to Mid-night" in Great Britain in 1981.* Early in his lecture Dr. Humphrey quoted Professor George Kennan, former U.S. ambassador to Russia, speaking in Washington earlier in 1981: "We have gone on piling weapon upon weapon, missile upon missile . . . like the victims of some sort of hypnotism, like men in a dream, like lemmings headed for the sea." Humphrey then went on to say:

> On the front cover of the Bulletin of the Atomic Scientists the doomsday clock, set at ten minutes to midnight some years ago, was advanced by six minutes last January: four minutes to go. I want to ask a simple question. Why? Why do we behave like lemmings? Why do we let it happen? In the words of Lord Mountbatten: "How can we stand by and do nothing to prevent the destruction of our world?"
>
> Mountbatten said in the same speech: "Do the frightening facts about the arms race, which show that we are rushing headlong towards a precipice, make any of those responsible for this disastrous course pull themselves together and reach for the brakes? The answer is no." I want to ask how the answer can be no.

* Broadcast on BBC-2 and printed in *The Listener*, Oct. 29, 1981.

Perhaps there is an obvious answer, which is that we are simply unaware. Is it possible that we either do not know or else discount the dangers of the arms race? That we think the bonfire which is being built around us will never catch light—indeed, that the larger it grows the less dangerous it becomes?

When I was a child we had an old pet tortoise called Ajax. One autumn, Ajax, looking for a winter home, crawled unnoticed into the pile of wood and bracken my father was making for Guy Fawkes Day. As days passed and more and more pieces of tinder were added to the pile, Ajax must have felt more and more secure: Every day he was getting greater and greater protection from the frost and rain. On 5 November, bonfire and tortoise were reduced to ashes. Are there some of us who still believe that the piling up of weapon upon weapon adds to our security—that the dangers are nothing compared to the assurance they provide?

From this beginning Dr. Humphrey goes on to examine the psychology of apathy, the psychology of passivity, the psychology of hypnosis, the psychology of reticence, and the psychology of helplessness as they all relate to the arms race. Humphrey is particularly eloquent in speaking of that root (among our other sins) of helplessness which he calls reticence. His words have a British flavor, but they are equally descriptive of American society:

In the old days it is said that kings would kill the messenger who brought bad news. Today, in the United States, the messenger may, as almost happened to the Plowshares Eight, be silenced by the law; in Russia he may get locked up in a mental hospital. But there are other and subtler ways of restraining those who might otherwise speak out. And in our own country none is better tried or more effective than the technique of the social pillory. Anyone who forces an unwanted confrontation on the subject of the Bomb is liable to be punished for his impudence by being mocked, snubbed, made the butt of sneers and ridiculed.

We all know the standard vocabulary of putdowns. "Idealist," "pacifist," "moralist," "holier-than-thou". . . . They have been with us a long time. . . .

. . . Hardly surprising if we sometimes persuade ourselves that, whatever we think privately, it is just not our place to make a public stand against the Bomb. Lords, philosophers, actresses, priests—they do that kind of thing. They can make exhibitions of themselves. But for the rest of us? Well, on the whole, all things considered, we like to keep calm. It is not our way to scream, or sing psalms, or call things the most important question in the whole history of the human race—even when the water is lapping round our feet. First one to panic is a wet.

The root of helplessness that I believe to be the strongest is ignorance or lack of knowledge. People feel most helpless in the face of the arms race, I suspect, simply because they do not understand it. And because they do not understand it, they cannot see the way out. It is not well understood by most psychologists and theologians because they lack the knowledge of politics and economics. Worst of all, it is even less understood by the politicians and business people who are primarily "in charge" of it because they don't understand the psychology or theology involved. And, finally, none of them has much understanding because most of them lack the knowledge of community. With that knowledge, combined with an understanding of the many interrelated factors that perpetuate the arms race, we need no longer feel helpless. There is a way out.

THE PSYCHIATRY OF FORCE

Much as it would make my life simpler, I am currently unable with integrity to be an absolute pacifist. There is evil in the world—both individual and group—and we have not yet discovered any way to contain it without at least the gentle use or threat of force. Other forms of less malignant insanity also seem to require the very occasional use of force for containment or healing. It does not take a psychiatrist very long to learn this unfortunate reality.

The first night I was on duty at the beginning of my psychiatric training I was called to the Emergency Room to see a soldier's wife who was extremely paranoid and obviously no longer capable of caring for herself. Had the case been that of a soldier, there would have been no problem. As an army physician I had the authority to hospitalize any soldier against his or her will. The relatives of soldiers, however, could be admitted to our hospital only voluntarily. They had to sign a form to that effect. I explained this to the soldier's wife. I told her that we had a first-class hospital, that there was no question about her need to enter it, that she would be very well cared for, and I asked her whether she wouldn't like to sign the consent form.

The answer was no.

I patiently explained to her that there was really no question about her need for hospitalization. She represented such a danger to herself that if she were not willing to sign into the hospital voluntarily, I would have no alternative except to call the police to the Emergency Room and have them take her to the city hospital. There she would be examined by two other psychiatrists. I told her that there was no doubt in my mind that the two other psychiatrists would also feel that she was desperately in need of hospitalization, and they would then admit her to the city hospital against her will. Since the city hospital was really something of a snake pit, I asked her whether she really wouldn't rather sign into our hospital.

The answer was again no.

I argued with this woman for the next three hours, championing what was obviously the only sensible decision she could make. From time to time she would look as if she were about to sign the form and would raise the pen only to put it down. Several times she would start to write the first letter of her first name but then would stop. Finally, at two o'clock in the morning, I gave up. Exhausted, helpless, and defeated, I lifted the phone, dialed the police, and told them about my patient. In the midst of my asking the police to come to the Emergency Room for her my patient suddenly picked up the pen, said, "All right, I'll sign," and did so.

Ten days later, when I was next on Emergency Room duty, this scenario was repeated in exact detail. All that was different was that it was a different soldier's wife—just as desperately in need of hospitalization. Patiently I argued with her, as I had before, from eleven at night until two in the morning. As before, the pen was picked up and put down, picked up and put down. As before, at two o'clock in the morning I finally called the police, and again, in the midst of my call the patient signed.

The third time I saw a similar patient I handled things differently. My arguments were the same, but I gave her exactly three minutes to make her decision. "If you have not made it in three minutes and signed the form," I said, "I will call the police." After three minutes, when she had not yet signed the form, I did phone the police, and in the midst of my conversation with them, the patient signed the consent form. What had previously taken three hours to accomplish now took twenty minutes. Neither the result nor the mechanics of achieving that result had changed—there had simply been a ten-fold increase in efficiency. I suppose that is partly what a psychiatric education is all about.

I have learned very well indeed that the threat of force is on relatively rare occasions required to deal effectively with individuals whose thinking is so disturbed that they represent a danger to themselves or to others. However, the use or threat of force can also be misapplied.

A year before I began my training, at that same hospital, it had been the custom to search the patients as they were leaving the dining hall to see whether they had secreted upon themselves knives or forks or other implements of potential destruction. In these searches a dozen table knives were discovered each week. Nonetheless, a number were missed, and fights on the ward using such implements ran around two a week. The policy did not seem to be working very well.

The staff decided on a bold experiment. What would happen, they wondered, if instead of searching the patients, they simply counted the silverware before they came in for their meal and counted it after they left? They bravely took this experimental leap of faith. By the end of the month the number of missing utensils had dropped to one a week. By the end of the quarter the number of fights on the ward using such kitchenware were fewer than one a month.

This sort of experiment has been repeated in mental hospital after mental hospital over many years across the nation and throughout the world. The results are always the same. Time and again, without fail, it has been demonstrated that as far as mentally ill individuals are concerned, the routine use of force or the routine threat of force actually causes far more violent and destructive behavior than it is designed to prevent. It is still another manifestation of an old psychiatric principle known as the "self-fulfilling prophesy." If you prophesy long enough and hard enough that a person will behave in a certain way, he or she will behave in that way. Tell your daughter one or two hundred times that she will become a whore when she grows up, and likely she will become one. Treat people as if they are violent madmen long enough, and sure enough, they will become violent madmen.

Where does this leave us? On one hand we know that the use of force or the threat of force is in rare instances required to contain evil or crazy behavior. On the other hand, we know that the routine use of force or threat thereof is dangerously self-defeating. Extrapolating this knowledge to nations, it is clear that the use of force or threat of force will at times probably be required to contain or help destructive nations, as it so clearly was in the case of Nazi Germany. It is also clear, however, that our current policy, which is that of the routine use of force or threat of force, will do more to create rather than ameliorate international havoc.

So it leaves us damned if we do and damned if we don't but apparently more damned if we continue our policy of the routine use or threat of force in traditional international relations. Still, I do not think we human beings are at all ready for a world without police. The question is: Whose police?

THE OBSOLESCENCE OF THE NATION-STATE SYSTEM

The political system according to which the world is organized is labeled by political scientists the "nation-state system." The world is divided into nation-states. A nation-state is defined as a "geographical territory, the government of which possesses both internal and external sovereignty." Internal sovereignty means that the government has the *sole* right to determine the internal affairs within its territory. External sovereignty means that the government has the *sole* right to determine how it is going to relate with other nation-states.

On the evidence of history it can be accepted as a given that nation-states and their governments, just like individual humans, can upon occasion become insane or evil. Since the use of force or threat of force is *occasionally* required to deal with human evil or insanity, individual or national, it would be naïve to advocate that the United States simply and unilaterally beat its swords into plowshares. Instead, our primary goal should be as rapidly as possible to turn our swords—and our guns and bombs and tanks and missiles—the whole kit and caboodle—over to the United Nations or another variety of supranational government.

The problem with that suggestion is, of course, that the United Nations is not constituted to maintain or wield an adequate supranational police force in the event that a nation-state commits an illegal or immoral act. It is not just a question of personnel and weaponry; it does not have the authority to pursue such a course of action. But the UN is not so constituted precisely because its member nation-states have not wanted it to be. They have been unwilling to relinquish their own authority. In fact, a supranational government is incompatible with the nation-state system.

Recently, when the International Court of Justice, an agency of the United Nations, declared U.S. intervention in Nicaragua illegal, our government simply responded that it was not obligated to heed the court's judgment. Within the confines of the nation-state system we were quite within our rights to ignore the court's decision. But how can there be an effective international police-keeping force unless nations agree to submit to it? How can there be enforceable international law as long as nations continue to possess—and insist on possessing—total external sovereignty? How can the United States, as it does, demand to maintain the sole right to determine how it will relate with other nation-states and do any more than simply pretend it desires an effective UN?

The nation-state system is the bedrock on which the arms race has been built. Two hundred years ago, when it took six weeks for a message to get from Washington to London and six months for one from Washington to Peking, it made sense for the world to be divided into nation-states. But in this technological age of instant global communication, as well as instant global holocaust, the system has become hopelessly obsolete. If we are to survive, it must at least be rapidly modified to the point where the nations of the world substantially relinquish their external sovereignty to a supranational government agency.

In 1984 many Americans were horrified by a television presentation, "The Day After," which depicted the human condition following a nuclear attack on a mid-American city. As a physician I had gone through that scenario in my mind so many hundreds of times that I found it, if anything, underdramatized. What did horrify me, however, was the panel discussion that followed, which some of us have termed "After the Day After." Here six somewhat elderly men, supposedly some of the nation's brightest and best, ranging from William Buckley on the political right to Elie Wiesel on the left—sat around mired in hopelessness. Not one of them, as they discussed the arms race, could propose anything beyond never-ending negotiations, any genuinely bold initiative clearly offering a way out. Each one of these presumably wise men knew that we humans have evolved out of tribes into city-states and out of city-states into nation-states, yet not one of them had the vision to suggest there might be any further evolution beyond the nation-state system. Not one had the temerity to propose what is seemingly obvious, that international peace ultimately requires the sacrifice of at least some external sovereignty of the nation-state.

Actually, Americans should be most comfortable with the notion of such sacrifice. Certainly, as individuals we have become quite used to handing over some external sovereignty to a supraindividual body. If my neighbor had begun dumping his garbage in my backyard and failed to stop despite my remonstrances, in the old days I might have pulled out my trusty six-shooter and shot him dead. But today, no matter how I felt, I would instead call my trusty lawyer to bring an injunction against my neighbor in the local county or state court—and perhaps even to bring suit for compensatory damages as well. In other words, when we are in disagreement we have long since handed over our right to hit our neighbor in the nose to a supraindividual agency—namely, the county, state, or federal court system. This is what we mean when we refer to ourselves as a "nation under law." Indeed, no longer living in the "Wild West," I could get into serious trouble by assaulting my neighbor and "taking the law into my own hands."

In fact, in addition to being a "nation under law" there is still another reason we citizens of the United States should feel comfortable with the notion of relinquishing external sover-

eignty. For it is precisely because we made such a relinquishment that we are the *United* States. Slightly more than two
hundred years ago, when each of the new states ratified the
Constitution, each was thereby relinquishing a substantial part
of its external sovereignty as a state to the whole. Had those
states not been willing to give up any external sovereignty,
there would be no United States—only thirteen or thirty or
three hundred separate "nations" within a strip across the
North American continent. Of all the nations of the world we
should be the one historically most acculturated to thinking in
terms of a United States of Earth.

Yet in referring to the concept of world government many
of our "intelligentsia" discount it as unworkable and pillory
those who believe it is feasible: "Oh, that's just the old ivory-
towered world federalism movement. Bunch of idealists who
never got anywhere. The reality is that the League of Nations
didn't work, and the United Nations doesn't work." These
people seem, however, to gloss over the fact that this country
refused to join the League of Nations and has done its best to
emasculate the United Nations. The reality is that, like Christianity, world government "has not been tried and found
wanting but hasn't been tried at all."

The relinquishment of sovereignty, while it means the end
of the nation-state system as traditionally defined, does not
mean the end of nations or national differences. As Golda
Meir once put it, "International government does not mean
the end of nations, any more than an orchestra means the end
of violins."* For we are speaking of only a partial, selective
relinquishment of sovereignty. The law says that I cannot shoot
my neighbor over a little matter like the garbage. It does not
say that I must be friends with my neighbor, have him over to
dinner, dress like him, or attend his church. In fact, it protects
his and my right to be different and interferes in our relationship only in extreme instances.

The same principle holds in matters of internal sovereignty.

* Quoted from Golda Meir, *New Age Journal* (Nov. 1984), p. 21.

Were we to develop an effective supranational government, it is not unlikely that such a government would seek to interfere in the internal affairs of a nation, such as Nazi Germany, demonstrably engaged in genocide. It is hardly likely, however, to attempt to dictate to a nation that it should be communist or capitalist, Christian or Muslim or Hindu. Similarly, the law may interfere with my internal sovereignty, my individual life style, but only under extreme circumstances. It may tell me that I must not sexually abuse my children or walk naked in most public places. It would not tell me what kind of clothes to wear or how to dress my children.

In fact, only that supranational government is possible that does respect—yea, celebrate—most national differences. For we shall not be able to arrive at supranational government until we have achieved some substantial degree of genuine international community. And the paradoxical requirements for supranational government are the same as the paradoxical requirements for community. On one hand, a community is a group that has become able to transcend its individual differences for the good of the whole. Such transcendence requires the sacrifice of certain attitudes, the emptying of prejudices, the submission to the rules of community-building and maintenance—a relinquishment of individual sovereignty of sorts. On the other hand, the primary aim of such sacrifice and submission is even greater variety, freedom of expression, creativity, vivacity and joy as well as peace.

Still, the hard part of the paradox remains: there must be some degree of submission. This requirement holds for each and every nation. Yet in a century that has seen us swing from isolationism to world power, our own nation (perhaps because it has been the most powerful and wealthy and hence had seemingly the most to lose) has apparently been more reluctant than any other to relinquish even a modest degree of sovereignty. Were we to be genuinely willing to submit ourselves to the requirements of international government and community, it might well become apparent that Russia or other nations are the real stumbling blocks to peace. Until such time, despite my real love for my land and my society, I suspect I, and increasing numbers of my countrypeople, will continue to have trouble distinguishing between the sheep and the goats and in which category we ourselves belong.

And until we make such submission to international government and community, it is inevitable that we continue to believe it proper for the United States to be "the world's policeman." It does not seem to matter to us that the USSR also believes it is required to be the world's policeman or that every other nation seeks to be the top cop within its sphere of influence. Better the United States than Russia, you may say, or Cuba or Libya. Perhaps. But how absurd! And how dangerous! I am not sure there is much less to fear from American arrogance than Russian arrogance. Assuming the right to be the world's policeman is for any single part of the whole arrogance indeed, and in all arrogance there is both evil and the possibility of greater evil. Certainly we must not submit to the USSR. But if we are to save ourselves we must learn to submit to humanity—and quickly. And until we accept that as our task, we do not truly want peace—only power.

THE ARMS RACE AS A GAME

As long as we nations of the world insist on preserving our "rugged individualism" as separate, totally sovereign states, it is probably inevitable that we will forever continue to play games with each other. The psychiatrist Eric Berne, in his famous book *Games People Play,* essentially defined a psychological game as repetitive interaction between two or more individuals in which there is an unspoken payoff.* Although there are analogies between "playful" games—Monopoly, for instance—and psychological games, it should be realized that there is always something destructive, almost evil, about those

---

* Eric Berne, *Games People Play* (New York: Ballantine Books, 1964), p. 48.

human interactions. They are miscommunications; they block community. The "unspoken payoff" means that something faintly illicit, hidden, underhanded, is going on. There is something ugly about a psychological game that the participants do not want to acknowledge publicly.

The arms race is a variant of the most frequently played psychological game of all. The name of the game is "If It Weren't for You." It is played by most married couples, often for a lifetime. For instance, Mary will say, "I know I am a nag. But that's because John has a shell around him. I have to nag in order to get through John's shell. If it weren't for John's shell, I wouldn't be a nag." John, of course, responds in this game by saying, "I know that I have a shell around me, but that's because Mary's a nag. I have to have this shell in order to protect me from Mary's nagging. If it weren't for Mary's nagging, I wouldn't have to build a shell." It is easy to see why such communication is repetitively dull and unconstructive; it admits no intervention of responsibility, initiative, or anything new.

America's principal "opponent" in the arms-race game is Russia. What we say is: "We don't like our huge defense budget and national debt, our CIA, and our ICBMs and our nuclear warheads, but we have to have them because the Russians play dirty. It is clear from their writings and their behavior they want to conquer the world. If it weren't for the Russians, we could start behaving much more decently." The Russians, of course, on the other hand, say: "We don't like our huge defense budget and suffering consumers, our missiles and our NKVD and our dirty tricks, but we have to have them because the Americans play dirty. They are imperialists with over a hundred-year proven history of trying to dominate the world. If it weren't for the Americans, we would be able to behave far more peaceably."

Eric Berne taught us something else about psychological games: the only way to stop playing them is to stop. Although that sounds simple enough—almost redundant—it is one of the most profound truths in human affairs. Anyone who has played the game Monopoly will recognize this truth. No matter how long a Monopoly game has gone on—no matter how much the players may complain about how boring it has become, how childish it is, and how many better things they have to do—as long as the players keep collecting their two hundred dollars when they pass GO, the game goes on. The game stops (if it is a two-party game—as the arms race mostly is) only when one of the players gets up and says, "I'm not going to play anymore." The other is likely to respond, "But Joe, you just passed GO, here's your two hundred dollars." The leader effectively ending the game will say, "No, I don't want the two hundred dollars. I told you, I'm not playing it anymore. I mean it. The game is over. Finished."

What this suggests is that negotiations are not going to work to end the arms race. Indeed, we might suspect that they are simply a part of the game. Experienced Monopoly players may be quick to realize this. How often have you seen the game extended—even made more interesting—by players saying, "I'll mortgage Park Place if you'll mortgage Boardwalk" or "I'll get rid of my hotels if you get rid of your hotels"? Negotiations are not going to work, because as we have traditionally practiced them, we have done so in the spirit of competitiveness and a determination to preserve rather than limit national sovereignty. We "negotiate" by giving up something we no longer need or want. We have to get rid of the whole game. The old system has to go.

THE UNSPOKEN PAYOFF

There is no clear evidence to indicate that the United States has ever truly recovered from the Great Depression of the 1930s. Despite the New Deal measures the economy continued to stagnate—even continued to go downhill—until the buildup for World War II began with the Lend-Lease program. We have been on a war economy ever since 1938, almost fifty years ago. No matter how healthy our economy might look, I wonder if we are not like a man walking around with an intravenous tube in his arm, carrying his life-giving IV bottle up and down a hospital corridor, proclaiming, "There's nothing wrong with me. I feel fine." There is considerable reason to believe that we are dependent upon the arms race to maintain our economic stability and our generally high standard of living—that, in fact, the military-industrial complex of this country behaves in such a way as *actually* to support the arms race in order to maintain the economy.

When he left office more than a quarter of a century ago, President Eisenhower warned us to beware of the military-industrial complex.* Why such a warning unless this man, in a better position to know than anyone else, recognized that the defense establishment—the military, the civilian Department of Defense, the military contractors, the defense-related industries, the weapons manufacturers and salesmen—represented a grave threat to peace and national health? It is strange. His warning has become almost a cliché, and yet it is as if we had never heard it. Year after year the military-industrial complex has only vastly increased in size and permanence.

It would be nothing but naïve to think that approximately ten million people totally dependent on the arms race for their livelihood—and another twenty million partially dependent—do not constitute an extraordinarily massive lobby in this country for war. Yet the vast majority of Americans believe us to be a thoroughly peace-loving nation. It is as if the lobby is so powerful and so effective that it can even go unnoticed—that in its very hugeness it has and uses the capacity to create a whole conspiracy of silence.

The hypothesis that the United States and other nations maintain the arms race (as predicted by George Orwell in his classic *1984*) in order to stimulate, manipulate, control, and sustain their economies and peoples is referred to as the "Classical Theory of the Arms Race" among many peace workers. Yet in major articles about the arms race over the past five years in huge-circulation periodicals such as *Time* and *Newsweek*

* Farewell Radio and Television Address to the American People, January 17, 1961, in *Bartlett's Familiar Quotations* (Boston: Little, Brown, 1980), p. 815.

there has not even been a passing mention of the "Classical Theory of the Arms Race." No matter how disputable (and there are some bases to question it), one would still expect the theory to see the light of day in the general media. But even the possibility is ignored. Why? Could it be that the avoidance of economic depression is a significant part of the "unspoken payoff" of the psychological game of the arms race? And that this payoff has to remain unspoken? Otherwise the game might collapse?

There are few moral rules so compelling as The end does not justify the means. Avoidance of economic depression might seem like a worthy end—but hardly one that would justify war or even the risk of war. And if that was not enough of a problem, it so happens that the avoidance of economic depression is a dubious end at best. Psychiatrists know not only that mania may be a defense against depression but also that mania is usually more dangerous and self-destructive than the depression it is designed to stave off.* Elaborating on Elisabeth Kübler-Ross's stages of death and dying, in relation to the task of emptiness, I pointed out that depression was a necessary part of the psychological change process itself. Moreover, it was made clear that people frequently fail to grow because they retreat from the pain of depression and are unwilling to do "the work of depression."

I believe that national economic depression is a societal analogue of psychological depression. A significant depression of the economy of a society is a signal that some significant change or adjustment needs to be made in that society. A society must be able to work through an economic depression in order to make the changes it needs to make to remain a sane and healthy society. But just as an individual may succeed in avoiding depression through unhealthy mechanisms, so a society may refuse to do the work of an economic depression to the detriment of its health and at the price of ever-worsening social pathology. I believe that the arms race is, in part and among

---

* Manic-depressive disease has profound biological determinants, but in some cases there are also obvious psychological dynamics.

other things, a symptom of the unwillingness of the United States to bear the pain of economic depression, which is the pain of constructive social change.

A twenty-year-old book, *Report from Iron Mountain,** is purported to be a "leaked" report of a secret high-level national commission to the president of the United States. The commission advised him, for social and economic reasons, against seeking peace. It stated that the changes required for peace would be too disruptive. Here again is the *refusal* to change. And that is evil. Remember the early Christian theologian Origen, who said, "The Spirit stands for progress, and evil then, by definition is that which refuses progress."

Economic depression is not welcome, but it is not evil. It is painful. I do not want breadlines more than anyone else— although we seem already to be seeing their recurrence. But there is a great deal of difference between a voluntary and an involuntary economic depression. The Great Depression of 1929 was involuntary, striking with sudden devastation, with no time for us to prepare ourselves psychologically and socially, much less economically. If we were willing to undergo an economic depression voluntarily, there would be time for planning, for gradual change, for innovative strategies that would minimize economic disruption. The key to large social change is *substitution*—not the demolition of institutions but their transformation.

In the process of achieving peace I would not, for example, suggest that we simply do away with our military. Not only would this make millions of people instantly unemployed but it would also unnecessarily destroy all the potential good the military might, if transformed, accomplish. Transformation, not demolition, is of the essence. So I would propose the transformation of our military into a national service corps, an idea that many of our best minds have long been espousing. Such a corps could work on the truly creative projects of slum clearance, education, and conservation. A branch could still be

* L. Lewin, ed., *Report from Iron Mountain on the Possibility and Desirability of Peace* (New York: The Dial Press, Inc., 1967).

maintained for the purpose of self-defense through nonviolent means: a cadre of brave men and women thoroughly trained in the techniques of passive resistance and nonviolent action.

Moreover, I would propose that the career personnel in such a national service corps be rotated from one branch to another. As our military is currently constituted, its career personnel have only a single raison d'être: the waging of war. One of the more bizarre aspects of our American culture is that we somehow expect and think that career military people are proponents of peace. The reality is that when there is peace, career military personnel have a very miserable time of it: mass firings occur, promotions are frozen, awards are not forthcoming, salaries are unreasonably low, and the whole role of soldier is denigrated. But let there be a war and suddenly prestige is regained, salaries are escalated, bonuses are available, medals pour in, and self-esteem is more than reestablished. To expect a career military person to want peace and not war is to expect that person to be a saint. What possible right do we have to expect or think that the military should be so much more than we are ourselves?

So I would propose the transformation of the military, as well as other institutions that are dependent on the arms race. In terms of organizational know-how and traditional discipline the military has, in fact, a great deal to offer our country which can be preserved to our lasting benefit—but only if we are willing to face the necessity for transformation.

Such substitution of purpose, such transformation, might also be applied to another institutional part of the military-industrial complex: the Central Intelligence Agency. Again I would not propose that we abolish the CIA but that we enlarge it. We need all the intelligence we can possibly gather about other nations, other cultures. But I do believe that we desperately need to transform the type of intelligence we gather, the ways we gather it, and the ways it is applied. So I would substitute cultural anthropologists for the spies who attempt to manipulate cultures without understanding them. Such substitution does not automatically require the disruption of the lives of the individuals involved. There is no reason that as part of their employment we could not retrain those spies who are willing and able, to be cultural anthropologists.

Still, change is change, and there is always some pain involved. "Willing and able" is not an entirely inconsequential qualification. There will be some spies who do not *want* to be cultural anthropologists, who have a thirst for excitement that cannot be satisfied by the cautious painstaking work of understanding a culture without manipulating it. Still others may lack the objectivity or other abilities required. Some people may be added, but some will have to be pensioned off or let go. There will have to be some disruption, some suffering.

The same principles hold true for the transformation of the largest, most powerful part of the military-industrial complex: defense or defense-related industry. Again, substitution is not only possible, it is essential. Those companies that currently manufacture napalm could, for instance, substitute the manufacture of better, safer fireworks. Those that concoct defoliants could turn to the production of better fertilizers. Those that make tanks could create superior road-building machines. In each and every case the weapons and machines of war can be transformed into the technologies of peace, and these sophisticated technologies can be shared for the betterment of humanity rather than secreted for the preservation of national sovereignty. Still, it will not be painless. Old equipment will become useless, and new machinery will have to be purchased. Capital expense will be required. And new learning. Those who already know how to make the chemicals of war will have to learn the new skills of making the chemicals of peace. New learning requires openness and effort. There will be some who do not want to make the effort. There will be some "dogs too old to learn new tricks." There will be some disruption, some pain.

This issue of voluntary economic depression raises a basic problem of the relationship between economic pain and capitalism. The central problem of capitalism is that it is, in and of itself, amoral. Its thesis is that the general welfare is best served by the individuals motivated by profit in a competitive environment. It does not speak of any other motives. Indeed, it places such faith in the profit motive precisely because it is the primitive motive of individual self-interest. But as such the profit motive requires no submission of the self to anything higher or beyond the self. It is unabashedly self-centered. And a will unsubmitted to anything higher than itself is, or will inevitably become, evil. So it is that capitalism, in and of itself, has a profound tendency to "refuse progress."

Thus the notion of a "voluntary economic depression" is an anathema to traditional capitalism. Why, for instance, should the capitalists running a profitable napalm-manufacturing business ever want to undergo the retraining and replanning and undertake the capital expense involved in converting the business to fireworks manufacture? Particularly when it looks less costly, more profitable, to lobby in Congress for the continued demand for napalm? Traditional, unsubmitted capitalism must be expected to resist any form of change or progress that cannot be demonstrated to be *individually* profitable in the relatively short run.

I doubt the wisdom of throwing out the profit motive or abolishing institutional capitalism. But how can it be appropriately *transformed*? How can capitalism possibly be willing to undergo voluntary economic depression? How can capitalists learn to submit their individual profit motive, when appropriate, to higher values of truth and love and peace? This is one way of stating the most crucial question of our times.

As with any problem that is overdetermined, a combination of answers is required. One is community. Businessmen must be brought into genuine community in order to learn experientially community values and the emotional profits—the joy— that come from operating with such values. There are a scant few who have already accomplished such learning. Most, however, fake it. It is fashionable for corporations to adopt an image of being community-minded, but that is all it is: an image. More often than not it is simply designed to hide the unabashed nature of the self-interest with which the corporation operates. We have a long way to go. But unless capitalism as a whole can become genuinely community-minded, it and the world from which it profits are unlikely to survive.

NATIONALISM: HEALTHY OR SICK?

We do not change that of which we are proud. It is because it resists change that we say "pride goeth before the fall." In the minds of many, capitalism, as we currently practice it, is all tied up with "Americanism" in a prideful bundle of self-satisfaction. Critics who argue for significant change are not welcomed. "Capitalism, Love It or Leave It," could be a subtranslation of "America, Love It or Leave It."

Pride has its time and place. There are times when and places where pride is not only normal but necessary. And other times, for groups as well as for individuals, when it is sick and destructive. Narcissism is the psychological side of our survival instinct, and we could not survive without it. Yet an unbridled narcissism—what Erich Fromm called malignant narcissism—is the principal precursor of either group or individual evil.

In particular, pride is a healthy and necessary part of the process of identity formation. Individuals and groups are engaged in the work of forming and refining their identities throughout their life spans. But it is in adolescence that the largest part of this work is accomplished. And look at the pride or narcissism that is involved! It is normal for adolescents, male or female, to be extremely preoccupied with how they look. Even though their clothes may appear either careless and slovenly or otherwise outrageous to their parents, to adolescents these clothes are extremely important. When they try them on or out, they are trying on various identities. They spend endless hours looking in the mirror, not only at their clothes but at their faces, their developing bodies, and their other features, good or bad. As they look in those mirrors they are in a very real way trying to figure out who they are, seeking to discern in those reflections an identity. That same pride or self-preoccupation before mirrors is quick to be wounded. Adolescents do not normally take kindly to criticism. And when the normal turmoil of adolescence becomes so extreme as to be abnormal, the underlying problem is generally that which we call an "identity crisis."

When a group is doing the work of developing an identity, the matter of pride is also very much in evidence. The example most familiar and dramatic is that of the struggle of black Americans, particularly during the sixties, to develop an effective identity. Before that time blacks largely lacked an identity of their own—many going to ridiculous extremes in an attempt to adopt a white identity, even to the point of efforts to straighten their naturally curly hair. But then, suddenly and properly, almost overnight, all that changed. The curly hair was allowed to grow out. The "Afro" was in. African history was searched in order that one might take pride in his or her roots. There was necessary "black rage" as the concomitant of the new "black pride." "Black is beautiful" was the catchword of the day.

This was good. It is a matter of respect. It is good that we should respect ourselves, just as it is good that we should respect others. In order for us to respect ourselves we must have some dignity and the kind of pride that goes with dignity.

The pride of a national group or nation is what we call nationalism. It is most natural and healthy at that point when the national group is developing an identity—when it is truly becoming a nation. Such a time occurs when tribes or city-states form themselves into nation-states or when colonies throw off the yoke of foreign dominion (as we Americans began to do in 1776).

The force of nationalism is formidable, as the United States discovered to its chagrin in Vietnam. Because Ho Chi Minh, the leader of the Vietnamese in their struggle to throw over the yoke of colonial imperialism, was a communist, we took sides against the Vietnamese in their fight for independence. The most serious of the many misjudgments we made in

Southeast Asia was to misinterpret Vietnamese nationalism as a communist movement. Had we sought to encourage Vietnamese nationalism instead of attempting to perpetuate colonialism, there is a wealth of evidence to suggest that Vietnam might have become a truly democratic noncommunist nation. Conversely, the same evidence suggests that by opposing the Vietnamese desire for national self-determination, the United States actually pushed the Vietnamese into alliance with Russia and into the very kind of communism and totalitarianism that we feared. In any case, in Vietnam it was the extraordinary power of nationalism, not communism, that brought the United States to its knees. To oppose legitimate nationalism is to do so at our peril.

There is, however, a kind of illegitimate nationalism, or national pride, that should be opposed, both in others and in ourselves. Just as there is a difference between "rugged" and "soft" individualism, so there is a difference between a healthy amount of independence and a state of being in which a nation insists that it be beholden to no one and that it will exercise its right to be a law unto itself. It is nationalism, for instance, that prompts the United States to proclaim that it need not be subject to any decision of the International Court of Justice in The Hague. But is this healthy nationalism? And what does this kind of nationalism mean in terms of making progress toward the development of world community?

There is a kind of pride of identity that is not only normal but even necessary for the health of any group, whether they are black Americans or Americans as a whole. Even in the process of community-building, a group will come to take a certain amount of pride in its real accomplishment at having moved out of chaos and through the gauntlet of emptiness. Yet this healthy pride of identity so easily and frequently slips into a sense of arrogant superiority. The genocidal Nazi concepts of the "master race" were also symptoms of nationalism in action. As is the apparent certainty of our own government that it knows what is best for Nicaragua. Somehow we must learn to draw the line between the nationalism that is required for reasonable self-respect and self-determination and the nationalism that leads to jingoism, enemy formation, and blind patriotism and thereby interferes with the development of world community.

How to discern between healthy and unhealthy nationalism is a critical task in our shrinking world. For the reality is that there are some places on the globe where the development of nationalism needs to be encouraged while simultaneously there are others where further development of nationalism needs to be vigorously discouraged. The nationalism of black South Africans, for instance, clearly needs to be encouraged as they move toward legitimate respect and true nationhood in which all citizens are enfranchised. Black South Africans *need* to forge their identity as a nation, with or without the cooperation of white South Africans. The USSR and the United States, however, have long since succeeded in forging their identities as nations. Further increases in their already immoderate national pride hardly seem necessary. To the contrary, it is clear that in the interests of peacemaking, Russian and American nationalism need somehow to be better bridled.

The key to the discernment between healthy and unhealthy nationalism clearly, then, centers around this issue of identity development, in which the notion of the self—the "I-entity"—as a separate entity is an illusion. We are all, in reality, interdependent. Throughout the ages the greatest leaders of all religions have taught us that the journey of spiritual growth is the path out of and away from narcissism, toward the mystical consciousness in which our identity merges with that of humanity and divinity. As it is with individuals, so it is with groups and nations. Ultimately we are called out of national narcissism and away from purely local identities toward a primary identity with humanity and a state of global community. Still, one must possess something before it can be given up. We cannot begin the work of forsaking our identity until we have developed one in the first place. So it is that the proper pattern for the development of nations is, first, growth into nationalism, then growth out of and beyond nationalism. The discernment between healthy and unhealthy nationalism, therefore, requires that we have an accurate sense of where a nation is in its historical course of development.

Beyond that, the tests for healthy as opposed to unhealthy nationalism are much the same as those to distinguish between good and bad thinking: What is missing? How integrated is it? How much has the person consciously tried to include all the relative variables into his or her thinking? The leader operating out of healthy nationalism will be quite conscious of that nationalism and how it fits into the larger scheme of things. At the time of the Vietnam War, Ho Chi Minh was quite conscious of what he was doing, whereas President Johnson was not. Johnson was operating out of a pathological nationalism to which Senator Fulbright gave the term "the arrogance of power"—a malignant kind of narcissism that, like most prejudice, is quite unconscious of itself.

An almost humorous example of unhealthy nationalism at work occurred in February 1964, when my wife, Lily, who had been born and raised in Singapore, became eligible for United States citizenship. The Immigration Department in Hawaii, where we were then living, asked her whether she would mind waiting until the first of May to receive her citizenship papers. They were planning that day to celebrate Law Day (America's answer at the time to Russia's celebration of May Day) with a mass induction of new citizens. Lily agreed. So on the afternoon of the first of May she and I assembled with approximately two hundred other new citizens and their relatives, along with appropriate dignitaries, on the ancient turf of a military post in Waikiki.

The festivities began with a parade. Together with a band, three companies of soldiers, rifles gleaming in the afternoon sun, marched four times around the parade ground before taking their positions at strict attention behind seven howitzers. These then were used to give a twenty-one-gun salute to the occasion. As soon as the noise subsided, the governor of Hawaii, a tall, distinguished-looking gentleman, stood up to begin the speechmaking. "We are gathered here this afternoon," he said, "to celebrate Law Day, although," he quipped, "here in Hawaii, with all our flowers, we might call it Lei Day! Be that as it may," he continued, "the point is that here in the United States we are celebrating this day with flowers, while the communist countries are having *military* demonstrations."

No one laughed. No one seemed to see the absurdity of it: this man with three companies of armed soldiers standing at strict attention behind him, his head still wreathed by the smoke of seven cannons, speaking utter nonsense. That was just harmless stupidity. Yet the same kind of unconscious nationalism was beginning to kill increasing numbers of people farther west across the Pacific.

The United States is no more guilty than Russia of unhealthy nationalism. To the contrary, from all I can gather, the Russian "man in the street" suffers even more from a "my country, right or wrong" mentality than does the average American. Indeed, a rather ferocious and mindless patriotism seems to be a part of the Russian character and does not make Russians any easier to deal with. But blaming the sick nationalism of the Russians without healing our own sick nationalism is as mature and constructive as the child who points to his younger sibling and cries to Mommy, "But *he* started it."

Unhealthy nationalism can either be encouraged or discouraged. I am told that when young Russian children go to school, there is a Mercator projection (rectangular) map of the world usually running across the top of the classroom blackboard. And at the very center of that map is the USSR. I know that when American children of similar age go to school, what they see at the center of the map at the top of their blackboard is the USA.

It does not have to be this way. I am grateful to my children for giving me a massive new world atlas this past Christmas. It is a rather extraordinary thing. It has no center. A roughly equivalent amount of space is given to the USSR, the United States, Central and South America, Africa, Europe, even the North and South poles. I have never seen an atlas like it before. Its publishers clearly went to great pains to make it a true and integrated depiction of the geography of the world community.*

We can change our maps.

---

* *Atlas of the World*, 7th comprehensive ed. (New York: Times Books, 1985).

CHAPTER XV

The Christian Church in the United States

We know that change is possible but also that it is always effected against resistance. And the changes required to dismantle the arms race and to achieve world community are far more profound than revising an atlas. We are talking about a veritable revolution. Revolutions begin in the hearts and minds of the people. If they are to be peaceful, however, they must be facilitated by the peoples' institutions. Yet the two most significant and relevant institutions in this country—the Christian Church and the federal government—are seemingly impervious to change, unable or unwilling to incorporate the principles of community that would facilitate this revolution and save our skins.

WHERE ARE YOU, JESUS?

The arms race is against everything that Christianity supposedly stands for. It stands for nationalism; Jesus practiced internationalism. The arms race stands for hatred and emnity; Jesus preached forgiveness. It stands for pride; Jesus said, "Blessed are the poor in spirit." It is supported by the weapons manufacturers and the bellicose; Jesus said, "Blessed are the peacemakers." Its central dynamic is the search for invulnerability; Jesus exemplified vulnerability.

Why then has the Christian Church not fought against the arms race from the beginning? How could Cardinal Spellman have worked for the escalation of the Vietnam War? How is it that the builders of weapons systems attend national prayer breakfasts? What is the American flag doing at the entrance to the sanctuary of my little Protestant New England church (and most every other Christian church across the land) when Jesus walked with Canaanites and Samaritans, and when, in imitation of Him, the very first decision of the Church was to be international? What happened to Jesus?

A bumper sticker put it quite succinctly a few years back: "After religion, try Jesus."

The absence of meaningful Christianity from institutionalized religion is hardly a recent problem. The history of the Church for the past 1600 years has innumerable instances of institutional blasphemy. It is the Church that marched off in crusades to murder Muslims in the name of Jesus. It is the Church of the Inquisition that killed and tortured in the name of Jesus. It is the Church of Rome that stood by during the Holocaust doing nothing in the name of Jesus.

Why? How could the Christian Church be so consistently blasphemous? At what point did Jesus get lost in the shuffle? When did the Church lose sight of what community is all about?

THE MAUNDY THURSDAY REVOLUTION

As a Christian, I consider the most important day of the church year to be not Easter, not Christmas, but Maundy Thursday. For the meaningfulness of this day I am indebted to a set of lectures, *The Holy Thursday Revolution,* by the Christian philosopher Beatrice Bruteau.* In it she points out that the greatest revolution in the history of mankind occurred on Maundy Thursday—or what she calls Holy Thursday, the day before Jesus' crucifixion.

She sees it as a two-stage revolution. The first stage occurred when Jesus washed the feet of his disciples. Until that moment the whole point of things had been for someone to get on top,

* Beatrice Bruteau, "The Holy Thursday Revolution," series of lectures held at Orr Forum in Religion at Wilson College, Chambersburg, Pa., Feb. 8–10, 1981.

and once he had gotten on top to stay on top or else attempt to get farther up. But here this man already on top—who was rabbi, teacher, master—suddenly got down on the bottom and began to wash the feet of his followers. In that one act Jesus symbolically overturned the whole social order. Hardly comprehending what was happening, even his own disciples were almost horrified by his behavior.

Bruteau then suggests that Jesus, having symbolically overturned the whole social order, gave us a new social order through the Last Supper, in the symbolic form of Communion. Through Jesus the early Christians discovered the secret of community. We know well from the history of the early Church that this is so. But since we ourselves have mostly lost the secret, we do not realize the power that it once had.

In his book *The Scent of Love** Keith Miller proposes the reason why the early Christians were such phenomenally successful evangelists. It was not because of their charisms—such as the gift of speaking in tongues—and not because Christianity was such a palatable doctrine (to the contrary, it is about the most unpalatable doctrine there is) but because they had discovered this secret of community. Generally they did not have to lift a finger to evangelize. Someone would be walking down a back alley in Corinth or Ephesus and would see a group of people sitting together talking about the strangest things—something about a man and a tree and an execution and an empty tomb. What they were talking about made no sense to the onlooker. But there was something about the way they spoke to one another, about the way they looked at one another, about the way they cried together, the way they laughed together, the way they touched one another that was strangely appealing. It gave off what Miller called the scent of love. The onlooker would start to drift farther down the alley, only to be pulled back to this little group like a bee to a flower. He would listen some more, still not understanding, and start to drift away again. But again he would be pulled back, think-

* Keith Miller, *The Scent of Love* (Waco, Texas: Word Books, 1983).

ing, I don't have the slightest idea what these people are talking about, but whatever it is, I want a part of it.

This might have seemed to me merely like one author's romantic imaginings had I not myself witnessed the phenomenon in action. I have led community-building groups in the most sterile hotels, yet desk clerks and barmaids will stop me or other members and say, "I don't know what you people are doing in there, but I get off duty at three o'clock. Can I join you?"

The Maundy Thursday Revolution began to be aborted at the time of Constantine, when Christianity became a legal religion. A short while later the abortion was virtually complete when it became the official religion. It then became safe to be a Christian. The crisis was over. And when crisis ends, community generally tends to fade away. So, as the time of martyrs largely passed, so did the life blood begin to flow out of Christianity and out of the Church.

What we desperately need to reunderstand is that it is dangerous to be a true Christian. Anyone who takes her or his Christianity seriously will realize that crucifixion is not something that happened to that one man nineteen hundred and fifty-odd years ago, nor was martyrdom the fate of just his early followers. It should be an omnipresent risk for every Christian. Christians should—need—in certain ways to live dangerously if they are to live out their faith. The times have made this apparent. Today the times demand of us that we take major risks for peace. And in combating the entrenched forces of the arms race—the principalities and powers of this world—that very much includes the risk of martyrdom. From time to time, since the days of Constantine, there have been occasional Christian martyrs. But this is no longer the time for an occasional isolated brave soul living out and dying for his or her faith. The crisis is too large. It is the time for communal, congregational action and corporate risk.

Another way of phrasing the most crucial question of our times, therefore, is whether the danger of the arms race can restore the crisis to Christianity and thereby restore to the Church Jesus' heritage of community.

When I think of the enormity of the changes required to bring about the end of the arms race—a veritable revolution not only in our economic and political thinking but in the way in which we relate to our neighbor in the pew next to us or down the street as well as on the other side of the tracks—it sometimes seems that a virtual Second Coming is required. I am not talking about a bodily second coming. In fact, I am profoundly pessimistic about a Church that would sit around passively waiting for its messiah to appear again in the flesh. Rather, I am talking about the resurrection of Christ's spirit, which would occur in the Church if Christians took him seriously. I am talking of the resurrection of the Maundy Thursday Revolution.

PSEUDODOCETISM: THE HERESY OF THE CHURCH

How could the Church so easily have lost Jesus' legacy of community and fallen away from his commandment that we love one another? With the legalization of Christianity it became safe to be a Christian. The time of danger was seemingly passed. The crisis was over. But was it really? The reality is that evil continued to stalk the world, even within the Church itself. The particular evil of being forced at knife-point to bow down and pledge allegiance to pagan gods had passed away. But all the other evil remained. How could the Church have deserted the battle almost the very moment it became acceptable to fight it? How could the Church have so quickly sold its soul?

The answer is fear. To be a true Christian one must live dangerously. The battle against evil is dangerous. Jesus said, "I am the way." But his way was obviously a dangerous one. It might very well end with crucifixion or some other form of martyrdom. And so, out of fear, Christians en masse deserted his way.

Yet how could they then still call themselves Christians? How could they call Jesus Lord and yet refuse to follow him? Jesus fought against his fear, and, in imitation of him, for three centuries the majority of his followers seemed to be able to do the same. But then they stopped. By what intellectual sleight of hand could they possibly still call themselves followers of Christ when they no longer attempted to imitate his courage?

What happened to Christian doctrine that allowed the ceremony of Communion to continue while community was lost? By what failure of Christian docrine did Christianity become largely empty ritual and no longer a way of life?

I cannot answer that question in relation to the entirety of Church history through its many centuries. But I can with certainty answer it in relation to the Church in the United States today. For it has become apparent to me that the vast majority of churchgoing Christians in America are heretics. The leading—indeed, traditional—heresy of the day I call pseudodocetism. It is this predominant heresy that intellectually allows the Church to fail to teach its followers to follow Jesus.

The majority of American Christians have had enough catechism or confirmation classes to know the paradoxical Christian doctrine that Jesus is both human and divine. What is meant by pseudodocetism, however, is that they then put 99.5 percent of their money on his divinity and 0.5 percent on his humanity. It is a most comfortable disproportion. It puts Jesus way up there in the clouds, seated at the right hand of the Father, in all his glory, 99.5 percent divine, and it leaves us way down here on earth scratching out a very ordinary existence according to worldly rules, 99.5 percent human. Because that gulf is so great, American Christians are not seriously encouraged to attempt to bridge it. When Jesus said all those things about being the way and that we were to take up our cross and follow him, and that we were to be like him and might even do greater things than he did, he couldn't possibly have been serious, could he? I mean, he was divine, and we're just human. So it is, through the large-scale ignoring of Jesus' very real humanity, that we are allowed to worship him in name without the obligation of following in his footsteps. Pseudodocetism lets us off the hook.

The great Quaker Elton Trueblood once said, "Jesus Christ can be accepted; he can be rejected; he cannot reasonably be ignored."* What the vast majority of American Christians have done, however, is to unreasonably ignore him. The intellectual defect in our thinking—the unreason that has allowed us this cop-out—is the heresy of pseudodocetism. Despite what Jesus told us, it enables us to worship both God and mammon. It is the unreasonable intellectual underpinning of a Church that in the name of Jesus can blasphemously coexist with the arms race.

To end the arms race Christians must become Christians. They must become true disciples—that is, followers—of Christ. As a friend once put it, "The problem for us is how to move from the saviorhood of Jesus to the Lordship of Jesus." If Jesus is truly to be our Lord, we must be willing to follow in his footsteps. And in order to follow in his footsteps we must envision such following as being quite humanly possible. For this to occur, the heresy of pseudodocetism must be rooted out of the Church. We must return to the understanding (still on the doctrinal books) that Jesus was and is *fully* human as well as fully divine. We must not only realize that he in fact suffered all that we suffer, we must also realize that we in fact *can* suffer all that he suffered. We must once again become his followers in deed as well as word. We must put ourselves back on the hook.

THE CHURCH AS BATTLEGROUND

In the early part of this decade I had the opportunity to participate in two major exorcisms. During each I had a vague, inchoate sense that something inappropriate was going on. I do not mean that the diagnosis was in question. To the con-

* Elton Trueblood, as inscribed on a plaque at the Yokefellow Institute, which he founded in Richmond, Indiana.

trary, those experiences convinced me of the reality of possession. Nor do I mean that the exorcisms were unnecessary. As far as I can ascertain, both of those patients are still alive today because of those procedures. What seemed to be inappropriate, rather, was that the being of each of these patients had become a battleground for a struggle between the forces of good and evil (or Christ and Satan, if you will).

Actually, each of us—every soul—is a battleground for a struggle between good and evil. But in these two cases the nature of the struggle was titanic. Cosmic forces seemed to be involved, and I wondered why. Finally, by the end of the second exorcism it dawned on me that the proper battleground for the struggle between good and evil is the Church. Each of these patients was so dreadfully torn apart in serving as such a major battleground precisely because the Church has failed in its role of being the battleground.

In fact, although very different from each other, both patients had become possessed partly as a result of a whole host of specific failures of the Church: the superficiality of the Church, the lack of community within the Church, the blasphemy of Church leaders, and other factors. But of all these failures the one that most made them sacrificial victims was the refusal of the Church to serve as a battleground.

This refusal is so traditional that even the very notion that the Church should be a battleground is likely to seem strange, almost bizarre. The Church is not a place to fight, is it? Indeed, we try to keep all fighting out of it. We try to keep it a pseudo-community where everything is all smiles and politeness, all sweetness and light. If any fighting is to go on, it should be restricted to vestry meetings—or better yet, to prevestry meeting political caucusing. The problem is that this has nothing to do with real community—only with a mannerly pretense.

We come here to the nub. Because Christ so clearly called us to peacemaking, the Church is the most important key to disarmament. But in order for the Church to get wholeheartedly behind the disarmament movement the issue of the arms race will have to be fought out within the body of the Church. And

I do not mean simply fought out within the councils of Church leaders. It must be fought, parishioner struggling with parishioner, in each and every congregation across the land.

The battle has not yet begun to be joined. Even in those churches where the leadership has had the faint courage to proclaim the arms race an issue with which Christians should struggle, nothing has been done to make the struggle a corporate one. The most they have done has been to bring in speakers to argue both sides. Individual parishioners have been free to attend or not attend such lectures as they pleased. Sitting in their individual pews they have been left to make up their own individual minds (which usually were quite made up beforehand) without any struggles with one another, without any struggle as a body. The Church has sidestepped its responsibility to *deal* with the arms race.

The Church likes to refer to itself as the "Body of Christ." But it behaves as if it thought it could be the Body of Christ painlessly, as if it could be the Body without having to be stretched, almost torn apart, as if it could be the Body of Christ without having to carry its own cross, without having to hang up on that cross in the agony of conflict. In thinking that it could be thus painlessly the Church has made a lie out of the expression the "Body of Christ."

What, then, must happen? The answer is not painless, but it is clear. One of the characteristics of a true community is that it is a body that can fight gracefully. The Church will not be able to fight out the issue of the arms race until it becomes a community. Currently the Church is not only not the Body of Christ, it is not even a body, a community. It must become a community before it can serve as the Body of Christ.

The process of community-building begins with a commitment—a commitment of the members not to drop out, a commitment to hang in there through thick and thin, through the pain of chaos and emptiness. Such commitment has not generally been required by the Church. Now the time has come to require it. For without that commitment community is impossible.

As I travel through the country I find many of the clergy in a state of near despair. Most are intensely aware of a lack of community in their congregations. They suffer it not only in their role as leaders but also as individual humans. They do not feel in community with their own congregations. They look for community outside their congregations but seldom find it. They virtually never feel free to speak their minds to their own flocks or wholeheartedly to preach the gospel in the light of their own understanding.

When they ask me what to do I suggest that they must begin by exacting from their congregations a commitment to stay there, to be faithful to one another. "How can you possibly feel free to preach the gospel," I ask them, "when you are afraid that it will drive them away? If it drives them away, the numbers will go down, the budget will be pared, and your bishop will be angry. You will be labeled a failure in your role. The first thing you must work on is to obtain a commitment from your parishioners to stay. That's where community must begin."

But such advice is not easily taken. We still live in the age of "rugged" individualism. Individuals should be free to come and go as they please, should they not? Should it not be left up to individuals to decide whether or not they attend a particular denomination, a particular church within that denomination, and, indeed, whether or not they will attend church at all that particular Sunday, that particular month, that particular season? How can loyalty be exacted like a pound of flesh in such an age when the individual is quite free to go down the road to another church, where loyalty is not a condition of membership? The reality is that exacting from the members a commitment to hang in there as a body is quite likely to drive a significant number of them away. It would be a risky business indeed.

But we must also return to the reality that faces us again and again: it is—or should be—a risky business to be a Christian in the first place. Perhaps there will be a start with a few brave individual clergy who are willing to take the risk of telling their

302 The Different Drum

congregations that the time has come for Christians to stand up and be counted. But I shudder at their sacrifice. It could be made much easier for them if they were encouraged by their bishops or other Church leaders in this risk. And ultimately their sacrifice will be in vain if their bishops and leaders do not also assume the risk. For just as the true Christian individual must live a life of risk, so the Church as a whole, as a body, must be willing to be at risk if it is going to be the Body of Christ.

The risks are large. Thinking at the level of a bishop or denomination president, I would have to ask such questions as these: "If it is the policy of the Church to exact a significant commitment in this age of individualism from its members, just how many members will we lose? Ten percent? Twenty-five percent? Fifty percent? What will this do to our financial structure? And where will these lost members go? Will they go to the other denominations, God forbid? And what will that do to the Church as a whole? Will it divide the larger Church into the committed denominations and the uncommitted denominations? Will it mean two Churches: a Church of the committed and a Church of the uncommitted? Besides, isn't community inclusive? Will not a policy that requires any commitment whatsoever be exclusive of those who are unwilling to make any commitment? Will we not be depriving them of the possible virtues of the sacraments and at least some exposure to the Gospels? Will it not be ultimately divisive when our task is to be reconciling?"

These are hard questions and should not be dodged. But for those Church officials and their congregations with a sincere interest in becoming a true community, those who are willing to take that risk, there are three things they must remember. The first is that the issue of inclusivity is one with which every community must struggle as it maintains itself. The inclusivity of genuine community is never total or absolute. In fact, the Church has failed in one dimension because it has attempted to be too inclusive. At the root of this failure, however, has been a failure of motive. The Church has tried to be as inclusive as it could, not in the service of community but in the service of numbers; it has not welcomed the stranger so much out of love as out of greed. It is not out of a desire for community that it has refrained from asking its members to stand up and be counted; it has been out of fear. It cannot argue that it has been undemanding of its members in the interest of community, because it has not had community in the first place. The plain reality is that by and large the Church has not been in the community game; it has been in the numbers game.

The second thing to remember is that there are vast numbers of uncommitted religious who remain uncommitted because they have never seen a church worthy of their commitment. What they have seen instead are churches in the numbers game, churches that are wishy-washy social clubs, churches that lack community and the spirit of community, churches where the gospel is glossed over, churches where the members don't seem as a rule to take Christ seriously, churches that seem to stand for everything and hence stand for nothing. If the membership is required to stand up and be counted, many old members will be lost. But that church will then attract some new ones. Maybe many fewer. Maybe more. I don't know which. Nor will the Church until it takes the risk.

The final thing to remember is the example of Jesus. Jesus was not unfailingly tolerant. He was amazingly tolerant of overt sinners. He included them in his company and was in community with them. But he was also remarkably intolerant of the self-righteous and the pretentiously pious and the money changers in the temple. He was not inclusive without conditions. He offered a young man discipleship. He invited this young man to travel with him, to be in the closest possible community with him. But he also instructed the young man that he would first have to get rid of his possessions—and hence his need for security and invulnerability—and that he would have to take up a cross and follow in his footsteps. Church leaders and their congregations—as they struggle over these very real issues of inclusivity and ultimately the issues of disarmament and community—must remember Jesus and ask what he would have done. The young man, we all know, decided that he did not want to meet the conditions that Jesus laid down. And that was sad. But it is also said that when he laid down these conditions, Jesus looked at the young man with love.

SIGNS OF HOPE

Although I have described my Church as being largely blasphemous, heretical, and a weak-kneed failure, there have always been occasional exceptions—a martyr here, a congregation there that did, at the risk of life, protect the Jews. There have always been some strange signs of the hand of God at work in this pathetic, miraculous institution. On the surface it would appear that the Church is currently impotent to implement the social revolution so desperately needed to achieve world peace. But it is not uncommon to find that when an old order is collapsing, the new is already beginning under the rubble, and that in the midst of decay there are the signs of new life. So it is that there are not only reasons for hope for the world but also that those reasons can be found today perhaps even more often than in other places amid the centuries-old corruption of the Church.

The most obvious sign of hope is that the majority of Church leaders have in fact begun, albeit timidly, to take up publicly the cause of disarmament. The thrust seems to be least timid in the Roman Catholic Church. The Pastoral Letter of the National Conference of Catholic Bishops of this nation is a careful but clear departure. By virtue of its authoritarian structure, priests of this part of the Church are beginning to convey the message to the faithful with some of the power of its magisterium. They can and should be even more forceful. Meanwhile Protestant clergy of that majority of denominations whose leaders have conjointly issued similar statements need to take their leaders at their word and begin to address their flocks on these matters with greater outspokenness and authority. The time for pussyfooting has come to a close.

Another—and perhaps even greater—reason for hope is that there are signs that the Church is moving toward community. The most obvious of those signs is in a congregation here or there that not only has stumbled on community but is seriously working at it. The most noteworthy is the Church of the Savior, whose central location is in Washington, D.C., and which exacts from its membership precisely the kind of commitment of which I was speaking earlier. It is becoming a model for the Church as a whole. But it is a demanding model. Consequently, relatively speaking, it is a very tiny church, and its imitators are few and far between. Still, they are there.

Still another sign of hope is a more subtle yet broader-based phenomenon. Mysteriously, the Church over the past decade has become more Eucharistic. The Eucharist, or Communion, has always and consistently been the center of the Roman Catholic service. In the Protestant churches, however, this liturgical representation of phase two of the Holy Thursday Revolution faded almost into oblivion over the first half of this century. Some Episcopal churches in the 1960s reached the point where they celebrated the Eucharist only once a month, and other Protestant churches at best did it quarterly. Yet for no readily apparent reason it is now rapidly returning to many Protestant denominations. Virtually all Episcopal churches celebrate the Eucharist at least once a week, and some have only Eucharistic services. Many Lutheran and Presbyterian churches generally have weekly Eucharistic services. More surprisingly, so do some Methodist congregations. Additionally, the Curcillo Movement, which originated in Catholic Spain, is also seeping into Protestant denominations, experientially teaching something about community and much about the passion of community worship.

Finally there is a quiet but massive movement in the Church best described as the "laicization of the ministry."* It is a very

* See *The Laity in Ministry: The Whole People for the Whole World*, ed. John Hoffman and George Peck (Valley Forge, Pa.: Judson Press, 1984).

simple movement. It has only one premise. The premise is that every Christian is a minister. This movement seemed to begin just about simultaneously in the Roman Catholic Church and in the Protestant denominations. In the Catholic Church it was spearheaded by Vatican II, which specifically allowed certain formal changes, such as granting permission to the nonordained to be chalice bearers or wine servers at Communion. No longer was liturgy something enacted solely by professionals at the altar in front of an unprofessional audience. Suddenly the common man and woman were allowed up in the pulpit as lay readers or around the altar or in the sacristy. The old specializations of priest and penitent, preacher and listener, pastor and flock began to break down. No longer were the clergy simply up there in their robes representing specialized spirituality while the majority were down there in the pews representing specialized unspirituality. Thus the church began to move out of excessive specialization into integration, and the old distinctions between who was and who was not a minister began to blur.

It was as if the Spirit was at work in the Church. While the laicization of the ministry began with Vatican II among the Roman Catholics, the same phenomenon was occurring in the Protestant denominations. Small support groups were started by Protestant businessmen who saw themselves as having a ministry to evangelize their fellow workers so enmeshed in the secular world. Housewives banded together to minister to the elderly and shut-ins. The nonordained started "house churches." Without a priest or ordained or even designated minister being present, Protestants began casually to celebrate Communion together in "Agape" meetings. It was as if a voice from somewhere else was simultaneously speaking to many Christians in many different churches in many different places, telling them in no uncertain terms, "You are ministers. Go and feed my sheep."

Still, in relation to the whole, exciting though they may be, these steps toward community remain relatively small and statistically insignificant phenomena. They are real. They are growing. But the reality remains that the Church still has a very long way to go. And there is not very much time left. I recently witnessed an awesome phenomenon: the largest bird migration I have ever seen. Not tens, not hundreds, not thousands, but hundreds of thousands of creatures winging their way south together. They know what to do for their survival. But do we? Even the government scientists at Los Alamos have researched the subject sufficiently to recognize "nuclear winter" as a reality. Yet society as a whole acts as if it were not, as if it could stay where it is without changing direction. The time has come for the Church to be on the march.

CHAPTER XVI

The United States Government

In the summer of 1970 my wife and I moved to Washington, D.C., so that I could go to work for the office of the Surgeon General of the Army. I chose this job out of a deep interest in the relationship between psychology and politics. I had two hopes. One was that I would learn more about how our government operates. This hope was fulfilled, although I did not necessarily like what I learned. The other hope was that as an idealist, I could give service that would somehow contribute toward improving the health of the government. That hope went very largely unfulfilled.

I arrived in our nation's capital fired with enthusiasm. It was exciting simply to walk along those marble corridors of power. I felt privileged to be there in a position to participate at the very center of our government. Twenty-seven months later I left with my spirit crushed.

Our last night there I wrote a poem, "Leaving Washington." Its beginning gives a sense of the state of my spirit at that time:

> The rugs are taken up; the cleansers
> Like wooden soldiers, in formation stand
> Waiting for action on a cardboard battlefield.
> Plymouth Van Lines will rescue us tomorrow
> From this soul-sucking sterile marble town.
> The sapless trees bear National Trust blossoms
> And the angry-real blacks mock it all.

The poem eventually ends:

> I know
> That if the fight must again be here

I will need better armor
Or greater love.

The state of my mind at the time would be of no great significance except for the possibility that the climate of our government might have a similar effect on the spirits of others like me. There are two possible hypotheses. One is that I deserved it. What was crushed was not so much my spirit as my pride. My dreams of accomplishing something—of having some beneficial influence—were immature and narcissistic. The problem was that I could not be content to be a little fish in a big pond. I did not possess the humility or otherwise have the temperament to be a bureaucrat, a simple cog in a huge but quite properly working machine. My idealism was naïve and unrealistic. I deserved to be disillusioned, and it was appropriate that I should leave the business of governing up to those tougher and more mature.

I think there is some truth in that hypothesis. There is also at least equal truth in an alternate hypothesis—namely, that our government is so constituted that it will crush the spirit of any idealistic and sensitive and humane person who seeks, as I did, to "work from within." If I am correct, we are in serious trouble. For it means that our government must be left to the cynical and insensitive, to the hard of heart, to those who thrive in an atmosphere of unending intrigue, manipulation, and total dedication to expediency.

BALANCE OF POWER OR CHAOS?

What politicians chiefly do in Washington, I came to learn, is fight. And they fight hard. I cannot fault them for being lazy in the usual sense of the word. The seventy-hour week—generally spent in fighting—is the norm in that town. They also fight dirty. And, finally, they mostly fight each other.

What they fight about mainly is money in the form of budgets. I do not mean to imply that these budgetary battles have nothing to do with ideas or ideals. A budget is a concretization of priorities.* But I also don't mean to imply that their fighting is commonly altruistic. Most of it is to preserve or enlarge one's own slice of the budgetary pie at the expense of someone else's slice. Deals may be cut, but otherwise I never saw a budget worked out cooperatively. Cooperation is not big in Washington.

Nor is communication. The very first thing I was taught on the job was the number-one unwritten rule: "Be very careful whom you communicate with. Generally speaking, it is all right to communicate with the people in your subdepartment. If any higher ranking officer in the Surgeon General's office asks you a question, you probably should reply honestly, but that doesn't mean you have to go around volunteering information. Except under the most extraordinary circumstances you should not communicate with any other branch of the Department of the Army without going through the Surgeon General. Still, there may be times you will have to talk with the Department of the Army, but for God's sake don't give any information to the people in the departments of the Navy or Air Force. If you have permission, however, it may occasionally be all right for you to talk with the officers of the other services, but there is no need to let the civilians in the Department of Defense know what you're doing. Now, while we cannot say that you will lose your job if you communicate with the Department of Defense, you had better go way, way out of your way to avoid communicating with the White House. And above all bear this in mind: you must never, never, under any circumstances, release any unsolicited information whatsoever to any member of Congress, because Congress is the ultimate enemy."

One of the few things that keeps our government even vaguely sane is the practice called leaking. One may think it

* For instance, a significant number of people in Washington have been fighting for over a decade to establish a national peace academy with a budget of less than 1 percent of that allocated to our national war academies. The ideas and ideals of war clearly seem to have consistently won a far greater priority than the ideas and ideals of peace in our government. Budgets are the reflections of political realities.

generally occurs when a government official leaks some piece of information to the press. That, of course, does happen and is important, but actually the major part of leaking consists of leaks within the government itself—when an official from one department sneaks across the territorial boundaries to provide information to another department. Indeed, there is a special name for this kind of leaking: "whistle blowing." Within the system it is regarded as the most serious offense and its commission is dangerous. The penalties can be severe.

Such is the overall pattern of communication within our government. As communication goes, so goes community. The rules by which our government operates, not only in relationship with other governments but also within itself, are the rules of anticommunity. There is no community within the government. It is pervaded by an atmosphere of constant competitiveness, hostility, and distrust. One of my superiors was not being in the least facetious when he advised me: "Here you had better be paranoid or else. Being paranoid is sane." I was not able to survive long in that environment.

Is that the way it has to be? Many would say yes. "That's just the way the world works," the so-called realists would proclaim. Indeed, they would argue that it is downright constitutional. When our founding fathers were working on the development of the Constitution they were quite explicit about the concept of the "balance of power." They not only foresaw that the three major branches of government—the judiciary, the executive, and the legislative—would frequently be at odds with each other but they also saw that this would be good. The friction between these branches, or powers, would serve to refine the behavior of the whole, check abuses of the parts, and create a balance of sanity and wisdom. They very deliberately built conflict into the system.

The concepts of "checks and balances" and the "balance of power," as our founding fathers intended them, are good. But I do not think the framers of the Constitution intended reasoned conflict between the three major branches of government to extend to chronic internecine warfare between departments and subdepartments within each branch. Nor do I believe they intended the flow of information to be obstructed between these major branches, much less within them. Nor, I suspect, did they desire to create a climate of government in which only a soulless, paranoid, bureaucratic mentality can survive.

No, the Constitution does not require us to have a government totally at war with itself, a government devoid of cooperation, staffed by the mindless at the bottom and the predators at the top. But does human nature require it? The answer again is no. For we return to the reality of community. People can and do live together in community. Not often. But it not only can happen; with an awareness of the rules of community it can be constructed to work that way.

Our government is oblivious to the rules of community. It is stuck in the task-avoidance assumption of fighting, the predominant style of that precommunity stage I have called chaos. It behaves in its international relationships as if its primary purpose was to fight with other nation-states. But perhaps even more dramatic on the domestic, internal level, government executives behave as if their purpose in being together in Washington is to fight with each other.

Yet that is not their purpose. Their task is to govern. And it can be presumed that their task could better be accomplished if they generally worked with rather than against one another. A group bogged down in a task-avoidance assumption—in this case fighting—is remarkably inefficient. Imagine how much more efficiently our government might operate if its employees were not incessantly engaged in infighting. There is a better way than the authoritarian, bureaucratized chaos that is our government. That way is community.

It may seem paradoxical, but I estimate that if government executives spent a quarter of their time community-building, they would not only operate with greater efficiency and effectiveness, they would also be able to cut their numbers in half. But government bureaucrats on whatever level will not be able to relate to each other with humanity and common purpose if they continue to believe that the name of the game is one-upmanship and power struggles. Community can be brought to the government only when government leaders are committed to its principles, from the president down.

In many ways the president has less power than the uninitiated may think. Often the range of possible options in decision making is remarkably narrow. On the other hand, the greatest power the president possesses is one that is usually underestimated: it is the power of spirit. The spirit of change and innovation pervaded the Kennedy administration. The spirit of manipulation pervaded the Johnson administration. Nixon's blindness to civil liberties that encouraged "dirty tricks" pervaded his administration. Community will come to our government only through the administration of a president who is committed, not just in name but also in spirit, to the principles of community.

THE UNREALITY OF THE AMERICAN PRESIDENCY

Like the nation-state system at the end of the twentieth century, the institution of the presidency of the United States has become obsolete. When that office was established by the Constitution two hundred years ago the population of the nation was less than one hundredth as great and the complexity of its problems was smaller still. Despite a hundredfold increase in the magnitude of the tasks it must accomplish, the basic structure of that office has remained unchanged. In this regard the Constitution requires no alteration. But the manner in which the president performs his or her role desperately needs to undergo a radical revision.

Americans currently expect the president to greet the Boy Scouts on the White House lawn, meet visiting heads of state at the airfield, make ritual speeches to the VFW and the National Press Club, twist the arm of each member of Congress on every important piece of legislation, campaign actively for any party member in trouble, know all about El Salvador and nuclear energy, and so on ad infinitum. And to make informed, contemplative decisions. It is all impossible.

It is hardly President Reagan's fault. Since the time of the Roosevelts we have developed a macho image of the president as a superman who can know everything, who can be almost everywhere at once, who can be single-handedly in total control of the entire ship of state. An image is exactly what it is, and it is utterly unreal. No wonder that in 1980 we finally had to elect an actor to fill the role.

Images worry me. When we go to the theater, no matter how engrossing the images, we know they are unreal. They are just theater, and when the lights go back on, our consciousness returns to the world of reality. But this is not the way it is with our presidency. A recent presidential seeker who had consistently voted for routine increases in the Pentagon budget attempted to portray himself as a proponent of disarmament. Reagan "acts" as if he wanted to balance the budget. Yet despite all the hype with which the candidates and the press and the networks attempt to create an entertaining spectacle out of politics, we must try to remember that politics is real. It should not be the drama of images. It is the drama of reality. Millions, billions of real lives are at stake.

When images are portrayed not as theater but as reality, they are lies. Perhaps the best definition of Satan is a "real spirit of unreality." I am afraid that our government to a considerable extent is pervaded and operates by a real spirit of unreality. It is descending into evil. Radical therapy is required for the presidency.

Radical change is ultimately not the responsibility of a democratic government itself. Whatever its other faults, our government does succeed in being responsive to the desires—not necessarily the needs—of the people. Consequently the healing required for the presidency must begin in the minds and hearts of ordinary citizens and anyone else whose eyes they might help to open.

The macho image of the president as a kind of superman has been created and maintained because the people have wanted it. We have wanted a Big Daddy who has all the answers, who will take care of the bully down the block, who will not only give us a safe and secure home but one that is luxurious and where we will be protected from all hard knocks. The American presidency is the reflection of the task-avoidance assumption of dependency, a creation of our own childish fantasies. And a vicious cycle has come into being. In order to be elected or reelected, candidates after candidates vie with one another as to whose image can seemingly best fulfill the unreal expectations of us, the people. Moreover, administration after administration uses the media to perpetuate the image and convince us of its realism.

Paradoxically, the presidency has become too strong and too weak. It is too "strong" because, in attempting to fulfill this macho image of superhuman strength, it tries to do too much, to meet too many needs, to manipulate too many factors, to meddle in the affairs of too many other nations. It is too weak in that it does not exercise true leadership. It lacks the courage to refuse to fulfill unrealistic expectations and direct the country toward greater health, realism, and spiritual power, no matter how unpopular such directions might be.

Two changes need to be made. The major one is in the peoples' expectations of our president. We must come to expect a leader, not a caterer; a real person, not a superman; a spiritual director, not a Big Daddy. We must prepare ourselves to accept—to celebrate—not an imperial presidency but a "poor-in-spirit" presidency.*

When he gave his one full sermon, the first words out of Jesus' mouth, the first of the Beatitudes, were "Blessed are the poor in spirit." We can debate what he meant by this, but we can be quite sure he did not mean an administration that

* President Carter had the courage to make an attempt at creating a poor-in-spirit presidency, but given the institutionalized nature of his role, he somewhat understandably lacked the courage, in several instances, to make it stick or work. This is a particular shame, because his failure suggested to people that a poor-in-spirit presidency must inevitably be a weak presidency and one that cannot work in the "real world." So with his successor we retreated with gusto to our primitive images and notions of power.

regards itself as the world's policeman, that pretends to have all the answers, that cannot admit mistakes, and seeks to maintain an image of both infallibility and invincibility.

I look forward to the day when, asked at a press conference something such as "Mr. President [or Ms. President], what do you plan to do in El Salvador?," our Chief Executive will be able to respond: "Frankly, I don't yet know much about El Salvador. I've been studying it for several months, but it's a complicated situation down there. The people have a long history and a culture very different from our own. To the best of my knowledge their situation doesn't seem to be critical, so until we have a more complete understanding of things we don't plan to do anything in El Salvador."

We are not, however, ready for that day. The world is ready, but the American press and the American consciousness are not yet ready. We still want a fantasy Big Daddy in Washington. But we must, for our own salvation, begin a concerted effort to educate ourselves out of the task-avoidance assumption of dependency toward greater maturity.

We are all confronted with the task of achieving maturity. And nowhere can this task be more effectively accomplished than in community, where all members learn to exercise leadership and combat their own tendency to depend upon an authority figure. But media professionals in particular should pick up this burden. In their hands lies the most critical power to decide whether to support or to ridicule a realistically poor-in-spirit presidency. It is the primary responsibility of journalists, TV, and radio commentators to educate the public toward political maturity and restrain its capacity to infantilize us.

TOWARD A COMMUNITY PRESIDENCY

The second change required is the development of a community presidency. It is the only way that the tasks of the office can be effectively distributed, that the president can be freed to be contemplative, that he or she can be expected to maintain his or her integrity, and that the faith of discerning people can be restored in the institution of the presidency.

All this can be done without any alteration in the Constitution. My dream of the reformation of the presidency begins even before the primary process of candidate selection. Let us think in terms of potential President X (and let us suppose this potential candidate to be a woman). Called by her gifts of leadership and those who recognize them, she would begin her extraordinary role by selecting her vice-president and cabinet. She would select these individuals not so much for their particular expertise as for their capacity to operate in community—that is, their maturity and capacity to transcend, when appropriate, any personal axes they might have to grind. The reality already is that cabinet officers are not technical experts but managers. In other words, our candidate would begin by developing an effective community.

She would then refuse, except for the most extraordinary circumstances, to "hit the campaign trail." Ninety-five percent of the campaigning would be done by the cabinet, or community members. This would unburden her so she could perform her two primary roles: the contemplation required for truly thoughtful policy making and the leadership required to assure the maintenance and integrity of the community.

In short, from the very beginning of the electoral process the people would be voting not simply for an individual but for a community. Again, this would require no constitutional change. It is true that the appointment of cabinet officers eventually requires the approval of Congress. As it stands now, however, such officials begin their duties before such approval is ever obtained.

The system I am proposing has the single disadvantage that the presidential candidate herself would be far less visible to the voters than she would be under the present system. But this is far outweighed by the advantages. Ultimately, campaigning should be more effective, since there would not be one but a dozen campaigners. The candidate herself would not need to be exhausted by the absurd rigors of the campaign trail. Moreover, despite her lack of visibility the voters would actually be in a position to know more rather than less about what they were getting. They would know beforehand who the secretaries of state, defense, and education would likely be, as well as the identity of the attorney general and the vice-president.*

The operation of the presidency would continue in the same manner, not only through primary elections to the party nomination but also through the national campaign to the election and the administration beyond it. At all times the presidency would function as a community. All major decisions would be made in community and consensually by it. The president's role would not be to make decisions single-handedly. Rather, her primary responsibility would be to facilitate the ongoing development of the presidential community and its decision-making process.

People who have never experienced genuine community might be inclined to think that the requirement for consensual decision making in community would weaken the potency of the presidency—that all decisions would be watered-down compromises. The opposite is the case. The presidency is currently too weak as it is. Operating single-handedly, the president is unable to exercise the courage required for true spiritual leadership of the country in directions that are healthy but unpopular.

Do not underestimate the cost of courage and integrity. No real single human being can possibly possess the integrity and courage to be a decent Chief Executive within the current system. He or she would be too overwhelmed by responsibilities, too fragmented by conflicting demands, too lonely and isolated to keep her or his balance and resist the temptations to sell out to the lobbyists and the image makers, to stand up for what is right, to have the strength of character to bear up with true no-

---

* In fact, one of the things leading to a loss of faith in our political process is the way in which vice-presidential candidates are presently selected—not on the basis of their qualifications to fill the role of the presidency, if necessary, with excellence, but merely on the basis of the crassest political considerations. Through knowing the people a candidate has selected for high office, the people would have far better reason to be able to judge the kind of president they are voting for than they do now.

bility under the demands of the presidency as it is now constituted.

It is not simply a matter of delegation. Under the current
system the president can theoretically delegate whatever tasks
he might choose to and thereby obtain whatever "tactical support" seems necessary. But I am not talking about tactical support. I am speaking of emotional support. I do not think that
any human being could possibly exercise the courage that the
presidency requires in this age of potential global holocaust
without the emotional support of an ongoing community.

Nor am I talking about community of "support group" intensity. Many presidents have had a support group of one
kind or another—cronies or kitchen cabinets. But these have
tended to give him the sort of support that is provided by the
yes-men of the world. Such support may be *encouraging* but
not necessarily wise. Indeed, it has the danger of giving the
president false courage.

No, I am speaking of a true intense ongoing community. A
community is not a group of completely like-minded, yes-
people. While it may be designed to include specific talents, it
must be designed to include differences—to be inclusive and
not a clique. In my imagination, the president of the future
will refrain from selecting yes-people for her cabinet. Beyond
choosing on the basis of emotional maturity, she will select the
members of her cabinet/community for their variety, for the
differences in their backgrounds, outlooks, and personalities.

She will also have a high tolerance for conflict. Genuine
community is a safe place where appropriate conflict is actually welcomed and faced rather than dreaded and avoided. It
is a group that has learned how to fight gracefully. Although
her primary role will be to facilitate the development and
maintenance of her cabinet/community, the president of the
future will not simply stand aloof from the fray. She will be a
member of the community, as responsible to the other members as they are to her. She will need their encouragement but
no more than she will need their doubt and disagreement,
criticism, and confrontation for her integrity. As a member of

a genuine long-term community once said: "We love one another too much to let anyone get away with anything."

The graceful fighting that occurs in genuine community will
not only provide the courage and integrity that is required of
a radically poor-in-spirit presidency but also its intellectual
foundation. It is my experience that working groups (that is,
ongoing true communities) consistently get down to the root
of things. Through struggling together over their differences
a community always gets down to the basic issues. It succeeds
in not being sidetracked by superficialities and thus will not
behave reactively, as the presidency has so often tended to
behave in recent years.

Although it would require no constitutional change, this
proposal of a community presidency is almost certain to arouse
outcries of "communism," as if community and communism
were the same. Indeed, does not a community presidency look
strangely like the Politburo? But the Politburo is not elected in
any true sense of the word. Moreover, we do not know how
the Politburo operates, because it operates in secret.

I see no compelling reason whatever why *all* cabinet/com-
munity meetings cannot be made open to a small rotating
number of representatives from the press. The press, however, would have to restrict itself to reporting on the action of
the community as a community.* Great harm could result if it
were reported that "Secretary So-and-So continually took pot
shots at the attorney general" or "The vice-president accused
the president of having a sexist outlook." On the other hand,
I think it could only be to the benefit of both the public and the
government if it were reported that "in today's cabinet meeting there was active disagreement over the correct policy to

---

* One of the roots of the community movement was what has been called the
T-group. Roughly thirty years ago some "trainers" who were training students to
communicate more honestly and effectively were challenged by their students:
"You talk about this as if it were easy, but maybe it's all talk. Why don't you let us
see how well you trainers communicate with each other?" The trainers agreed and
communicated with each other over an extended period of time while their students looked on. The experiment was sufficiently successful that this trainer group,
or T-group, became the model for the sensitivity-group movement.

take in relation to Nicaragua. The major focus of this disagreement centered upon the degree to which the communist movement in Nicaragua is indigenous or externally inspired. No consensus was reached beyond the conclusion that the situation in Nicaragua does not represent an emergency and that the subject would be made the major agenda item for next Tuesday's meeting."

Here again we can see the reciprocal relationship between a healthier presidency, healthier press, and healthier general population. If the demand of the people for a "cult of personality" is sufficiently great, the press will give in to it, making disagreement between so-and-so newsworthy and will thereby force much government decision making into necessary cloaks of secrecy. On the other hand, if both the press and the people can transcend their fascination with the strengths and foibles of individual public figures (or restrict that fascination to rock stars and ballplayers), we can have a much more open government. Secrecy is never healthy for either the government or the people. It would be good for both if it could be made public knowledge that the administration is in conflict over this issue or that. But such health ultimately requires a more mature public outlook.

Still, it is neither desirable nor necessary for enlightened political leaders to wait for the maturation of the public and the press. For one thing, in their reciprocal relationship political leaders have their own responsibility for educating the press and the public. Just as there can be no vulnerability without risk, politicians will not be able to establish a community presidency without being willing to suffer the throes of being radically innovative. If our political leaders insist on waiting around until the press and public are totally ready for it, we will never achieve a community presidency.

We do not have that much time to wait. If the current relationship between the people, the media, and the presidency continues, we will inevitably sink deeper and deeper into the morass of image making, with its potential for ever greater evil. The need for a realistic, poor-in-spirit community presidency is now.

This very specific proposal for a community presidency is in
no way naïve. I am not a romantic. The business of community
is not easy or some cheaply bought experience of unending
warm fuzziness. True communities are often places of great turmoil and struggle. There are some who are not qualified for either the struggle or the love involved. Like any community, a
presidential community will have its own trials and tribulations.
Some members will have to leave it in pain and anger, and new
ones will have to be arduously trained. Community will not relieve the presidency of its agony. To the contrary, what it will do
is make the presidency strong enough to bear fully the agony of
leadership without deserting integrity.

The proposal of a community presidency cannot be evaluated
by one who has never experienced community. This is doubly
tricky because some people think they have experienced
community when, in fact, they have not. I am reminded of a
tough-appearing retired army colonel who, early into a community-building workshop, proclaimed: "I feel sorry for all of you.
You're all talking about the lack of community in your life.
There's been lots of community in my life. For more than twenty
years in the army I had community." A day and a half later this
wonderful man had the courage to say with tears in his eyes: "I
need to apologize to you. I told you I had experienced lots of
community in the army. Today I know I was wrong. You have
taught me that what I experienced in the army was not community. In fact, I now realize that the very reason I joined the army
in the first place was that I was searching for community, but the
reality is that I never truly found it there."

Finally, what is naïve is to expect the current system to work.
It is naïve to expect that a single person can do a job that carries
twenty times the responsibilities it did when the job was created.
It is naïve to think that a single person can truly understand what
is going on in two hundred different nations. It is naïve to think
a person can be wise and contemplative when burdened down
with all manner of ceremonial as well as innumerable other responsibilities. And should you think to yourself, But it all seems
to be working pretty well, perhaps you should wonder if you

have not been so naïve as to have swallowed the unreal images that have been prepared for your consumption. For the reality is that we live in a world extremely different from the world of two hundred years ago, and it is naïve to expect that we, in terms of the presidency or other political realities, can effectively operate in the same old ways.

The presidency is the center of all political power in our country. But the change in mode of government operations from a disintegrated, specialized, and bureaucratized style of dehumanized competition to a cooperative—even nurturing and loving—level of functioning according to the principles of community needs to occur throughout the political process. The change is called for at every level of the executive branch. It is called for in Congress and the judiciary. It is called for in the state governments. It is called for in every county and town. But more than any other single political segment, the presidency has the power to set the tone for government. It would be the easiest way to begin to change the climate. But the change could begin in other places. It could even occur despite an outdated presidency. In the end, the point to bear in mind is that however it is accomplished, the whole climate of our government must change.

It is difficult to govern. Domestically, the special-interest groups are not just going to go away. Agonizing decisions will always have to be made as to which of those interests are truly worthy and which should be courageously resisted despite public outcry. The USSR does not have an easy culture to relate to. Internationally, no matter how much it might offend the nationalism of the constituents, the federal government must take weak-seeming true initiatives of vulnerability leading toward effective world government. At the same time our leaders must be able to say "No" very forcefully to atrocious behavior of other nations. They must truly be as wise as serpents and innocent as doves. They must be strong enough continually to strike and restrike paradoxical balances.

Such spiritual as well as political strength is far beyond that of any individual. The strength for real servant leadership can be found only when people work together in love and commitment. It can exist only in a climate in which leaders are emotionally sustained in community. It cannot exist in a climate of competitive isolation in which idealism and humaneness are crushed. Only through community will our officials be strong enough truly to be our leaders, truly to be peacemakers.

Such a climate is so radically different from the traditional climate of Washington as to require a revolutionary shift of spirit. Yet it is exactly such a shift in spirit that is needed in our government, just as it is needed in the Christian Church, to make possible the revolution required for genuine peacemaking, for saving our skins. The gulf between what is and what needs to be is so great as to make these proposals seem like a dream. The so-called realists may call it "naïve." The prophets of the old brain* will scream "impossible." "It is a mere feckless vision," they will say. Indeed, "visionary" is one of their traditional pejoratives for discounting the real prophets. But they, the prophets of the old brain, are the prophets of death. For as our Jewish forebears instructed us: "Where there is no vision, the people perish."†

---

* Richard Bolles, *The Land of Seven Tomorrows* (Ten Speed Press, P.O. Box 7123, Berkeley, CA 94707; $1.00, which is the cost to Bolles).
† Proverbs 29:18

CHAPTER XVII

Empowerment

We know there are rules for good communication. These rules work. Yet they are seldom either taught or practiced. Consequently most people, including government, business, and religious leaders, do not know how to relate to each other. And we Americans are hardly likely to be able to relate decently to the Russians or peoples of any other culture when by and large we do not know how to communicate with one another.

The rules of communication are best taught and only learned through the practice of community-making. Fundamentally, the rules of communication are the rules of community-making, and the rules of community-making are the rules for peacemaking.

The behavior of our government leaders who are responsible for international relations consistently—almost unfailingly—violates all the rules of community-making. Their behavior guarantees international misunderstanding, war, and the chronic threat of war. The traditional rules under which they operate are the rules of anticommunity. There is no way we can move toward peace until these rules are changed.

The changes required in our churches and government necessary to support the revolution needed in our international relations will not be easy to accomplish. But Church and government leaders arise from the people and to a considerable extent do represent the people and reflect their cultural norms. The rules of government, therefore, can be substantially changed only when the rules by which the people relate to each other are substantially changed. Peacemaking—community-making—ultimately must begin at a grass-roots level. It begins with you.

WHAT TO DO NOW?

Start communities.

Start one in your church. Start one in your school. Start one in your neighborhood.

Don't worry for the moment about what to do beyond that. Don't worry about which peace group to join. Don't worry about whether to withhold taxes, blockade a missile plant, march in a demonstration, or write a letter to your congressman. Don't worry much yet about feeding the poor, housing the homeless, protecting the abused. It is not that such actions are wrong or even unnecessary. It is simply that they are not primary. They are not likely to succeed unless they are grounded, one way or another, in community. Form a community first.

You are not likely to be able to contribute much to peacemaking until you yourself become a skilled peacemaker. And then you are not likely to be able to undertake concerted social action on behalf of peace without a community to empower you.

Start your own community.

It won't be easy. You'll be scared. You will often feel that you don't know what you're doing. You'll have a difficult time persuading people to join you. Many initially won't want to make the commitment, and those who are willing to will be as scared as you. Once you get started it will be frustrating. There will be chaos. Most will consider dropping out, and some probably will. But hang in there. Push forward into emptiness. It will be painful. There will be anger, anxiety, depression, even despair. But keep going into the night. Don't stop halfway. It may seem like dying, but push on. And then suddenly you will find yourself in the clear air of the mountaintop, and you'll be laughing and crying and feeling more alive than you have in years—maybe more alive than you've ever been.

That will just be the beginning. After a while the mists will come back, and you'll lose the beauty. The chaos will return. But do not be disheartened. Look at it. Figure out what needs to be changed, be emptied. And the mists will clear again, more quickly than before. After a while your community will feel solid. Then you may want to turn your eyes outward as a community. Then you may want to consider how to expand your community gifts into the larger society. Then is the time to think about social action.

But don't feel you have to do anything. Remember that being takes precedence over doing. If you concentrate simply upon making your community beautiful, its beauty will shine forth without your having to do anything at all—as long as you don't hide its light under a bushel. If your community is a part of a church congregation, hold your meetings in the church. If it is in a business, hold them in the offices. If you are town leaders, meet in the town hall. You will not have to advertise. But leave the door open. Leave it open so that passersby can hear you laugh, can hear you cry, can get glimpses of your faces and the way you touch each other. Leave it open so they can walk in and join you.

Whom will you find to join you in forming community? I don't know. There is no formula. Some people you think are right will be too afraid, and they will conclude they do not have the time. Others you doubted would be interested will suddenly get a little gleam in their eyes, as if they glimpsed a distant vision you thought they had never had and they thought they had forgotten. There will be many surprises. There is a kind of unpredictable "grace" to it.

But as you search for people to join you, there are two guidelines. One is to be wary of people who have a very big axe to grind. All of us have our little axes, and it is proper that we should have pet causes and projects. We do not have to give these up to form community, but we do have to have the capacity to lay them aside, "bracket" them or transcend them, when appropriate, in the interests of community. A person who lacks the maturity for such bracketing or transcending will not make a good candidate. This is a very weak guideline, however, because it is difficult to discern beforehand just who does and who does not, when the chips are down, have that maturity. You will find that some who seem to have the capacity actually do not once they are in community. And others who seem to lack the capacity will learn it in community. So it is a guideline only for gross selection.

The other guideline is to seek out people who are different from you. If you are white, look for blacks. If you are black, look for whites. If you are a dove, try to find at least one hawk for your community. You need hawks. If you are a Democrat, you will need a Republican; if a Christian, a Jew; if an Episcopalian, a Baptist; if rich, some who are not. Since birds of a feather tend to flock together, it will not be easy to find women and men different from you. You will not be able to achieve perfect variety. Only remember that genuine community is inclusive and that if you are a wealthy white Democrat, you have the most to learn from the poor, the blacks and Chicanos, and the Republicans. You need their gifts to be whole.

Once your community is established, there is yet another guideline: remain inclusive. Be on guard against using enemy formation to invigorate yourselves. Watch out for tendencies to elitism—thinking in terms of "us" and "them" or, even worse, "us against them." Focus your energy and being on what you are for (peace, love, community) rather than what you are against (military industrialists, child abusers, organized crime). It is not that you should be Pollyannaish. Hardly. There is evil in the world, and community is its natural enemy. It is not that your community should ignore evil but that it should avoid being contaminated by it. Leave the door open to everyone, including other organizations and communities. Do not be exclusive. Relate with other groups rather than set yourselves apart.

So start community. Don't be afraid to fail. I know you are likely to be frightened by the prospect. Remember that I learned everything I know about community through flying by the seat of my pants. In fact, whenever I am in community I am flying by the seat of my pants, but that's where some of the excitement comes from. True community is always, among other things, an adventure. You will always be going into the unknown, and you will often be scared, particularly at the beginning.

But you will not be alone. You will be entering this adventure with others as scared as you, and you will be able to share not only your fear but your talents and strengths. Out of the strength of your community you will be able to do things you never thought you were capable of.

People are called to peacemaking in different ways. It is rare that God will call a mother of two young children to go to jail as a peace activist. On the other hand, I have an acquaintance, whose children are grown, who regards it as a bad year if she doesn't go to jail at least once a month. Remember, however, that there are some ways in which we are *all* called. We are all called to be peacemakers, whether we like it or not. And as peacemakers, we are called to community. Finally, out of the strength of community, we are all called to be individuals of integrity.

One of the things a calling to be an individual of integrity means is a calling to speak out, to be outspoken. We are called to overcome the psychology of helplessness, of reticence. If we see a lie, we are called to name it a lie. If we see insanity, we are called to name it as such. If you are a preacher, you are called to preach the gospel, no matter how unpalatable it may be to your congregation. Don't avoid the subject of the arms race at a party just because it might be divisive. Yes, there are some who may find it upsetting, but perhaps they need to be upset. There are others who will respond to your outspokenness with gratitude for that leadership that gives them the courage to speak out in turn.

The call to fight against our reticence is neither an easy nor a simple one. There is no point in buttonholing a hawk already known to be intransigent. On the other hand, there is a point to working specifically on that person to get into community with you. For community is the only catalyst that softens intransigence. Yet this does not mean you should shy away from any kind of resistance. As the saying goes, you can't make an omelet without breaking eggs. You are going to have to discern just how much resistance it is constructive to take on and to what extent you are willing to be wounded in the process. You will also need your community to return to in order to lick your wounds and have them bandaged and healed by those who love you before you can venture forth to be wounded again. You will need to use strategy in your outspokenness.

Does all this talk of strategy and wounds and resistance make it sound as if there is a war going on? Yes. We are talking of a war, a struggle that is just beginning to heat up. Since the arms race is an institution that must be actively torn down, peace-making is a call to action. But remember that you are marching into this battle to the beat of a different drum. It is a battle to change the rules of human communication. We cannot change the rules through playing by the old ones. When I speak of strategy I am also speaking of tactics that are revolutionary. Yes, the hawks, the merchants of death, the blasphemers, are all targets, but they are not our enemies; they are our beloved. It is not just a matter of wooing them. The keystone of the strategy required to win this war is community, and the weapons can be only those of love.

Postscript

In December 1984 nine of my colleagues and I met together to form The Foundation for Community Encouragement (FCE). The purpose of this tax-exempt public foundation is "to encourage the development of community wherever it does not exist, and to assist existing communities, whether secular or religious, to strengthen themselves and their relationships with other communities, ultimately thereby fostering the movement toward world understanding."

Because community is inclusive, FCE has been deliberately designed not to be specifically Christian or even religious. However, because community is invariably spiritual, it would be fair to say that FCE does possess a spiritual quality. It does not embrace any particular ideology in the usual sense of the word. But one thing that all of the board members have in common is a commitment to peacemaking—a commitment to community at all levels.

It is not the purpose of FCE to supplant any existing organization. To the contrary, it exists to support all other true community organizations and encourage new ones. It is unique in that it is perhaps the only organization that has as its focus community per se. Other organizations exist to develop community within a certain city or among alcoholics or between Americans and Russians. FCE exists to strengthen all such organizations. But it also exists to help people get into community without having to be an alcoholic, without needing to belong to a particular Church, without requiring a specific task or crisis, wherever they may live.

There are a number of avenues through which FCE works. One is through individuals who are seeking some kind of personal help. Requests for such help usually arise out of a lack of community and simultaneously represent opportunities to build community. Wherever possible, and free of charge, FCE seeks confidentially to link up any such individual with an

appropriate community in his or her local area—a specific
church, an AA chapter, a Beginning Experience group, or any
other suitable resource. In so doing FCE also seeks to serve
with increasing effectiveness as a data bank of existing community organizations. Such networking is an important part of
FCE's mission.

FCE is also developing an increasingly large body of carefully selected, highly trained community-building leaders.
These men and women, working under contract with FCE, in
turn are helping to lead church congregations, colleges, and
other organizations into deeper levels of community. They go
out to where you are.

In addition, these leaders are conducting workshops open
to the general public either in Knoxville, Tennessee, home of
FCE's headquarters, or at selected retreat centers across the
country. Some of these workshops last two days and are designed to give interested individuals an experience of community and the community-building process. Others are longer in
duration and are designed to train individuals additionally in
the skills of community-building—although not to the same
degree that FCE's own leaders have been trained.

Among its future plans is the development of a scientific
research arm, not only for the purpose of improving FCE's
own direct activities but also to add to the general body of
scientific knowledge about communities and their development.

In response to my call to start communities, some of you will
find that you are able to do this without assistance. On the
other hand, if a group of you want community but feel unable
to lead yourselves into it, or if you have already started but are
floundering in some situation from which you cannot extricate
yourselves, then write or call:

The Foundation for Community Encouragement, Inc.
P.O. Box 449
Ridgefield, CT 06877
(203) 431-9434

Or call if you want to network with other communities. Or if you simply want to learn more about FCE. Or if there is some other manner in which you think we might assist you.

We want to help you in any way we can to build community—if you need that help. While the foundation was established to help you, it was not created to make you dependent upon it. For one thing, that would be harmful to you. We cannot carry you on the adventure; you must do your own adventuring. The most we can do is to serve as a guide when necessary. Moreover, we are not a "fat" foundation. You will be charged for its services if they are extensive. Thanks to philanthropy, the charge will be very reasonable, but we will need continued philanthropy to keep it that way. FCE needs you as much as you may need it. We are interdependent.

FCE is not "fat," because philanthropy for it is not easy to come by. Its few donors thus far have been pioneers, and we desperately need more of them. It is virtually impossible to describe our work to a possible contributor who has never personally experienced—tasted—community. The wealthy and powerful are generally the least likely to have had such experience and the most likely from whom to draw a blank when we try to explain ourselves. The usual response from traditional organizations, institutions, and individuals is that FCE's programs are too "soft." Some, trying to be helpful, have suggested that the word "encouragement" is itself "soft" and that our title should be changed—as if the world did not need more softness.

The problem can best be elucidated by a simple story. Recently a man repesenting a potential source of funds attended a community-building training conference conducted by FCE. Toward the very end this man said with visible agony, "I feel torn apart. On one hand this has been a most moving experience for me. I have personally benefited from it more than I dreamed. I am very glad that I came and surprisingly sad to be leaving. But as I think about what has happened here, about the essence of the experience and what you are trying to do, I cannot help but conclude that it is really about nothing more than love. And how on earth can I go back to my board of directors and sell them on love?"

That man's problem is ours and yours. It is our task and yours to sell the world on love.

More Inspiration from M. Scott Peck